W9-BMY-199

SCOTT HIGGINS

Harnessing the Technicolor Rainbow

Color Design in the 1930s

University of Texas Press

Austin

Publication of this book was made possible by the generous support of Wesleyan University and Technicolor.

Printed in the United States of America
First edition, 2007

♾ The paper used in this book meets the minimum requirements of ANSI/NISO Z39.48-1992 (R1997) (Permanence of Paper).

Library of Congress Cataloging-in-Publication Data
Higgins, Scott, 1968–
Harnessing the Technicolor rainbow : color design in the 1930s / by Scott Higgins. — 1st ed.
p. cm.
Includes bibliographical references and index.
ISBN 978-0-292-71627-8 (cl. : alk. paper)
ISBN 978-0-292-71628-5 (pbk. : alk. paper)
1. Color cinematography—History. 2. Color motion pictures—History. I. Title.
TR853.H54 2007
778.5'342—dc22

2007005799

FOR MY PARENTS

Contents

Acknowledgments

This book is a testament to the generosity of countless people, only a few of whom I can recognize here. I initiated this study during my doctoral work at the University of Wisconsin, Madison, and I owe a profound debt to the faculty of the Film Studies program. Lea Jacobs, my advisor, offered meticulous criticism of my work, asked challenging questions, and helped open my eyes to color. David Bordwell graciously shared his encyclopedic knowledge of film style and inspired the direction of my thinking about cinema. Tino Balio and Vance Kepley Jr. commented on my research, helping me refine the argument. Ben Brewster and Kristin Thompson reminded me of the facts and kept me honest, historically speaking.

At Wesleyan University I found another community of colleagues who supported the revision and completion of this book. Jeanine Basinger provided expert counsel on how to transform my research into a book and became a steadfast ally in supporting its completion. Leith Johnson was an inexhaustible problem solver, going miles beyond his duties as curator of the Wesleyan Film Archives. Lisa Dombrowski's encouragement kept me focused during my writing, and Lea Carlson kept the rest of my departmental duties on track. This book was also shaped by the insights of students in my seminars on color at Wesleyan. Among them, Marc Longenecker, Meghan McCarron, Lana Wilson, Heather Heckman, and Liz Collier revealed the rewarding complexity of cinematic color.

In pursuing this project, I discovered a network of experts who were tremendously forthcoming. Michael Friend, Richard May, Robert Harris, and John Belton all gave me access to rare materials and inspired me with their passion and matchless understanding of color processes and aesthetics. Dr. Richard Goldberg patiently shared his lifetime of knowledge about Technicolor and tracked down some essential pieces of the puzzle. Robert Hoffman, at Technicolor, guided me through the intricacies of digital intermediate and made possible the illustrations in this book.

The book reached fruition because of the generous financial support of several institutions. My early research was made possible by a fellowship from the Wisconsin Alumni Research Fund. Wesleyan University provided a project grant to help defray expenses during the final stages of this project. The color illustrations in this book were supported by a grant from Technicolor Incorporated.

It is a fact of writing that friends and family inevitably become colleagues, helpers, and enablers. I was fortunate that my circle of friends was not only supportive and tolerant of my obsession, but also very smart. Paul Ramaeker, Michael Walsh, Teresa Becker, Kevin Heffernan, and Dorinda Hartmann indulged, humored, inspired, and distracted me in all the correct proportions. Tara McPherson and Robert Knaack opened their home to me as a base for my work in Los Angeles. John and Beth Ross gave me a home in Madison and managed the unlikely feat of being both friends and in-laws. My very first teachers, Bob and Diane, nurtured my love of film and were surprisingly unquestioning and supportive when I decided to turn that love into a career. My brother, Sean, was unstinting in his encouragement and in his humor. Jack and Bess have inspired me to work and reminded me to play. They have also been uncommonly patient, allowing me to finish a project that has lasted all their lives. Finally, I could easily fill another volume expressing my gratitude to Sara Ross, my wife and intellectual partner. Without her ceaseless devotion, keenness for finding joy in life, and, well, her cooking, I would never have finished this project, or have done much else.

Harnessing the Technicolor Rainbow

ONE

Introduction

The Challenge of Technicolor

Watching a Technicolor film from the classical era is a perceptual luxury. We are impressed with the abundance of color, and we sense that it has been carefully organized, shaped into compositions that feel complete, polished, and dramatically nuanced. Compared to our contemporary experience of color as a necessary, automatic, and all-too-often mundane aspect of the moving image, a Technicolor production engages us in the unfolding of a complex and determined design. Color is an active and significant visual element, ebbing and flowing across the film. Yet the system of color design, though sensed, remains just out of reach. Immersed as we are in the classical narrative's forward momentum and deluged with shifting visual cues, we probably find it nearly impossible to track color's moment-by-moment contributions or to grasp its overarching orchestration.

This book aims to capture color's undeniable role in shaping our experience of the classical feature film by detailing Technicolor aesthetics during the crucial era of the 1930s. In the following pages, I seek to answer several questions: What functions did color serve during the classical era and how did these functions develop? How did commercial imperatives, stylistic norms, and technological constraints shape filmmakers' options for designing in color? How does color work, generally and specifically, to guide the viewer and tell the story? Most basically, I strive to articulate the "Technicolor look," that quality of design that helped make images feel perfectly organized, correct, and inevitable. The 1930s present a crucial intersection for addressing these questions because color was so carefully attended to and so openly discussed and debated. The period gives us a window onto the process by which color was brought into contact with America's most popular visual medium. The conventions developed in the 1930s had consequences for later cinema and our visual culture at large.

Of course, efforts to join color to the moving image are as old as cinema itself. Three-color Technicolor's precursors set the stage for the 1930s. Spectacular hand coloring was an important aspect of the magic-lantern tradition, and filmmakers had been painting frames at least since the release of Edison's *Annabelle's Dance* in 1895. Georges Méliès achieved astonishingly intricate hand-colored effects, most famously in *Le Voyage à travers l'impossible* (1904), which offers four hues in at least ten shades and tints simultaneously on screen. The importance of color as an effect, and the labor involved in achieving it, are on ready display in costume details, including narrow stripes of alternating color. Pathé Frères rationalized the technique with the refinement of stencil tinting between 1905 and 1908. Prints were mechanically colored through a series of stencil cutouts, one for each hue. Though largely limiting such effects to trick films and prestigious historical subjects, Pathé continued stencil coloring until the 1930s, achieving a look that resembled hand-tinted postcards.[1] Color in these films is an extravagant embellishment; it captures the eye and inspires wonder because of its obvious artifice. Tom Gunning aptly describes color in early cinema as a "superadded feature" aimed at "sensual intensity" rather than realism.[2] As we will see, these are associations that three-color Technicolor design will both seek to exploit and overcome.

By far the most common method of bringing color to cinema before the Technicolor era involved tinting and toning. Common estimates hold that between 80 and 90 percent of all prints were tinted or toned by the early 1920s.[3] Both processes achieved more or less uniform coloring by running release prints through baths of dye or toning agents. Tinting involved dyeing the gelatin of a release print so that the entire image was veiled in color, while toning replaced the silver image so that highlights remained clear.[4] Less spectacular than hand or stencil coloring, tinting and toning varied the viewing experience, and colors were quickly codified. By 1914 the standard conventions were in place: blue signaled night, red indicated fire and passion, magenta designated romance, green was used for nature and gruesome scenes, amber indicated lamplight, and so forth.[5] The prevalence of these techniques decreased with the coming of sound because the dyes interfered with the optical sound track, but in the late 1920s Eastman Kodak introduced Sonochrome release stock, which allowed the practice to continue. As late as 1937, MGM released *The Good Earth* in 500 prints toned red-brown.[6]

Tinting, especially, was fairly inexpensive, and during the silent era it became absolutely standard. At their height, tinting and toning likely became a transparent convention, going relatively unnoticed by the casual spectator. This formed another inherited context for the Technicolor look; the dominant kind of color cinema in the silent era had achieved familiarity and a clear semantic function. Three-color Technicolor designs strove to remain "new" while maintaining a margin of familiarity that would allow the fact of color to fade into the background of the viewer's experience. Moreover, they attempted to capture and enhance some of color's power to code dramatic events.

While artificial color dominated the silent era, natural, or photographic, color processes also vied for adoption. The successful commercial use of these processes remained rather rare until the late 1920s, and so they tended to crop up as briefly lived novelties. The earliest photographic color processes were additive, meaning that white light would be created by adding various densities of red, blue, and green. Additive processes included Gaumont's Chronochrome (an experimental three-color system in use between 1912 and 1913), and Technicolor Process Number One (in use around 1917). The most resilient and earliest additive process was Kinemacolor, a British venture successfully exhibited between 1908 and 1915. All additive systems required specialized projection equipment that could mix the colors of two or more distinct images on the screen. This requirement, as well as severe technical deficiencies such as color fringing and low illumination, doomed additive color to the status of a "special attraction."[7] The films, most of them documentary subjects, might thrill audiences as technological demonstrations, but they never successfully crossed over into the mainstream.

Much more successful were two-color subtractive systems, of which Technicolor Process Number Two (1922–1927) and Number Three (1928–1932) were the most lucrative. The Technicolor Corporation was formed in late 1915 by Herbert Kalmus, Samuel Comstock (both graduates of the Massachusetts Institute of Technology), and W. Burton Westcott. The three had previously formed an engineering consulting firm (KCW), which received a slew of patents, developed commercial processes, and launched at least three profitable corporations that, according to Kalmus, "enabled us to stick with Technicolor through years and years of experimentation."[8] The Technicolor Corporation, taking its name from Kalmus and Comstock's alma mater, was formed specifically to produce an engineering solution to the problem of color in motion pictures. The first Technicolor process was an additive system that required special projectors. It failed after the release of only a single Technicolor-produced feature, *The Gulf Between* (1917), but the experience convinced Kalmus to undertake the development of subtractive color technology.

Subtractive color systems solved the problem of special projection by layering some combination of cyan (greenish blue), yellow, and magenta (hues that create color when they are filtered or subtracted from white light) on a single piece of release stock. Since these films could be shown on any standard projector, they were more easily accommodated by mainstream distribution channels, and this adaptability facilitated the production of full-length color features (including *The Toll of the Sea* [1922] and *The Black Pirate* [1926]) as well as black-and-white films with color sequences (*Phantom of the Opera* [1925], for example). Before three-color Technicolor, or Technicolor Process Number Four, the subject of this book, subtractive systems were limited to reproducing a narrow slice of the spectrum. Based on two colors, usually cyan and magenta, these processes translated the mise-en-scène into compositions of bluish green and pinkish orange. Flesh tones and saturated primary hues were problematic. However, extremely careful and clever color designs could work within the process for beautiful effects. Technicolor's *Toll of the Sea,* in particular, balances pastels with soft browns for subtle and gently graded compositions. During one stunning sequence, in which Anna May Wong's character meets her lover in a rose garden, strong red flowers in the fore- and background complement the green of her dress in center frame. The image is strongly stylized as romantically glamorous, and careful composition lends it a sense of completeness—it militates against the feeling that something is missing.

The overwhelming bulk of two-color productions, though, exploited color as a temporary novelty. This was especially the case during the brief boom in two-color Technicolor production that coincided with the transition to sound. Musicals like the Paul Whiteman revue *The King of Jazz* (1930) managed a series of brilliant color effects, but they never developed schemes for integrating color into the basic vocabulary of narrative filmmaking.

Before the 1930s, color tended to offer novel embellishment or, as in the case of tinting, a simple and expedient method of signification. Color was very much present in both artificial and photographic forms, but none of these processes launched the far-reaching attempts to harness color to narrative that three-color Technicolor did. This book takes up the story of color cinema at the critical historical juncture when Technicolor became a significant option for classical filmmaking. During the 1930s, filmmakers and studios tempered color's novelty and developed practical methods for managing it. Studio personnel labored to balance the loss of flexibility entailed by the technology against the added resources of color. They found methods and motivations for foregrounding or restraining color and assigned it specific tasks to perform. This is the period in which color was defined as a cinematic device and assimilated into the classical system. Many Technicolor conventions seem obvious or common because we have inherited them, like so many aspects of our moving-image culture, from the era of classical Hollywood cinema's dominance.

But getting a grip on color requires an approach to film form that allows us to seek functions and patterns and avoid the pitfalls of random observation. My methods are broadly informed by neoformalism, an approach based on the work of Russian formalist theoreticians, including Boris Eikhenbaum and Victor Shklovsky, and best exemplified by Kristin Thompson's volume of film analysis *Breaking the Glass Armor*. Chief among the Russian formalists' contributions was to view form as constitutive of art rather than as merely instrumental in its communication. Our contact with an artwork is our experience *of* its form, as opposed to an abstracted understanding of "content" delivered *by* form. This view places a quality like color at the center of an artwork's identity rather than as a superfluous embellishment of a more fundamental message.

As described by Thompson, the neoformalist approach assumes that films are artificial constructs that engage viewers in nonpractical perception and function to defamiliarize, or transform, material that has become habitual or routine.[9] The goal of art is to renew perception, but different art forms work at different levels. In the case of classical Hollywood cinema, stylistic devices are apt to perform functions that support narrative. In this book, I take color to be a formal device, and I offer a detailed account of how functions were assigned to this device within the systems of classical style. In this framework, we might say that 1930s filmmakers feared color would so challenge narrative's dominance that it would shift the game of defamiliarization away from story and toward the image as a graphic. Color, rather than story, might govern the viewer's attention.

One goal was to make color in cinema more "familiar," or transparent. At the same time, Technicolor designs almost inevitably announce their novelty, engaging us in perceptual renewal.

Like all aesthetic works, the classical Hollywood feature is an artificial construct, but one designed to mask its construction. Neoformalism uses the concept of motivation to explain how works justify their devices. In a Hollywood movie, motivation tends to cover over the arbitrariness of devices, providing the viewer a rationale for accepting the formal choices. Roughly, an element within a classical Hollywood film can be motivated as necessary to the development of the story (compositional motivation), as plausible for the story world (realistic motivation), or as conventional for a particular genre (transtextual motivation). Neoformalism also allows room for devices that do not appear so easily justified, that call out as displays of technical virtuosity or spectacle. In this case, we may conclude that the element helps draw attention to the artfulness of the work (artistic motivation).[10]

One benefit of this typology is the way it highlights classical filmmakers' reasons for choosing color and color effects. A tightly crafted color design could show off a film's production values generally (artistic motivation), and genre might justify a degree of color stylization (transtextual motivation), but such rationales were tempered by a devotion to story development and plausibility. In the 1930s, justifying the use of color was especially important because it was an obtrusive device in a world of black-and-white filmmaking.

Finally, neoformalism contains an important historical implication for the study of film form. The approach holds that both functions and devices shift historically, but that devices are inclined to change more rapidly. The classical Hollywood cinema tended to sustain a set of narratively oriented functions for film style, but favored different devices at different times. In the 1930s, color was a new device, but the functions it performed were time tested. In instances where lighting, composition, or music might have highlighted a dramatic development, color could now be counted on as well. The task of neoformalist analysis is to unweave the patterns of function and motivation in the artwork. In this book, the approach gives us a consistent set of questions to ask as we chart historical change. Developments in technology and in Technicolor's market position conditioned the functions with which color was entrusted. Further, filmmakers were engaged in a historically bounded program of trial and error in which functions and motivations were tested and abandoned or revised according to reigning aesthetic norms.

By working from a neoformalist perspective, I in no way wish to deny the value of other frameworks that have been used to approach color in cinema. Questions of ideology, realism, and the split between spectacle and narrative are certainly worthwhile with regard to color, and this book will cover much shared ground.[11] My main concern, though, is to probe color's contribution to the moving image with new precision and to place it in a technological, industrial, and aesthetic context. A historically sensitive neoformalist approach offers tools and ideas specifically suited to the task of close analysis. Questions of how filmmakers have used color, of which kinds of palettes and designs came to prominence, or of how the components of color (hue, value, saturation) were controlled and varied for specific effects are well served by talking about devices, functions, and motivations.

This book will illustrate that the basic trajectory of Technicolor in the 1930s was toward integration and assimilation, toward the construction of norms for binding color to the tasks of style in the classical paradigm.[12] Though filmmakers worked quickly to develop a Technicolor style, the path to assimilation was neither direct nor easily traversed. As we will see, the earliest three-color films attempted to so load the device with functions that color became intrusive, and it was judged too strong a player among the elements of form. Yet this served a more proximate goal for Technicolor: it helped introduce the potentials of color to a reluctant industry. Similarly, color's generic range was in development during the 1930s. Though musicals (*The Goldwyn Follies*) and adventures (*The Adventures of Robin Hood*) formed an important strain of production, three-color was also tested in contemporary drama (*A Star Is Born*) and in rural, "outdoor" melodrama (*The Trail of the Lonesome Pine*). This was a decade of experiment and exploration, and the paths not followed can tell us much about the pressures that shaped film style in Hollywood.

The Prospect of Historical Color Analysis

Given the importance of color to cinema and the significance of Technicolor in shaping the norms of design, we might ask why the topic has received such scant attention. In fact, film scholars are not alone in more or less neglecting color's contribution to form. Art historians, particularly John Gage, have only recently sparked a contemporary dialogue about the problems and potentials of color. In the mid-1990s, Gage's groundbreaking volumes *Color and Culture* and *Color and Meaning* gave renewed attention to the historical determinants and characteristics of color in painting.

If we have lagged in studying color in the cinema's comparatively brief history, it may be partly because color itself is such a slippery subject and partly because we lack adequate methods for capturing the complexities of the moving image. This book is a study of Technicolor design, but I hope it is also a step toward meaningfully analyzing film color, an attempt to answer color's challenge.

In writing about color in art, it has become tradition to begin by acknowledging its elusiveness, its resistance to study. Joseph Albers opened his seminal volume *Interaction of Color* by proclaiming that color is "the most relative medium in art" and that "color deceives continually."[13] Similarly, in his foreword to Augusto Garau's treatment of color harmony, Rudolf Arnheim acknowledged that "the serious study of color, as compared with that of shape, faces almost insurmountable difficulties."[14] More recently, Charles A. Riley II began his investigation of color theory, *Color Codes,* with this apparently discouraging assessment:

> The first thing to realize about the study of color in our time is its uncanny ability to evade all attempts to codify it systematically. . . . Color behavior does not conform to one paradigm, chart, or episteme. The topic of color has become a watershed for thinking about models and about art that is created by systems simply because it is such a devourer of models and systems. It has attracted and ultimately confounded systematic innovators in philosophy and psychology, as well as writers, painters, and composers who attempt to use precompositional systems.[15]

Color has repeatedly proved one of the most challenging elements of art to theorists and historians. It throws up obstacles to description and to the uncovering of a system or logic of design. Yet writers like Gage, Albers, Arnheim, and Riley, to name a few, have found the challenge of color provocative and inspiring. The rewards of coming to terms with color far outweigh the difficulties of study.

Art historians and artists recognize several challenges to the detailed study of color. Albers identified two issues: "First it is hard, if not impossible, to remember distinct colors. . . . Second, the nomenclature of colors is most inadequate. Though there are innumerable colors—shades and tones—in daily vocabulary, there are only about thirty color names."[16] The imprecision of color memory and vocabulary is compounded by the fugitive nature of the object itself. Arnheim termed color "a capricious medium" and pointed out the "false testimony" of reproductions.[17]

The colors of original artworks are subject to deterioration and change. Finally, the sensual immediacy of color poses a particular challenge to the historian. Gage notes: "I may recognize from the style of the work that it belongs to a particular time which is not ours but how can I say the same for its colours? Is not red the same whenever and wherever it is seen?" To understand color historically, Gage concluded that he "had to look at artifacts and at the colour-language of the periods in question."[18] The task is stimulating. Gage's work repeatedly demonstrates that different historical eras mapped and understood color in strikingly different ways. Artists of Greek and Roman antiquity, for example, granted more prominence to value than hue; luminosity and luster carried more weight than the spectral identity of a color.[19] Our contemporary perspective, which emphasizes difference of hue, might fail to grasp artworks based on such a system. The historical analysis of color involves not only determining the artwork's original properties, but also ascertaining how the artist conceived of color and how that conception influenced the choices the artist could make.

Though movies are hardly as old as the paintings that Gage discusses, film scholars also have the opportunity for historical reconstruction of color choices and effects. In most cases for films of the 1930s, the original artwork, as presented at the time of its release, no longer exists, and what remains is a compromised form. The history of *Gone with the Wind* (1939) strikingly illustrates how precarious the color image can be and how changing aesthetics can influence a film's look. A victim of its own success, *Gone with the Wind* underwent a long line of reissues and rereleases, all of which sought to "improve" on earlier versions.[20] For this book I studied two noticeably different versions of the film: MGM's 1954 reissue, approved by producer David O. Selznick, and Warner Bros.' Technicolor restoration, released in 1998. Neither version can claim to recreate the colors of the 1939 original; each is a creature of its aesthetic context.

Richard May, Warner Bros.' vice president of film preservation, explained that each reissue attempted to increase the saturation and vividness of the production's color in order to keep up with audience expectations. If a contemporary audience were presented with a print that duplicated the 1939 version, he speculated, "I think they would see that absence of color and ask what we did to the picture."[21] For the 1954 version, in keeping with the then-current standards of spectacle, MGM released the film in "widescreen." Several key compositions were cropped, and projectionists masked the film so that it appeared to have a CinemaScope aspect ratio. The handling of color, though, in this version is not without merit. Robert Harris, the film restoration expert renowned for his work in color and large-format films (most famously *Lawrence of Arabia* and *Vertigo*) calls the 1954 version "the Rosetta stone for *Gone with the Wind*."[22] This version was processed to emphasize the design's rich, warm reds and browns. Scarlett's prayer dress in the opening scene, for instance, is reproduced in a sumptuous pearl white, very warm, with a soft near-yellowish cast. One effect of this printing choice is to accentuate the warm glow of simulated candlelight that Selznick had worked so hard to achieve in 1939. The fact that Selznick also supervised and approved this version of the film lends authority to its look.

The 1998 Technicolor reissue renders colors quite differently. This version was derived from a 1989 Eastmancolor restoration. May explained that the 1989 restoration team timed the new print to achieve good flesh tones and neutrals, and that the colors probably approximated those of the original scenes as staged before the Technicolor camera. Scarlett's dress, in that version, is a crisp, clean white. The aim, May suggests, was to create a print that would meet contemporary standards of color rendition and quality. The look clearly departed from the 1954 version and almost certainly was different from the 1939 original. In all, the colors are cooler and clearer, and perhaps they are truer to the original staged scenes. This technical polish raises questions, however, if we assume that *GWTW* was designed with the capacities of the 1939 Technicolor process in mind and that Selznick may have viewed that process as a creative tool to help stylize the film.

The 1989 restoration was fairly well received, but the 1998 Technicolor release met with harsh criticism. The film was meant to be a showcase for Technicolor's reintroduction of dye-transfer printing, a system that hadn't been used in the United States since the 1970s. Unfortunately, Technicolor distributed a set of reels with registration defects (errors in keeping the yellow, cyan, and magenta components properly lined up), and had to recall them.[23] Technicolor's president, Ron Jarvis, pointed the finger at Warner Bros. for relying on the 1989 restoration as a source, which "contaminates the color because you're now introducing another process: Eastmancolor."[24] Even the areas in which this version is said to excel can cast doubt on its accuracy. Jarvis touted Technicolor's new work by claiming that "the colors, the contrast, the blacks, the shadow detail, the lack of grain are big improvements over the '39 original."[25] Improvements, of course, amount to imposing current standards on the historical artifact, and they chip away at aesthetic credibility.

If technology stands between the historian and the film's original look, so too does culture. Hardly anyone was satisfied with the 1998 version, because it departed from expectations. Some critics complained that the colors were too intense, others that they were too muted.[26] The reactions said more about the variety of preconceptions of how *GWTW* should look than they did about the film itself. These preconceptions, though, were rarely grounded in history or in an understanding of color's status in a 1930s motion picture. Rather, critics measured the film against its reputation as a "Technicolor classic" and against their own previous viewing experience, likely limited to videos and prints from the 1970s and 1980s. Technicolor, for contemporary viewers, has come to mean bright, saturated, garish color. A historical reconstruction of the aesthetic context demonstrates that nothing could have been further from the truth during the 1930s.

The case of *GWTW* magnifies a historiographic issue that affects all fine-grained analyses of color film style.[27] This book is based on an examination of the best available materials, including nitrate studio prints. Even so, cultural, economic, and technological pressures continue to shape our contact with color. As in most historical practice, we must be aware of the bounds of our knowledge as we pursue our subject. Acknowledging obstacles need not mean giving in to them.

A full discussion of the kinds of prints that I studied, and their status with regard to color reproduction, is included as an appendix. Video, however, deserves special consideration here, since it is the viewing medium available to most readers. Indeed, standard-definition DVD and videotape are the primary media through which these works are experienced today. Unfortunately, standard video is a notoriously unreliable record, so it is important to understand exactly how its images differ from those of film. The relative poverty of image information in an NTSC (National Television System Committee) video image, as compared with that in a 35 mm print, has been widely recognized. One recent estimate suggests that 35 mm positive film presents color resolution equivalent to over 2,000 video scan lines, whereas domestic video can offer a maximum of 525 lines.[28]

Video introduces particular problems for color. Color film is a subtractive medium; that is, color is generated by placing a filter (the film) before a white light source. Video, by contrast, uses additive color. In a typical CRT (cathode-ray tube) television set, three electron guns scan discrete red, blue, and green phosphors that line the inside of a video monitor's screen. This mosaic of phosphors generates color by adding together various quantities of these primaries. Yellow, for example, is created by the juxtaposition of green and red phosphors.[29] Look closely at your television and you will see the separate elements that, at a greater distance, optically mix to form the hue. While televisions can yield highly saturated primaries by activating one set of phosphors, they have trouble rendering very saturated secondary colors like cyan, magenta, and, especially, yellow.[30] Put simply, film reproduces a far greater range of colors than video.[31] Video also has trouble producing hard separation between colors. Saturated reds, especially, can appear to bleed over the boundaries of the object that carries them. Similarly, the boundaries between adjacent hues may seem to vibrate. My experience has been that video versions of Technicolor films tend to average colors, flattening out the finer distinctions of value and saturation in closely related hues.

A brief example can illustrate how colors translate from print to video. Consider a single frame from the Munchkin sequence in *The Wizard of Oz* (1939). The image frames two figures in highly contrasting costumes. At the left stands a man in a high-value, saturated Fuchsia Purple waistcoat over a shirt with white and Stratosphere blue-gray stripes, and a blue-gray cummerbund with a pure Lemon Drop yellow daffodil (the capitalized terms refer to official Pantone colors, described below).[32] The woman next to him wears a mid-value Cobalt blue blouse with a dark Deep Lake blue-green hat. She holds a piece of Flame Scarlet ribbon.[33] On the video monitor, these colors can shift considerably.[34] When color and tint controls are set in the middle position (which renders good flesh tones), the man's waistcoat appears soft Violet, losing its strong red-purple bias. The woman's blouse and hat, contrasting blues in the print, take on a uniformly soft, Capri blue-green appearance. The purer colors of the Flame Scarlet ribbon and the Lemon Drop yellow flower fare better at this setting. Increasing the tint and color controls to near maximum brings the man's coat closer to Fuchsia Purple and restores some of the contrast between the woman's hat and blouse. The yellow flower, on the other hand, takes on a distinctly green cast, and the red ribbon gains saturation to the point of bleeding and obscuring details on its surface. Flesh tones become orange.

The Munchkin sequence, with its dynamic play of color, is an unforgiving test for video, but this is a general problem for those of us analyzing color in film. Careful manipulation of tint and hue controls can render an image that roughly approximates some of the key colors in a scene, but other colors are likely to be compromised. Video transfers of Technicolor films provide only an approximate sense of color design, of how color was generally handled in a production. They are certainly useful for teaching and learning about films that are otherwise impossible to screen, and for checking composition, editing, and camera movement. Indeed, I hope that this book will motivate readers to look at these films afresh, and video allows that. However, viewers should be aware that video and film provide distinct experiences of color.

Given the vagaries of film color, we are fortunate that 1930s Hollywood saw a thriving discourse on the subject. Nineteen-thirties film artists' ideas about color are undeniably less alien to us than, say, the color concepts of Greek and Roman antiquity explored by John Gage. Yet as the case of *GWTW* suggests, the historical procedure is much the same. Contextual research—an understanding of the color language of the time—can help restore color's historical specificity. The 1930s were a watershed because color was so openly and thoroughly debated. The industry's trade and technical presses provided a forum for color consultants, directors, cinematographers, and critics to discuss the proper and effective uses of color in film. This discourse on aesthetics, shaped by technological and industrial concerns, provides the foundation for a historically sensitive analysis. We can anchor our viewing in the terms by which the filmmakers themselves understood their engagement with color. Aesthetic discourse provides a map to help navigate the uncertainties of color reproduction.

Color Concepts and a Vocabulary for Analysis

Challenges of color memory and notation affect all considerations of color in visual culture, but confronting them opens up a vastly fascinating realm of study. Human memory is notoriously poor when it comes to color, and in everyday use, our color categories are rather crude. Prevailing estimates are that humans can distinguish between seven and ten million colors.[35] However, good observers can identify only around thirty colors when they are not given a reference standard for comparison, and our everyday color vocabulary contains about ten general terms.[36] Our ability to recall colors also seems relatively unreliable. Cognitive research suggests that color attributes are harder to remember, or retrieve, than other characteristics of an object.[37] Shapes tend to stick better in our memories, probably because color information is not required for many categorical or recognition judgments.[38] Remembered colors generally tend to be brighter and more saturated than those in the original stimulus, and they gravitate toward the colors most typical for the object in question.[39] Again, shape takes precedence over color.[40]

The facts compel us to find a more precise way of talking about color. We need tools to help us retain, describe, and communicate some very complex perceptual material. Since 1905, when Albert Munsell first published *A Color Notation* to combat "the poverty of color language," modern industry has developed a range of color notation systems.[41] Some, like Munsell's, specify colors by alphanumeric codes, which, though precise, are rather unwieldy for capturing the intricacies of a Technicolor composition. Color names, on the other hand, tend to be vaguely defined and fail to draw clear distinctions between closely related colors. Film analysis calls for a middle ground, a method of designating colors with precision while retaining some of the legibility of color language.

To specify important colors in the analyses that follow, I rely on names from *The Pantone Book of Color*. The Pantone Matching System was developed in 1963 to specify gradations of printer's ink. To serve other fields, such as fashion, industrial, interior and set design, the company developed the Pantone Professional Color System, consisting of 1,225 color standards.[42] The *Pantone Book of Color* collects 1,024 of these colors and identifies them by their Pantone number and a unique color name. The names draw on common descriptive language, and are designed to be easily visualized by the reader. Moreover, they allow the particularly obsessive among us to look the color up in a Pantone Professional Color System publication.[43] In this text, names from the *Pantone Book of Color* are capitalized. When it has been necessary to supplement the Pantone names with conventional color terms, those terms have not been capitalized. A list of the Pantone numbers that correspond to the color names is provided as an appendix.

Admittedly, this is an imperfect solution. Printed inks are more limited than even video in the range of hues they can reproduce, and the gamut of colors in a Technicolor film would certainly overwhelm the list of Pantone standards.[44] Still, the Pantone system significantly increases our descriptive vocabulary. It enables distinctions to be made between relatively similar colors, and it provides a way to compare colors as they appear across a film. The Pantone standards certainly do not guarantee the definitive identification of a film's original colors. Nonetheless, they do offer a somewhat higher level of descriptive precision. Where there is dispute about a particular color, at least the Pantone names provide a concrete reference about which to argue.

Analyzing color is not simply a matter of naming hues; we can reach a far greater understanding by considering the various components of colors and the relationships between them. Here, the ideas and terminology of conventional color theory help tremendously.[45] Technicolor designers, particularly Natalie Kalmus, referred to traditional color theories when defending and explaining their aesthetic, and even a cursory overview of color theory provides insight into how filmmakers control and systematize color. Since the rest of this book is invested in color analysis, we should familiarize ourselves with this concept set. A brief discussion will illustrate the leverage that color theory grants us for analyzing cinema.

Color is generally understood to have three characteristics, formalized by the widely adopted Munsell color system as hue, value, and chroma (or saturation).[46] These variables establish three dimensions of color relationships. Hue refers to a color's characteristic wavelength as designated by a common color name, such as red, blue, green, or yellow. The lightness or darkness of a color is its value: the addition of white generates a higher value, or tint, while black decreases value to create a shade. Saturation indicates the purity or intensity of a given color. Often, this quality is described in terms of the amount of gray in a given hue. Roughly, colors can be said to converge or contrast according to variations in these three qualities. Moreover, these variables are interrelated. For example, different hues reach maximal saturation at different values.[47] Yellow is most saturated at a very high level of lightness and quickly loses purity when it is darkened—a quality that led Johannes Itten to dub it "the most luminous of colors."[48] Purple and blue, on the other hand, become most saturated at low values. Differences in hue can be accentuated by attendant contrasts of saturation and value. These characteristics were important to Technicolor designs that sought to maximize contrasts of saturation and value around a scene's major players.

The most common way of representing relationships among hues is a color wheel. There are various methods of arranging color wheels, but the dominant Western tradition uses the "painter's" or "pigment" primaries of red, blue, and yellow.[49] A circle of twelve hues based on these primaries has been taken up as standard in works as diverse as Johannes Itten's *Art of Color* (1973), *The Pantone Book of Color* (1990), Faber Birren's *Principles of Color* (1969), and Walter Sargent's popular color primer of the 1920s and 1930s, *The Enjoyment and Use of Color*. Hollywood color designers also relied on the system, and when commentators within the industry discussed specific color relationships, they derived their observations from this basic arrangement.[50]

This ordering of hues generates the familiar color terms. The primaries are so called because they are not mixtures of other hues, and they can combine to form all other colors on the circle.[51] They mix to form the three secondary colors: green, orange, and purple. Mixtures of primaries and secondaries render the tertiary colors: yellowish green, green-blue, yellow-orange, and so forth. Complementary colors are those set directly opposite each other on the wheel. When juxtaposed, complementaries present a maximal contrast of hue, and when mixed, theoretically, they should create a neutral gray because, together, they combine all three primaries.[52] Finally, the wheel may be split down the middle into warm and cool colors, with red-orange and blue-green as the respective poles. Generally, and this is a central assumption in Technicolor design, warm colors are held to advance, appear nearer the viewer, or be active, whereas cool colors are said to recede, appear more distant, or be passive.[53]

These terms and ideas are probably already familiar to the reader as basic principles. Yet even this rudimentary vocabulary helps us discuss color style with some precision. For example, Natalie Kalmus, head of Technicolor's Color Advisory Service, recommended designs that centered maximal color contrast on the key narrative elements of a scene. Most often, this meant placing warm accents against cool backgrounds, but the warm-cool opposition left considerable room for variation. A significant development in Technicolor design involved a shift in the kinds of color contrasts that were favored. As Chapters 2 and 3 illustrate, early productions in three-color Technicolor employed broad palettes that consistently emphasized bold contrasts of hue. As filmmakers sought to subordinate color more fully, and to develop a restrained mode of design (considered in Chapters 4 and 5), they underplayed differences between hues and began to emphasize gradations of value and saturation. Broadly, we can specify a change of color style by tracking the set of color variables that designers chose to take up for contrast.

In conventional color theory, questions of how colors behave in combination are dealt with through the concept of harmony. The canonical ideas of color harmony, based on the red, blue, and yellow primaries, trace back to the work of French chemist Michel-Eugène Chevreul, who published *De la loi du contraste simultané des couleurs et de l'assortiment des objets colorés* (*The Principles of Harmony and Contrast of Colours*) in 1839.[54] Chevreul observed that complementaries seem to reinforce each other, each making the other appear more brilliant.[55] Based on his findings, he specified the types of color combinations that resulted in "agreeable impressions."[56] These combinations, or harmonies, were grounded in either closely related or strongly contrasting colors. Chevreul's assumptions inform long-held conventions of color harmony.

For a concise summary of conventional color harmonies, we can turn to Paul Zelanski and Mary Pat Fisher's primer for artists, *Color*.[57] They describe traditional color schemes, based on similar or dissimilar hues, which have generally been held to produce satisfactory combinations. Arrangements that depend on closely related colors include monochromatic and analogous schemes. While monochromatic combinations employ single hues with variations of saturation and value (sometimes broken up by neutrals and browns), analogous schemes are built out of hues lying next to each other on the color circle.[58] This definition of analogy depends on the number of divisions on a color circle, but it remains a useful way to characterize varied yet relatively low-contrast combinations.[59] Chevreul offered another possibility for low-contrast harmony, suggesting that a common tint injected into an array of colors would give the impression that they were viewed "through a slightly coloured glass."[60] Artists can also reduce contrast by toning down colors or reducing their saturation.

It becomes apparent in Technicolor design that low-contrast options such as these were generally preferred as a means for subordinating color. Natalie Kalmus warned against a "super-abundance" of color and recommended neutrals to provide a "foil for color," ideas that will be discussed in Chapter 2.[61] These prescriptions point toward a conception of harmony as the avoidance of high contrast. By the same token, the practice of repeating similar colors to coordinate costumes and other mise-en-scène elements draws on a definition of harmony that favors combinations of like colors. As we will see, analogous color schemes proved particularly important to the restrained mode of design.

Yet Chevreul famously proclaimed: "In the harmony of contrasts, the complementary assortment is superior to every other."[62] The equation of successful combinations with a balance of dissimilar colors forms an equally important trend in thought about harmony. Standard schemes based on high contrast include complementary, split-complementary, and triad combinations. Complementary schemes draw on hues directly opposite each other on a color circle. Like Chevreul, Zelanski and Fisher note the power of this combination. Complementary hues "hold each other in equilibrium" while they "intensify each other's appearance."[63] Equally powerful are triad combinations, which array hues lying equidistant on the circle: red, blue, and yellow, for example.

Contrasting harmony assumes that colors work well together if their combination presents a balance of the primaries. Johannes Itten suggested, "The idea of color harmony is to discover the strongest effects by correct choice of antithesis."[64] Toward this end, he laid out possible "color chords," combinations of two to five colors on the color wheel (including complementaries and triads), which, by presenting elements of all three primaries, could generate "harmonic equilibrium."[65] Thinking along similar lines, but from the perspective of Gestalt psychology, Rudolf Arnheim wrote that the "completion attained by complementarity" involves "not only maximal contrast but also mutual neutralization."[66] Arnheim argued that "the eye spontaneously seeks out and links complementary colors" and that painters could connect portions of a painting via this response.[67] Both authors were writing after the era of Technicolor design. However, in developing their observations from the premises of the red-blue-yellow color circle, Arnheim and Itten articulated ideas about the power of complementarity that were inherited from Chevreul and that held some force for Technicolor designers as well.

In the main, Technicolor features of the 1930s favor harmonies of similar colors and depend on general contrasts of warm and cool, light and dark, or of a hue against a neutral, to offset key areas. In the restrained mode especially, the careful balancing of primaries does not appear to be an operative principle of harmony. When Kalmus discussed complementary contrast, she did so as evidence that designers must practice restraint.[68] Still, as we will see, filmmakers did draw on complementaries, triads, or other "color chords" for momentary, punctual effects. After 1938, combinations of contrasting hues become particularly important. *The Adventures of Robin Hood* (1938), a film with a highly dynamic color design, relies more heavily on complementaries and triads as tools for guiding attention and delivering graphic flourishes. Chapter 6 suggests that many choices in this film follow from the notion that harmony could be achieved through a balance of chromatic contrasts. Both conceptions of harmony, whether founded on combinations of similar colors or strong contrasts, advance our grasp of color design in the cinema.

As might be expected, the notion that there are rules of color harmony has been severely criticized and, more or less, rejected by artists and scholars.[69] I must, therefore, emphasize that my intention is not to resurrect an embattled theory of absolute harmony. Rather, I hope to introduce a set of terms that seem useful for describing color motion pictures and to indicate some general conventions that inform Technicolor design. In fact, as the critics of color systems might expect, Technicolor designs rarely embody textbook principles. A hallmark of Technicolor design as it developed in the 1930s was that it did not betray a rigid or fixed system of harmony. If anything, the aesthetic draws on conventional ideas of harmony to fashion rather broad and flexible guidelines. Still, traditional color ideas offer a way to begin untangling the guiding principles of color design in Hollywood cinema.

Case Studies and Modes of Design

I argue that as filmmakers began to integrate color into their repertoire during the 1930s, they worked through a series of related modes of design. Each mode was a flexible set of conventions for handling color, conditioned by industrial, technological, and aesthetic currents. I identified these modes by closely studying all available Technicolor features produced during the period, being guided by contemporaneous aesthetic discourse. The reader will find references to diverse films of the decade, including *Ramona* (1936), *The Garden of Allah* (1936), *God's Country and the Woman* (1937), *Wings of the Morning* (1937), *Vogues of 1938* (1937), *Jesse James* (1939), *The Private Lives of Elizabeth and Essex* (1939), and, of course, *The Wizard of Oz* (1939), but this book is structured around close analyses of seven case studies. By this method I hope to rectify the overly general view of Technicolor that histories have thus far offered. While film scholars have provided technological surveys and broad-spectrum discussions of style, we have generally shied from the problems of how color is handled moment by moment, what specific duties it serves with respect to narrative, and how it helps shape visual perception. Only case studies, supported by extensive background viewing, can afford the opportunity to examine precise details of color style and to consider how color develops across films in their entirety.[70]

The selected case studies represent both key aesthetic and technological turning points in the 1930s and the norms of more routine productions. Chapters 2 and 3 examine the first three-color short, *La Cucaracha* (1934), and the first feature, *Becky Sharp* (1935). These prototype films, produced in close cooperation with Technicolor, demonstrate and test the possibilities of three-color technology. Robert Edmond Jones, color designer for *La Cucaracha*, Rouben Mamoulian, director of *Becky Sharp*, and Natalie Kalmus argued for an aesthetic that would make color an integral and expressive element of film style. These demonstration films employ color in particularly forceful ways, displaying the process's chromatic range and drawing attention to its potential for underscoring drama. They are films inspired by a fleeting belief that color would usher in a bold new form of cinema.

After 1935, Technicolor designers searched for a more conciliatory aesthetic, one that would help color cooperate with other stylistic devices. The result was the restrained mode, a subtle and nuanced approach to color that assisted Technicolor in developing a market with the major studios. The driving goal was to make Technicolor production practices, and color itself, approach the standards of black-and-white filmmaking. Chapter 4 details how cinematographers attempted to handle the technological constraints of three-color and how color designers sought to subordinate color. The restrained mode of design reduced hue contrast in favor of an emphasis on tone and value. *The Trail of the Lonesome Pine* (1936), the first major-studio three-color feature, well illustrates how the restrained mode helped open a space for color in classical Hollywood style. Chapter 5 examines how restraint informs two markedly different films, Selznick International's drama *A Star Is Born* (1937) and Samuel Goldwyn's musical comedy *The Goldwyn Follies* (1938). These productions stretch the limits placed on color and build on its capacity for amplifying drama without veering far from the ideals of tasteful moderation. At its best, the restrained palette was a finely tuned instrument, capable of directing attention and underscoring action with minute adjustments.

Hollywood's color landscape shifted once again in 1938 when Warner Bros. used three-color for their top-budgeted film, *The Adventures of Robin Hood.* Increasing commercial acceptance of Technicolor corresponded with a loosening of restraint. Chapter 6 explores *Robin Hood*'s premiere of the assertive mode of design. The palette is unshackled, reinstating hue as the key player in color design. But the assertive mode is not a simple reversion to the demonstrations of *Becky Sharp* or *La Cucaracha.* Rather, *Robin Hood* deftly handles a rich mosaic of color by extending and broadening methods founded in the restrained mode. The sheer variety of color may overwhelm some of Technicolor's subtler effects, but *Robin Hood* shifts the way color functions across the film, allowing both bold display and nimble underscoring. Spurred by the film's ornate complexity, this chapter, more than any other, delves into the fine grain of color's contribution to the cinema.

My final case study is of *Gone with the Wind,* perhaps the most popular and successful classical Hollywood Technicolor feature. Selznick's 1939 production did not inaugurate a new mode of design; rather it was something of a laboratory for exploring the possibilities of Technicolor's new film stock. Chapter 7 examines how *GWTW* took advantage of technological advances to produce a higher cooperation between color and the tonal elements of light and shadow. *GWTW* was both the culmination of the 1930s trend of emulating black-and-white cinematography in color and an audacious experiment in color cinema. By pushing the process's limits for handling low-key lighting and by exploiting new possibilities of precise facial modeling, the cinematographers of *GWTW* helped close the distance between monochrome and Technicolor style. At the same time, they manipulated color temperature and employed colored lighting to fundamentally extend color's expressive reach.

The concluding chapter synthesizes observations about the nature of color in the classical style and looks beyond the 1930s. To a large extent, the 1930s set the terms under which Hollywood would engage with color. Modes of the 1930s were sedimentary, each becoming a viable option for films of the '40s. The restrained and assertive modes lived on, but rather than distinct styles, they formed loose bodies of conventions and guidelines that filmmakers played with. The lessons and techniques of Technicolor design didn't fade with the end of the studio era. The advent of digital technologies for manipulating color has once again brought the problems of color design to the surface. I end this book by suggesting how its methods and arguments can shed light on the most recent developments in color technology. My hope is that this work will bring color's contribution to the moving image within our reach, making tangible what has previously been only sensed.

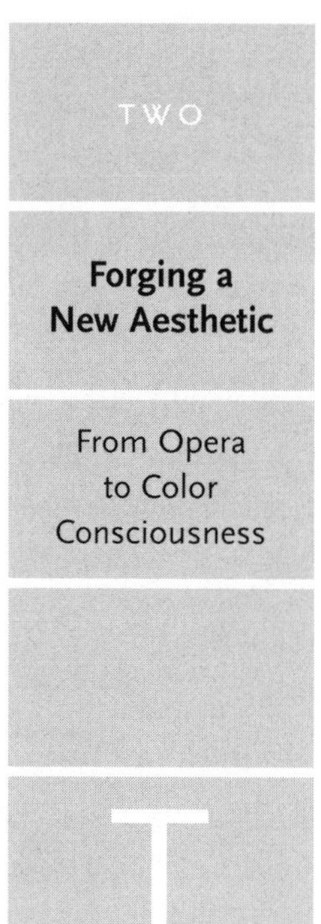

TWO

Forging a New Aesthetic

From Opera to Color Consciousness

The first three-color films, and early arguments about color aesthetics, trumpeted color to the Hollywood studios. The first live-action three-color short, *La Cucaracha,* and the first feature, *Becky Sharp* (considered in the next chapter), demonstrated color's formal possibilities to a skeptical industry by way of an aesthetic that I call the demonstration mode of color design. As prototypes, they used color forcefully, displaying three-color's chromatic range and drawing attention to its potential for underscoring drama. In retrospect, it seems inevitable that this approach would pass from favor quickly. The very goal of demonstrating color style is ultimately at odds with the famously unobtrusive classical Hollywood form. Nonetheless, the demonstration mode and the views that supported it are fascinating as both foundational and eccentric ways of thinking about and using color. Moreover, they played a critical commercial role for Technicolor in winning the interest of studios, even if not the popular audience.

Production and discourse formed two fronts of a single corporate strategy to showcase the new process. In their writings, Robert Edmond Jones, color designer for *La Cucaracha,* and Natalie Kalmus, head of the Technicolor Color Advisory Service, argued for an aesthetic that would make color an integral and expressive element. Their discussions in the trade press constituted a unified view of color that framed the terms under which filmmakers would work with Technicolor. The theories of Kalmus, Jones, and other commentators advocated for a bold vision of color as the major device of film form. *La Cucaracha* and *Becky Sharp* give us the chance to see this aspiration in action.

The Technology and Development of Three-Color Technicolor

Hollywood color aesthetics were formed in the shadow of Technicolor's earlier processes. Before turning to questions of color design, we should consider three-color's development and the process's technological basis. Three-color Technicolor was the company's fourth process. The previous three systems had been based on two color components, and they had met with varying success.[1] After the failure of additive Technicolor, the company developed a subtractive system. Red-orange and blue-green positives were cemented back-to-back to create a single print that combined colors before they reached the screen.[2] The cement-positive process was introduced in 1922, and it found limited application until 1928, most famously in Douglas Fairbanks's *Black Pirate* (1926). Technicolor brought two-color dye-transfer printing to the market in 1928. In this last version of two-color, engineers printed both colored images onto a single piece of release stock, thus solving the problems caused by the cemented prints buckling and drifting out of focus.[3] Two-color dye transfer, the process most commonly referred to as two-color, served Technicolor well during the early sound era, 1929–1931, but its novelty quickly declined. Twenty-eight Technicolor features were produced between 1929 and 1931, but only four were produced in 1932 and 1933, the last being Warner Bros.' *Mystery of the Wax Museum*.[4]

Color rendition by the two-color processes was necessarily a compromise between the available blue-green and red-orange. According to James Arthur Ball, who engineered the three-color camera, Technicolor had always considered these earlier processes to be preliminary and transitional:

> In the earliest days of Technicolor development we recognized that the ultimate goal . . . must be a process that would add a full scale of color reproduction to existing black-and-white product without subtracting from any of its desirable qualities, without imposing complications upon theater projection conditions, and with a minimum of added burden in the cost of photography and in the cost of prints.[5]

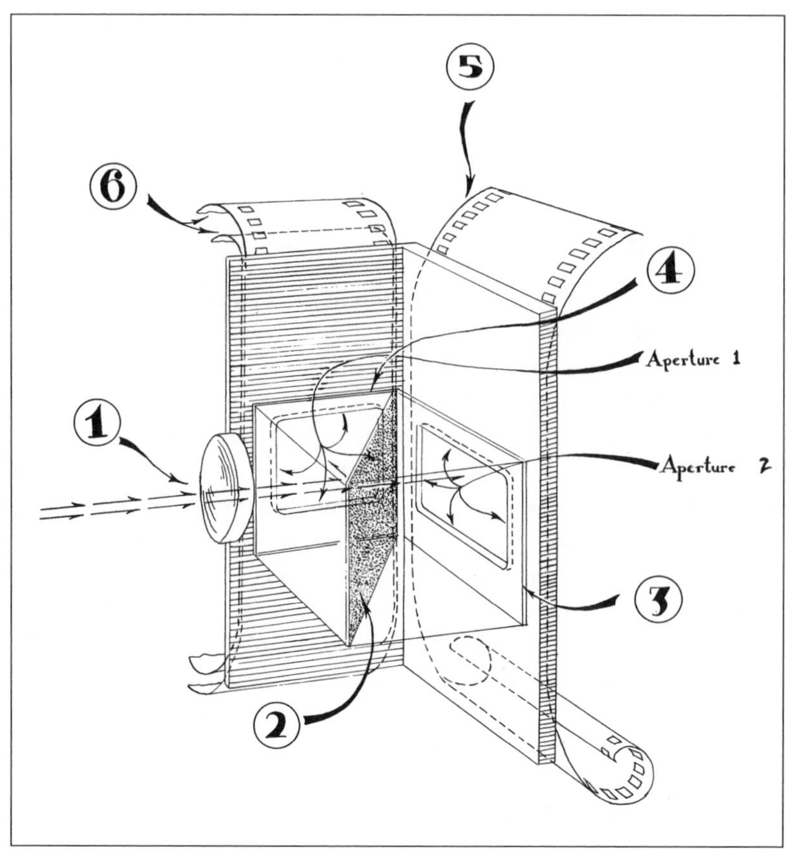

2.1. Diagram of the path of light within the three-color camera. Courtesy of Photofest.

As Ball explained it, each process offered a set of technical solutions upon which the next could build. Ball solved the final major problem, that of adding a third color component to complete the range of reproduction, in May 1932 with the completion of the three-color camera.[6]

Three-color Technicolor was a mechanically complex answer to the question of full-color cinema. Even a brief overview of the process helps us grasp its intricacies and how the elaborate system would influence film form. The three-color camera exposed three negatives, each registering a different portion of the spectrum. A prism-and-mirror combination behind the lens split the incoming light between two apertures (Figure 2.1). One-third of the beam passed directly through the prism and a green filter to expose a strip of panchromatic film with green light. The other two-thirds of the beam was deflected ninety degrees to expose a blue and red bipack of films, placed emulsion to emulsion. This light first passed through a magenta filter, which absorbed green light. Then the light exposed a blue-sensitive stock that was also equipped with an orange-red filter layer. The remaining light reached the second part of the bipack and generated the red negative.[7]

Each negative was then optically printed onto a special stock carrying a thick layer of emulsion that would harden where it was exposed. When the soft, unexposed emulsion was washed away, it would leave a gelatin relief image represented as a range of peaks and valleys of that color record. This was the matrix stock, and it had been developed as part of the two-color dye-transfer process.[8] The matrices performed like rubber stamps in transferring a color image to the release stock, known as the blank. Each matrix positive was saturated with a subtractive primary dye corresponding to the color complementary to that registered by the negative. In other words, the matrix made from the red negative would carry cyan dye; the green negative, magenta dye; and the blue negative, yellow.[9]

Prints were then made on an elaborate contact printer, or transfer machine. After traveling through a dye tank, the matrix came into contact with the blank on a 206-foot pin belt.[10] The blank was pressed down onto the matrix in a heated pathway for nearly a minute, after which the two were peeled apart and the blank was dried.[11] A system of nineteen water jets placed between the dye tank and the point of contact served to wash the dye away to a specified density. This wash-back mechanism was an essential strength of dye transfer since it allowed for the precise and independent manipulation of each color's density and contrast, a level of control that has only recently been regained by way of digital technology.[12] The order of the color transfer was yellow, cyan, and magenta.[13] Before applying the colors, the blank was pretreated with a halftone exposure, or gray ghost, generated from the green record. This black-and-white image, often referred to as the "key image," served to improve the shadow detail and contrast and to increase the picture's apparent sharpness.[14]

The three-color dye-transfer process would dominate color film production in Hollywood until the 1950s. In 1932, however, Technicolor's president, Herbert Kalmus, faced the problem of enticing a doubting industry to reconsider color production. According to Kalmus, because it would take some time to build enough three-color cameras and convert the plant to the new process, and because producers were unwilling to invest in the untested system, Technicolor first turned to animation.[15] In fact, three-color animation did not require a fully functional three-color camera. Rather, the animation cels were filmed using the successive exposure of frames through filters of red, green, and blue onto a single roll of black-and-white film. A step printer could then derive the three matrices.[16] Kalmus found a customer in Walt Disney, who entered into a two-year exclusive contract for three-color animation, and premiered the process in the Oscar-winning short *Flowers and Trees* late in 1932.

Disney's *Silly Symphonies* series provided a platform for promoting three-color to the industry and the public. Kalmus recalled using the animated shorts to persuade producers of Technicolor's potential for features.

> Producers were willing to admit they had been wrong about color cartoons now that the color cartoons were being held over for weeks, or even months and earning several times their costs, but they still began every conversation about color in feature films with the question of costs.
>
> I liked to confound them with the following reply. "Do you remember the huge rainbow in Disney's *Funny Little Bunnies?* Do you remember the bunnies drawing the colors of the rainbow into their pails and splashing their paints on the Easter eggs? Don't you agree that it was marvelous entertainment? Now I will ask you this: How much more did it cost Mr. Disney to produce that entertainment than it would have in black and white?" The answer, of course, was that it could not have been done in black-and-white at any cost.[17]

Rather than prove that color could enhance conventional techniques, Kalmus positioned it as something entirely new, a fundamental advance beyond the possibilities of black-and-white. This idealist rhetoric had aesthetic implications for the first live-action three-color productions.

Merian C. Cooper, former production chief of RKO, and millionaire financier John Hay (Jock) Whitney took up the cause of three-color feature production. Whitney, whose family fortune originated in New York's street railway system, had been interested in investing in motion pictures, and saw Technicolor as a worthwhile venture. In early 1932 he and his cousin Cornelius Vanderbilt Whitney purchased a block of Technicolor stock, generating $180,000 in cash for the company's expansion and securing the Whitneys an estimated 15 percent interest in Technicolor.[18] In the spring of 1933, Cooper and Whitney formed Pioneer Pictures, and in

August 1934 they signed a contract to produce eight Technicolor features, to be distributed by RKO.[19]

With the formation of Pioneer Pictures, Whitney and Cooper set out to bring live-action three-color to the theatrical market. Though feature production was the company's goal, it would be faster and less expensive to first produce a short subject. According to Herbert Kalmus, Pioneer's decision to make *La Cucaracha* was propelled by lingering questions about the process's color rendition and makeup requirements. Specifically, the producers wanted to know whether a "dark-haired actress with olive complexion" would "photograph attractively against light backgrounds," or whether a blonde "would virtually disappear against the stronger colors."[20] The two-reel short was a low-risk way for Pioneer and Technicolor to gain experience with studio production.

La Cucaracha became a prototype for color filmmaking. Kalmus described it as "a very practical and complete test of the process."[21] At a cost of $65,000, the film was relatively expensive for a short subject, but it still managed to gross a reported $250,000.[22] Given Whitney's financial interest in Technicolor, the profitability of *La Cucaracha* itself was probably a secondary concern. More importantly, the film could promote the new technology to the industry and boost the value of his stock. In this respect, the production was successful. It garnered Technicolor positive attention, culminating in an Oscar for best comedy short subject at the 1934 Academy Awards.

Robert Edmond Jones and Operatic Color

La Cucaracha is not simply a technical demonstration. The film is also an experiment in color aesthetics, in making color support narrative development and in organizing it for pictorial effects. Whitney, Cooper, and producer Kenneth Macgowan, hired the famous Broadway designer Robert Edmond Jones as color designer at $1,000 a week.[23] Jones claimed that black-and-white films had never interested him, but with three-color Technicolor, "something living had been brought into the world that was not there before."[24] In his stage designs, Jones championed assertive color. He proclaimed, for instance, to a critic for *Theatre Arts Monthly* that "color is emotion."[25] The prospect of color lured Jones to Pioneer, and *La Cucaracha* presented him with an opportunity to experiment with Technicolor.

In his articles, which verge on idealistic rants, Jones continually stressed color's implications for drama. He declared to the *New York Times* that with Technicolor, "We are standing on the threshold of a thrilling adventure into a new form of dramatic art."

> Color on the screen is not only more natural than black-and-white, it is more stimulating, more exciting, more dramatic. Color, properly selected and composed, can immeasurably enhance the dramatic value of the screen story. Here is the dynamic force that lies behind this extraordinary new invention. The promise that color holds out to the producers of motion pictures is that their films (in the proper hands) may become not only more beautiful but incomparably more powerful than ever before.[26]

Jones was justifying the employment of color designers ("the proper hands") to integrate color and drama correctly, to make color an essential component of film production rather than an added ornament.

Jones captured the nature of color's relationship with narrative through an analogy to opera. In "A Revolution in the Movies," an article for *Vanity Fair,* Jones asserted: "As a matter of fact, the difference between a black-and-white film and a Technicolor film is very like the difference between a play and an opera."

> Color on the screen, shifting, flowing from sequence to sequence—*largo, allegro, fortissimo, scherzo, grave*—is an orchestral, symphonic accompaniment to the melody of the drama. Color enlarges the drama, supports it, enhances it, actually impels it; becomes an organic part of it, just as Wagner's music becomes an organic part of the great emotional surge of the love motif of *Tristan*. . . .
>
> . . . A marvelous new instrument is given us, by means of which we may combine the beauty of painting and the emotional flow of music. This instrument must be *played upon.*[27]

In his vision, design could organize color across a film like a score that accompanies and accentuates the action. Jones's notion of color as an orchestral accompaniment presumes a high level of stylization; beyond verisimilitude, color must be manipulated, "flowing from sequence to sequence just as music flows from movement to movement."[28] The analogy to Wagner suggests that color should be patterned to form motifs and that it should act as a register for emotion: "Color on the screen—mobile color, flowing color—is really a kind of visual music."[29]

In Jones's discussions and in his experiments, he was rather literal about the expressive powers of color. For example, when describing color's "significance," Jones rehearses a set of extremely broad cultural conventions: "Light bright colors make us feel gay. Dark somber colors make us feel sad. We see red; we get the blues . . . we become purple with rage; green with envy."[30] If his analogy to opera gives the impression that color should be richly textured and delicately varied, Jones's ideas about color and emotion suggest an approach of much less nuance or intricacy. *Popular Science* described a series of tests Jones made using "the technique he had built up in the theater—the throwing of 'mood lights.' "[31] Changes in colored illumination corresponded to precise changes in the mood or emotion of the scene:

> At first the actress was enveloped in cold, tragic blue. This drab color literally painted her in gloom as she contemplated the loss of her lover. Then she heard footsteps and turned expectantly, hoping for his return. As she smiled the screen changed to the colors of dawn, her face flooded with rose and yellow.[32]

In another test, John Barrymore read the ghost scene from *Hamlet.* At first, blue moonlight modeled the actor's face, then when his father's ghost appeared, greenish blue lights "painted Barrymore's face with a forbidding fear."[33]

Through tinted lighting, Jones sought a one-to-one correspondence of color and emotion. The diegetic motivation (moonlight, dawn) for this light is a thin contrivance for the expressive, "emotional" effect. Admittedly, these were only tests; they were not subject to the limitations and demands of style in a feature-length film. Yet in them and in *La Cucaracha,* Jones exercised a peculiarly obvious approach to color. His solution to the challenge of blending color with story and drama was to foreground color and link it in a mechanistic manner to discrete developments in the scene. In a sense, this conception is equivalent to the practice of "mickey mousing" in a musical score, in which a sound directly mimics an on-screen action. Color is wholly redundant given the already broad, pronounced emotional shifts. Jones envisioned an operatic role for color, but he didn't have on hand a system that could codify hues and emotional states with much complexity or subtlety. If anything, his tests recalled the motivations for tinting and toning during the silent era.

Though bizarre in its literalness, Jones's approach to color was not entirely idiosyncratic. In fact, it conformed to the tenor of discussions about color aesthetics in the professional press. The relationship of color to drama was at the forefront of most attempts to conceive of a new Technicolor style. For instance, one of the earliest attempts to lay the groundwork for discussing norms of three-color design was offered by Henri Coulon in the May 1934 issue of *American Cinematographer.* Coulon acknowledged that the "advent" of Robert Edmond Jones "portends a greatly increased interest in the artistic use of color by the industry," and he set out to offer advice about properly employing color. According to Coulon, previous two-color films exhibited "a tendency to overdo with splotches of irrelated colors in order to make a visual flash—this is neither good art or good judgment and will not prevail when the correct use of color is understood."[34] In addressing the problem, Coulon recommended his own vaguely defined system for balancing the "vibratory intensities" of colors to create visual harmony.[35] He also invoked the musical analogy to explain that color must be in accord with a scene's expressive requirements: "By correctly relating color to mood, action and plot, and by using less color, vast improvements may be accomplished. Color, in itself, has vast potential advantages for the screen and through its proper use can be as dynamic and effective in conveying the message of the picture as sound or music."[36]

The idea that style should support drama is common enough in professional and technical journals. With color, though, the most interesting point of discussion was *how* it could be brought to serve such narrative functions. A few months after Coulon's piece, *American Cinematographer* ran an essay by L. O. Huggins, ASC, "The Language of Color," adding to the ongoing dialogue about color film aesthetics. Like Jones, Huggins viewed color as carrying specific emotional associations:

> Red, for instance literally shouts at us. It is an energetic and aggressive color, at times brutal and angry. Whenever we see a brilliant red color we are reminded, consciously or sub-consciously, of fire, blood, war, passion.
>
> Orange is another active color, it is gay and jolly, suggesting ambition and progress.
>
> Gold is ostentatious, proud. The "language" it speaks is very definite. It always reminds us of money, riches, palaces.[37]

Huggins extended his system of signification to basic color mixtures. Tinted colors suggest "youth, gaiety, informality"; hues toned with black "speak of dignity, reserve, seriousness, stability"; and hues of low saturation, mixed with gray, represent "more restraint, refinement."[38] In this view, color carries with it an abstract emotional value that should accord with the content of a scene. Huggins concluded that, as for cinematography and dialogue, "in the judicious use of color we can express a complete range of emotions and associations which will enhance the value of our story."[39] This required specialized knowledge of its specific associative values. Huggins's taxonomy of color meanings presented a way to control the emotional potential of hue.

When placed in this context, Jones's ideas about color appear as variations on a more general trend of thought. If color were to become a legitimate tool, these authors suggest, filmmakers must avoid simple decoration and carefully tailor color to a film's dramatic needs. This emphasis on color control likely stemmed from industry perceptions of the failure of two-color. Though it was readily acknowledged that Technicolor had lost control of quality by overreaching its plant's capacity during the two-color boom of 1929–1931, commentators also placed blame on poor designs in the films themselves. Of the bust that occurred in mid-1931, *Fortune* explained:

> The good early pictures were succeeded by mediocre and bad. Not that the fault was entirely Technicolor's. The producers themselves had very little color sense, either from the standpoint of getting esthetic compositions or from the standpoint of acquiring color-picture technique. A color picture is not a black and white in color; the whole staging and shooting job has to be designed from the beginning with reference to its colored nature.[40]

The perception that the two-color process had suffered from thoughtless design helped explain Technicolor's emphasis on the aesthetic control of three-color. In retrospect, Herbert Kalmus recalled that with two-color, "many producers chose to film in the gaudiest colors, simply proclaiming that their product was in color instead of black-and-white, but doing little to explore the aesthetic capacities of color."[41] Whether this was actually the case, Technicolor's spokespeople sought to protect the new process by stressing that it must be carefully handled to serve drama. Aesthetes like Jones claimed to hold the secrets of taste and of directing color's emotional power.

2.2. Title card for *La Cucaracha.*

La Cucaracha: A Complete Test

La Cucaracha was designed as a demonstration of Technicolor's technical and dramatic potential (Figure 2.2). The film is a sort of false start, an attempt to slot color into a ruling position rather than negotiate its place among established techniques of visual expression. It insistently juxtaposes strong hues, showcasing three-color's expanded chromatic range. As a comedy-musical-melodrama, it also illustrates how color might support a range of narrative situations. The short's plot is a trifle. Chatita (Steffi Duna) and Pancho (Don Alvarado) are entertainers at the out-of-the-way El Oso Café Contante. One evening, Señor Martinez (Paul Porcasi), a talent scout from Mexico City, arrives to hire Pancho for his theater. Chatita, in love with Pancho, tries to aggravate Martinez and drive him from the café before he sees the act. When she fails, Chatita begs Pancho to take her with him to Mexico City. They quarrel, and he calls her "*la cucaracha,* a cockroach creeping into my life." Angry, Chatita sings "La Cucaracha" for the café's audience, and then uses the song to interrupt Pancho's dance. They dance an impromptu duet briefly before Pancho pulls Chatita backstage and threatens to murder her. Martinez, however, has been charmed by the act, and offers both of them jobs at his theater. The film ends with a reprise of "La Cucaracha" featuring the café's chorus of dancers.

La Cucaracha's palette is wide and bold, with red, blue, yellow, and green accents continually intermingling. The first few moments launch Jones and director Lloyd Corrigan's display of three-color's gamut. The title credit features text in Magenta, Lemon Drop yellow, and Baltic blue-green (near cyan), juxtaposing the fundamental three-color hues, colors that would have been compromised in the two-color process. Moments later, the frame erupts with red, green, and blue, each modulated in value and saturation, showcasing a range within each family. Martinez and his friend Esteban pause outside the café, and the primaries leap forward. At the right, cold blue light highlights Esteban's sombrero and back, while his shirt introduces a soft Willow green accent along his shoulder. These colors are of relatively low saturation and value, helping center attention on Martinez. His costume features a deep Moroccan Blue cape with a Bright Green satin lining turned outward on his shoulder. The vivid green complements his Geranium Red tie, while a Blossom pink carnation provides softer contrast. Over Martinez's shoulder, in the far left background, standing outside the café's door, Chatita completes the composition with a splash of Bachelor Button blue carried by her shawl and the Poppy Red and Citrus gold of her dress. The touch of gold adds a fourth color family. But greater emphasis is placed on the sharp complementary contrast between Martinez's green cape, his red tie, and the red of Chatita's dress, which is set directly against his shoulder in the background (Color Figure 1).

Variety of hue remains a key principle of the film's color design. As in the shot described above, Jones often includes representatives of at least three families of hue in the color schemes. This variety is virtually guaranteed by Chatita's costume, which combines vivid accents of red, yellow, and blue, the primary triad. With the main character so clad, Jones manipulates the surrounding mise-en-scène either to isolate her against a more or less neutral background or to coordinate her with a range of accents. For example, at the start of the film, the major colors of her costume are echoed across the mise-en-scène. When Chatita watches Martinez enter the café, she is framed in medium close-up against a wall. The basic color scheme is carried by her blue shawl, draped over her head, and the strong Flame Scarlet bow, with a bright Lemon Drop yellow accent, in her hair. Her dress reiterates the gold and red, but the wall behind her also joins in the pattern of color. The right half of the wall is bathed in strong blue light, and the left is suffused in yellow, effectively surrounding her with a coordinating mise-en-scène. Nearly every region of the frame participates in this play of triadic hues, rendering a composition that resembles a color test pattern.

The dances, of course, provide occasion for even more vigorous color foregrounding. The first number features women in Purple Orchid blouses, Banana yellow skirts with purple and metallic gold stripes near their hems, and Poppy Red shoes. The chorus of male dancers wears deep Strong Blue capes over Tabasco (brownish red) jackets, and Stone Blue (bluish gray) sombreros. The dance is choreographed to exploit the contrast between the women's yellow, purple, and red costumes and the men's blue capes. For example, one shot frames a solitary female dancer on the right while six male dancers form a diagonal along the left. The men keep their backs to the camera, creating a line of solid blue against which the soloist's reds and yellows stand out (Color Figure 2). Then the men swiftly turn, whisking their blue capes from sight and revealing a line of five women who step forward to join the soloist. In an instant the colors have changed, the reds and yellows overtaking the blues. The moment is typical of the film's manipulation of color: graphic contrast is the formal dominant of the performance and choreography.

Color foregrounding, the showcasing of color for its graphic power, is clearly central to *La Cucaracha*'s design. Jones mixes strong hues by juxtaposing them within the frame or by alternating colors across shots. This flamboyance makes color into something of an attraction, and the final shot acknowledges this directly. A low angle frames the cheering café audience as the men throw their sombreros over the camera, in the direction of the dancers. A single Orchid Purple sombrero, conspicuously perched on a table at the center of the frame, draws attention to itself as the strongest warm color in a generally cool composition. After a moment, Esteban seizes the sombrero and tosses it toward the camera, where it blocks the lens, leaving the screen black for an instant before the end credits appear. The moment is exhibitionist in the manner of early cinema; it self-consciously confronts the viewer with the primacy of color.

La Cucaracha asserts color by laying stress on the contrast of hue. Yet as Jones was at pains to point out in his writing, he was vitally concerned with making color dramatically significant. Toward this end, he employed colored figure illumination, what *Popular Science* called his "mood lights," to underscore character emotions. As in his test films, Jones relied on very broad cultural conventions to coordinate color with emotion. For example, in the first use of the device, Chatita spies Martinez across the café and steps backward into blue light, signifying her sadness at the thought of losing Pancho; she has the blues. She steps forward, back into neutral light, and her expression brightens, indicating that she has settled on a plan for dealing with Martinez.

The other cases of colored figure lighting involve red illumination to suggest anger, passion, and rage. When Martinez boils with exasperation, the camera dollies into a close-up as a red light gradually illuminates his face. The red light mimics a physiological reaction that is in keeping with Paul Porcasi's exaggerated comic performance. The effect when Chatita and Pancho argue in his dressing room is more symbolic. The couple is staged on either side of a table lamp with a red practical (a light source) hidden inside. As their argument intensifies, the camera cuts inward, and the couple is staged progressively closer to the lamp. The third cut brings them into medium close-up, and both actors lean down toward the red light as Pancho calls Chatita "la cucaracha." In this case, the colored illumination is broadly expressive of passion and anger. The same is true for the final instance of the device, when Pancho pulls Chatita backstage and threatens to kill her for ruining his career. This time, the entire frame is flooded in red light, expressing the intensity of Pancho's wrath (Color Figure 3).

Jones's attempts to bind color to narrative are thus bold and conspicuous. They also illustrate a problem with using color to signify exact meanings. In the arguments between Chatita and Pancho, because the red illumination coincides with peaks of dramatic intensity, it is redundant given the tone of the scene as established by dialogue and performance. In terms of Jones's analogy to opera, the color score swells to underline the drama. The blue light that bathes Chatita as she watches Martinez is less redundant; there are fewer cues to reinforce its meaning. In fact, Jones relies on color alone to communicate Chatita's state of mind, that she is "blue." Because this meaning is not repeated by other stylistic registers, the color's significance remains ambiguous; one must take an interpretive leap to assign it an emotional value. *La Cucaracha* reveals the limits of constructing an independent signifying system from color. Either the color cues are redundant and become too obvious, or they are obscure and ill defined.

In either case, by aligning expressive color so directly with characters' emotions, Jones lays considerable stress on the device. As we will see, when Technicolor was taken up for regular studio production, designers tended to avoid such emphatic coordination between color and dramatic tone. Extreme stylization of color, especially colored lighting, would generally be relegated to transitional sequences, bracketed off from the main line of narrative development.

John Belton makes similar observations about the film in relation to cinematic realism. He suggests that *La Cucaracha*'s tendency toward an abundance of color "over-shadows the story."[42] On one hand, the film fails because "the color range is so extensive that it gives us too much to look at."[43] On the other hand, Jones's attempt to give narrative functions to color is disruptive because it relies "entirely on extra-filmic coding to do its work for it." Rather than approximate the expressive conventions of black-and-white, Jones relies on the "arbitrary imposition of extra-filmic color codes" that are "so banal as to distract from the narrative."[44] The lack of strong diegetic motivation for the colored illumination, according to Belton, contributes to its apparent arbitrariness, "rupturing the coherence of its illusion of reality."[45]

Belton's broad point is that Technicolor did not automatically confer a sense of realism on cinema; instead, conventions had to be developed whereby color films duplicated the "monochromatic range" of black-and-white.[46] These observations are important because they position *La Cucaracha* as part of a path not followed in bringing color to the classical style. Jones attempted to solve the basic problem of making color serve drama, but he did so too obtrusively, pushing style too much to the foreground and invoking conventions that seemed too far afield of accepted black-and-white norms. Indeed, throughout the 1930s, efforts were focused on integrating color into conventional film style, on finding ways to let color cooperate with established and respected techniques, not dominate them.

Yet it would be misleading to overemphasize *La Cucaracha*'s failure to make color unobtrusive. The prototype film's main function was to demonstrate color, and toward this end Jones's design continually highlights and draws attention to it. Suffusing the frame in colored light not only helps make that color pronounced, but also emphasizes the reemergence of varied hues when characters return to neutral illumination. Similarly, though Belton rightly suggests that compositions threaten to "scatter attention" by combining primaries, strong hues can also reinforce one another, helping jar the spectator into awareness of Technicolor. In its emphasis on color foregrounding, the demonstration mode is essentially a novelty-based approach to color design.

La Cucaracha systematically runs through a range of possibilities for bringing color to cinema. It lays out a field of applications in an experimental fashion, testing whether colored illumination, for example, should be taken up as a standard option. The technique is varied: blue light on a single figure, red light combined with a dolly to a close-up, red highlights on two figures against a neutrally lit background, and strong red light tinting the entire frame. Function also varies from situation to situation: projected color communicates Chatita's sorrow, reinforces Martinez's comic expression, and emphasizes Pancho's rage. The short subject allowed Pioneer and Technicolor to take risks with devices that might not work in a feature production, and the fact that these devices rendered color obvious should not necessarily be regarded as a weakness.

Though colored lighting did not survive as a regular formal option, *La Cucaracha* does demonstrate several devices that became part of the developing Technicolor style. For example, even within the busy palette, color contrast guides attention around the frame. In the opening compositions, Chatita creates an eye-catching blue and red accent in the far background, activating the depth of the shot beyond the plane of focus as a zone of important visual information. Planting significant color in the background proved a lasting technique. Jones also places accents within the frame to reinforce the prominence of important characters. Compositions around Martinez's table repeatedly frame him against the Orchid Purple curtain that hangs at the back of the dining room. Here, the device appears somewhat clumsy; the color of the curtain does not coordinate with any details of Martinez's costume, but it matches exactly the dress of his waitress. Still, the effect is to help highlight his area of the frame, a technique that will be refined in the assertively designed *The Adventures of Robin Hood* (1938).

Likewise, locating the strongest colors within the frame in Chatita's costume while using blue or gold light to generate coordinating background accents anticipates what would become a general rule of Technicolor design: color schemes should be harmonized around the lead female character. The task of beautifying women already received priority in costume design and lighting, so it comes as no surprise that color would follow suit. Again, as Technicolor style developed, the degree of coordination and contrast would become less prominent, but the basic principle would remain.

The same could be said for emotionally punctual color. Though we have emphasized Jones's use of emotional lighting, he also underscores action during Chatita and Pancho's dance by employing a colorful prop. Pancho whips his serape through the air to enwrap Chatita. The action is carried over a cut, so the serape suddenly appears as a vivid swath of red, jetting across the frame before settling on Chatita's shoulders (Figures 2.3, 2.4, and 2.5). The flourish signals a turning point in the dynamic of the dance. Pancho, filled with rage, gains control of Chatita and quickly ends the performance. Like the projected mood light, this is a stylized use of color that relies on broad associations of color and feeling. Yet, because it involves the manipulation of a costume accent, a piece of the mise-en-scène firmly rooted within the diegesis and controlled by a character, the effect is not as obtrusive as colored lighting. Here, Jones hits on a way of exploiting color for dramatic effect that has greater potential for integration into the classical style. Indeed, it is on this level of design that most Technicolor productions worked to achieve color scoring.

Finally, cinematographer Ray Rennahan's lighting schemes suggest the possibilities for incorporating color into figure illumination without re-

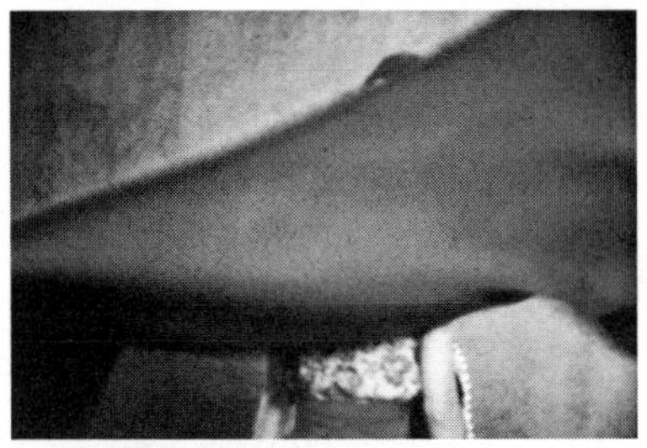

2.3, 2.4, and 2.5. Pancho's red serape jets across the frame.

sorting to wholesale, more intrusive, mood light. In the play of shadow and highlight, certain shots emulate the kind of modeling available to black-and-white. Facial light would remain an area of concern for Technicolor cinematographers throughout the 1930s, and not until *Gone with the Wind,* and a revised film stock, would three-color obtain something like the precise tonal control so prized in monochrome. *La Cucaracha* serves to demonstrate that even with arc lights and extremely slow stock, Technicolor could accommodate some of the expressive techniques made familiar by black-and-white. The film not only experiments with methods that foreground color, but also, perhaps to a lesser extent, seeks to demonstrate how three-color might serve monochrome conventions.

The film's broad and wide palette impinges on its ability to grant color finely tuned functions. As Henri Coulon recommended, and subsequent productions would bear out, using less color could be dramatically more effective. But while the constant foregrounding may have kept Jones from realizing his ideal, making color an "organic" part of the drama, it did not block him from experimenting with narrative functions. As his use of colored light attests, Jones had envisioned a mode of filmmaking in which color would be so integral as to forge "a new form of dramatic art." If the specific technique failed, the intention to bind color to story remained central to three-color aesthetics. Perhaps Jones's mistake was one of emphasis; instead of creating a *new* dramatic art, color would have to be integrated into *existing* conventions and stylistic norms.

Color Consciousness: Setting the Rules for Color

Though color experts like Jones, Coulon, and Huggins offered guidelines, the job of articulating and enforcing an official Technicolor color aesthetic fell to Natalie Kalmus (Figure 2.6). Natalie had been married to Herbert Kalmus from 1903 to 1921, and after their divorce she headed the Technicolor color-control department, also referred to as the Color Advisory Service. Natalie Kalmus's experience in studying art recommended her for the position. Reportedly, she had studied art at the University of Zurich, the John B. Stetson University in Florida, the Boston School of Art, the Curry School of Expression in Boston, and Queen's University in Ontario.[47] Drawing on her background, Kalmus set stylistic boundaries for the use of color, and she helped position the Color Advisory Service as a liaison between Technicolor and the studios' production teams. If there was a single voice behind the Technicolor look, it was likely Natalie Kalmus's.

When it was formed, in the 1920s, the department was meant to aid production personnel in designing for the limited range of the two-color process. With the advent of three-color, Technicolor promoted the department as a means of avoiding the purported excesses of the late 1920s and early 1930s. Natalie Kalmus emphasized the importance of her department in the mid-1930s by pointing to "the early two-color pictures" in which "producers sometimes thought that because a process could reproduce color, they should flaunt vivid color continually before the eyes of the audience."[48] Technicolor publicity suggested that the department was vital because the three-color process had "greatly increased the demands of precision in color control in order that the fine gradations of color now available on the screen may comprise a pleasing harmony."[49] The basic argument was that since three-color had so substantially increased the filmmaker's palette, the regulation of color design now became more essential. If color were to provide more than a vivid novelty, it would have to be carefully crafted, and the Color Advisory Service provided guidance.

From the 1930s into the 1950s, Natalie Kalmus and her crew of consultants oversaw the color design of every major-studio Technicolor production. Kalmus's contract stipulated that she receive screen credit as color

2.6. Natalie Kalmus. Courtesy of the Academy of Motion Picture Arts and Sciences.

consultant on each of Technicolor's features. However, beginning in 1937, credits indicate that work was parceled out between Kalmus and her associates Henri Jaffa and Morgan Padelford. During the late 1930s and early 1940s, both associates worked on films for Paramount and Fox, while Jaffa also handled MGM and some United Artists releases, and Padelford was responsible for Warner Bros. Kalmus, Jaffa, or Padelford would consult on most of the features during the period, although *Technicolor News and Views* reported that altogether there were six associate consultants.[50]

According to Kalmus, the department reviewed scripts and generated a "color chart for the entire production," accounting for "each scene, sequence, set and character." The goal, wrote Kalmus, was to produce a color score, like a musical score, that "amplifies the picture" by matching color to the "dominant mood or emotion" of a sequence, thus "augmenting its dramatic value."[51] For his excellent overview of Technicolor style, Richard Neupert interviewed Leonard Doss, a Technicolor consultant during the late 1940s and early 1950s, and, in 1989, the department's lone survivor. Doss recalled that the color consultants' responsibilities involved five major steps:

> First, they read the script, then researched and planned out the appropriate color schemes (meeting occasionally with Kalmus). Second, they met with the producers to set up a budget and schedule. (A larger production budget would warrant several consultants being assigned to a film.) Third, they met with the costume department, since the interior set was generally designed around the colors worn by the protagonists. Fourth and fifth, they met with the studio's Art and then Props Departments to guarantee that the props and sets would reinforce the color schemes planned for each shot and scene.[52]

As Neupert notes, the Color Advisory Service was strongly invested in guiding the preproduction and design of a feature, but the consultants would continue to advise the studio during the production and postproduction stages.

Natalie Kalmus's department secured Technicolor a degree of aesthetic control over its process, helping ensure that productions conformed to certain design principles for linking color to drama. Kalmus explained these principles in a lecture entitled "Color Consciousness," presented to the Technicians Branch of the Academy of Motion Picture Arts and Sciences in May 1935. The lecture, read in Kalmus's absence by Kenneth Macgowan, was part of a panel about three-color Technicolor and *Becky Sharp,* and it was reprinted in both the academy's *Technical Bulletin,* and in the August 1935 issue of the *Journal of the Society of Motion Picture Engineers.*[53] Though her comments were originally framed as part of an early discussion about the possibilities of the three-color feature, they also defined what became her department's long-term approach to color. In 1938, Kalmus revised the essay only slightly for inclusion, as a chapter entitled "Colour," in Stephen Watts's anthology *Behind the Screen: How Films Are Made.* "Color Consciousness" has been a touchstone for historians seeking to reconstruct Technicolor aesthetics, and so it merits detailed consideration.

In his analysis of the piece, Richard Neupert quite justly points out that Kalmus's comments played an important role in promoting Technicolor to studios and critics. In justifying her principles of design, Kalmus referred to nature, high art, and human perceptual psychology. Each point of reference helped her build a case that color must be carefully controlled and harmonized. On one hand, she argued, "If the color schemes of natural objects were used as guides, less flagrant mistakes in color would occur."[54] At the same time, like Holbein, Bouguereau, Rembrandt, or Velázquez, the motion-picture colorist must follow "the principles of color, tone, and composition [that] make painting a fine art."[55] Finally, she suggested that the human nervous system "experiences a shock when it is forced to adapt itself to any degree of unnaturalness in the reception of external stimuli," and so it was "important that the eye be not assailed with glaring color combinations, nor by the indiscriminate use of black and white."[56] As Neupert observes, Kalmus's message was "that color is already theorized in terms of nature, art, and psychology; the job of the Technicolor consultant is simply to ensure that those pre-existing rules are fully exploited by [the] film's color schemes."[57] Further, he notes that Kalmus sought "to convince the industry that her advisory department was not so much dictating a color style as enforcing established aesthetic norms."[58] "Color Consciousness" was a bid to persuade producers that Technicolor could bring with it a tested aesthetic of quality. All of these claims were also bound up with a basic teleology. Cinema, Kalmus argued, had been "steadily tending toward more complete realism," and after the addition of sound, color became "the last step" of perfection.[59] Color was cinema's destiny, and Kalmus offered the means of properly harnessing it for artistic expression.

Beyond promoting her office, Kalmus was also interested in explaining her conception of color's role in the cinema and laying out specific standards for ensuring that color could function within a feature film. Like Jones, she sought to demonstrate the power of color, but she couched her claims in terms of restraint. In this regard, she responded to Jones's excesses. Kalmus's writing points in two directions. On the one hand, she offered a fairly literal approach to color that, though not in keeping with classical Hollywood standards of subtlety, could be easily grasped and visualized by potential customers for Technicolor. On the other hand, she provided guidelines designed to check the kind of chromatic play that Jones had indulged in.

One might abstract four general principles for the use of color from her comments. Kalmus's broadest directive was that color should support the mood or tone of the story. In this first principle, she echoed Jones and the other commentators, suggesting that color carries with it an emotional valence. The main goal of creating color charts, according to Kalmus, was to ensure that from the beginning design would suit the tone of the script. Yet, unlike Jones's supremacist rhetoric, Kalmus's discussion implies that color's role should be supportive of action and dialogue, suggestive of mood rather than an equal partner in its communication. In Kalmus's words, the director's "prime motive is to direct and control the thoughts and emotions of his audience. The director strives to indicate a fuller significance than is specifically shown by the action and dialogue." Color should aid the director in achieving this "fuller significance:"

> We have found that by the understanding use of color we can subtly convey dramatic moods and impressions to the audience, making them more receptive to whatever emotional effect the scenes, action, and dialog may convey. Just as every scene has some definite dramatic mood—some definite emotional response which it seeks to arouse within the minds of the audience—so, too, has each scene, each type of action, its definitely indicated color which harmonizes with that emotion.[60]

In this model, color buttresses the mood carried by performance and script; it helps prime the viewer for the scene's dramatic import, which is realized more explicitly in dialogue and action. The claim that color could communicate emotion was still quite strong, but Kalmus stopped short of Jones's predictions of a "new form of dramatic art." Color would augment rather than dominate.

Like Jones and Huggins, Kalmus rested her assertions about color's dramatic significance on a rather literal vocabulary. As they did for Huggins, the large categories of color theory provided Kalmus with a means of specifying expressive properties. Warm hues were "advancing colors" that "call forth sensations of excitement, activity, and heat." Cool colors were "retiring," and they "suggest rest, ease, coolness." Similarly, colors of low saturation, or mixed with gray, "suggest subtlety, refinement, and charm." Higher-value hues "indicate youth, gaiety, informality," while colors at a lower value, or mixed with black, could "show strength, seriousness, dignity, but sometimes represent the baser emotions of life."[61] Because this kind of signification is rather broad and flexible, it could well provide a color consultant with a general guide for color scoring. In her own example of how costumes might reflect character, Kalmus relies on these distinctions. She describes two sisters. One, "vivacious, affectionate, and gay," was costumed in "pink, red, warm browns, tan, and orange," and the other, "studious, quiet, and reserved," was clad in "blue, green, black, and grey."[62] By this method, Kalmus explained, "colors were kept in unison with their film characters." The level of correspondence, however, is quite general: warm and light colors suited the extrovert, and cool and darker hues would be selected for the introvert; we are far from Jones's "mickey mousing."

Kalmus also presented a detailed catalogue of the emotional values of specific hues. Here, she verged on the more mechanistic approach to color exemplified by Jones's mood lighting. Each color possessed a set of associations, and Kalmus suggested that through careful design these associations could be narrowed into rather precise meanings:

> For example, red calls to mind a feeling of danger, a warning. It also suggests blood, life, and love. It is materialistic, stimulating. It suffuses the face of anger, it led the Roman soldiers into battle. Different shades of red can suggest various phases of life, such as love, happiness, physical strength, wine, passion, power, excitement, anger, turmoil, tragedy, cruelty, revenge, war, sin, and shame. . . . Whether blood is spilled upon the battlefield in an approved cause or whether it drips from the assassin's dagger, blood still runs red. The introduction of another color with red can suggest the motive for a crime, whether it be jealousy, fanaticism, revenge, patriotism, or religious sacrifice. Love gently warms the blood. The delicacy of strength of the shade of red will suggest the type of love. By introducing the colors of licentiousness, deceit, selfish ambition, or passion, it will be possible to classify the type of love portrayed with considerable accuracy.[63]

Kalmus was surely hyperbolizing, but her intent was to demonstrate that color *could* be reined to narrative through a system of classification.

Because such treatment of hues as concrete semantic signs did not fit with the more flexible and fluid kinds of expressiveness favored by the classical Hollywood style, it is surprising that she retained this discussion of color meaning in her subsequent versions of the paper. In practice, Technicolor designs would intermittently stress connections between the narrative and color by building motifs within a film rather than constantly accessing an external set of associations. At this stage in three-color's diffusion, though, it was in Kalmus's interest to demonstrate that color had the potential to become an essential stylistic element, that it offered very specific and concrete gains for the expressive range of Hollywood cinema.

Natalie Kalmus's other principles were more directly prescriptive of the way color should be arranged on screen. Her second general rule held that excessive use of bright, saturated color should be avoided in favor of more "natural," harmonious, and less intense color schemes. In Kalmus's words: "A super-abundance of color is unnatural, and has a most unpleasant effect not only upon the eye itself, but upon the mind as well." She recommended "the judicious use of neutrals" as a "foil for color" in order to lend "power and interest to the touches of color in a scene."[64] Successful design would balance assertive hues with an array of neutrals.

This principle is related to the rule for coordinating color with mood, since significant colors might more readily be recognized within a field of neutrals; the neutrals themselves could take on expressive force through a juxtaposition "emphasizing the severity of the black, the gloominess of the gray, the purity of the white."[65]

The third principle of "Color Consciousness" links this mode of harmony to the problem of directing attention with color. Warmer and brighter shades should emphasize only narratively important information; otherwise, Kalmus advised using neutral colors. According to Kalmus: "The law of emphasis states in part that nothing of relative unimportance in a picture shall be emphasized. If, for example, a bright red ornament were shown behind an actor's head, the bright color would detract from the character and action."[66] The maximum point of color contrast should be associated with the principal players in a scene; those who play "relatively unimportant roles" should blend with the background.[67] Further, because flesh tones are usually warm, Kalmus explained, "we usually introduce the cooler tones into the backgrounds; but if we find it advantageous to use warmer tones in the set, we handle the lighting so that particular section in back of the actor is left in shadow."[68] In general, then, the warmest colors should be associated with the main action, whereas background and incidental information should be carefully blended and carried by cooler and unobtrusive hues. Where color might distract, other components of style, such as lighting, could intervene.

Finally, elements of the mise-en-scène should be coordinated to avoid the occurrence of any distracting juxtapositions when characters move through space. According to Kalmus, it was vital to "consider the movement in the scene in determining its color composition because the juxtaposition of color is constantly changing due to this movement."[69] By "color juxtaposition," Kalmus meant to invoke the problem of complementarity. She explained that, for example, orange would "appear more red than it really is" next to a blue-green because "each color tends 'to throw' the other toward its complement."[70] Restraint and attention to color harmony were the keys to avoiding unwanted juxtapositions. More specifically, the kind of harmony that Kalmus encouraged would limit complements and play contrasting hues against neutrals to avoid generating any distracting apparent changes in color. This rule would seem especially important to the restrained mode of design that was initiated with *The Trail of the Lonesome Pine* in 1936, but even films with more assertive palettes, like *The Adventures of Robin Hood* (1938), exhibit attention to juxtaposition, sometimes revealing complements to underscore a moment of action.

The primary goal of these principles was to align color with the normal functions of film style. Harmonizing color to avoid striking juxtapositions, concentrating assertive hues on the protagonists, and associating color with mood would prevent Technicolor from becoming intrusive or distracting. Natalie Kalmus's rules were drafted to guarantee that color, like lighting, sound, camera movement, and editing, would keep the viewer's attention on the narratively important elements of the moving image and suit the expressive demands of feature production. At the same time, the principles were broad enough to encompass a range of design modes or color styles. Color could more or less explicitly underscore narrative development, and color harmonies could run from the sparing use of accents against a background of neutrals to the rich play of stronger hues, carefully handled to keep the key contrast centered on the action. The strength of Kalmus's formulation is that it did not posit a single, inflexible mode of design.

Conclusion

Their views were distinct, but together Kalmus and Jones waged a campaign for color's legitimacy in the cinema. In hiring Robert Edmond Jones, Pioneer had invested in a name associated with quality. Jones's writings and interviews were, in part, a promotional effort on behalf of Technicolor and Pioneer to give the process some aesthetic clout. Kalmus's vision for three-color was somewhat more conciliatory toward actual film practice, but she too proposed a color language that seems rather naïve or simplistic. Their ideas, though, were easily grasped and had rhetorical force as evidence that color could play an important role in film.

La Cucaracha participated in the campaign for Technicolor by boldly, and clumsily, granting color dramatic functions. But we should not lose sight of its more modest achievements. Ultimately, as a prototype, it was the production's mission to rehearse a spectrum of possibilities or, as Herbert Kalmus noted, to perform "a complete test" of the process. The short introduced techniques for guiding attention and punctuating action with color and for blending color with cinematographic conventions. These were areas of experimentation that would be important for bringing Technicolor to feature production.

Natalie Kalmus's ideas would prove far more durable than Jones's, partly because her model was so versatile. Though different commentators specified and extended "Color Consciousness," those four principles set the pattern for most discussions of the proper and tasteful use of color into the 1950s. Proof of the principles' longevity can be found in the 1957 manual *Elements of Color in Professional Motion Pictures,* published by the Society of Motion Picture and Television Engineers as an aid to production personnel in the early era of Eastmancolor. Not surprisingly, the manual's suggestions for color design follow closely those propagated by Kalmus decades earlier. In fact, the book goes as far as to suggest that productions employ "color coordinators" to take the place of the now absent Technicolor consultants.[71]

Natalie Kalmus's legacy was a set of long-standing aesthetic criteria for the correct use of color in motion pictures. It established that color was to be channeled toward the subtle expression of drama through careful harmony and coordination. At the same time, her literal chromatic vocabulary and her arguments for color's expressive power seem more in line with an aesthetic that emphasized color demonstration. These elements serve as reminders that "Color Consciousness" had its roots in Technicolor's efforts to gain the attention of a wary industry. *La Cucaracha* had effectively introduced three-color, but the first feature film would offer a more important trial of Technicolor, and of Kalmus's and Jones's aesthetic proposals.

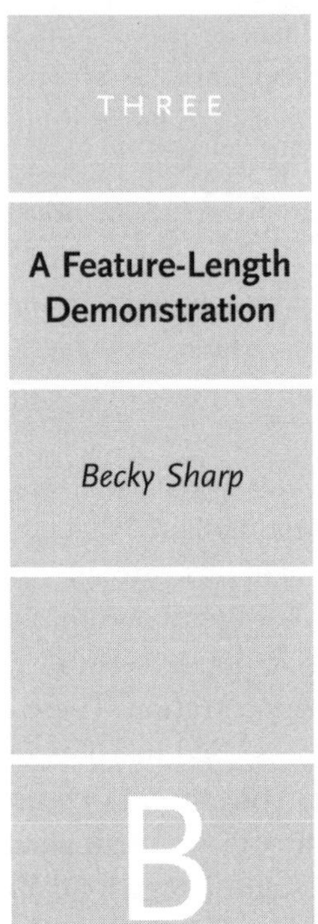

THREE

A Feature-Length Demonstration

Becky Sharp

Becky Sharp offered the first practical test of three-color's aesthetic and dramatic potential for feature production. Herbert Kalmus declared, "As a laboratory of the new process, *Becky* turned out to be an expensive proving-ground" (Figure 3.1).[1] The production cost nearly $1,000,000 and grossed only $672,000 domestically.[2] Pioneer's first feature was plagued by setbacks. The original director, Lowell Sherman, died of pneumonia a month into production, and when Rouben Mamoulian took over, he opted to reshoot Sherman's material.[3] Miriam Hopkins also fell ill with pneumonia, causing further delays. A work print for the Duchess of Richmond's ball sequence, the film's color showpiece, was destroyed in a projection room fire. Finally, because portions of the dialogue were unintelligible, RKO had to transfer the sound track of the finished film from RCA's Photophone process to Western Electric's variable-density system, and back again, delaying release another month.[4]

All these setbacks were willingly absorbed by the producers because like *La Cucaracha, Becky Sharp* was a prototype: the goal of production was as much to demonstrate the possibilities of three-color as to create a profitable or popular film. *Time* explained that Jock Whitney "was not particularly excited" about whether RKO could help turn a profit on

3.1. Title card for *Becky Sharp.*

the film: "If *Becky Sharp* fails to make production costs, the Whitneys still have their shrewd 15% of Technicolor, Inc., which *Becky Sharp* is sure to boom."[5]

Rouben Mamoulian and Robert Edmond Jones shared credit for *Becky Sharp*'s color design in the popular and technical press. William Stull, in *American Cinematographer,* reported that Jones served as "a sort of chromatic supervisor of every detail of the production," adding, "Not only did he design the settings and costumes and plan the coloring of every scene: he outlines the chromatic composition of every shot, and serves on the set almost as a co-director and co-cinematographer."[6] Mamoulian, though, claimed authority by explaining that, as in the theater, he "tried to make the dramatic and emotional use of color play a vital part of my work."[7] Similarly, in "Some Problems in Directing Color Pictures," his oft-reprinted lecture to the Technical Branch of the Academy of Motion Pictures Arts and Sciences, Mamoulian explicitly took credit for the design, pointing to the Duchess of Richmond's ball as an example of how he "tried to take advantage of the mental and emotional implications of color."[8] In interviews with the *New York Times,* both men explained their views on color in association with *Becky Sharp.*[9]

Surprisingly, Natalie Kalmus was absent from discussions of *Becky Sharp*'s design. Anthony Slide reports that Mamoulian managed to dismiss Kalmus from the set with an ultimatum to Whitney and Macgowan: "Look, tomorrow, either she is not there or I am not there."[10] One of the promotional functions of Kalmus's essay "Color Consciousness" must have been to reinforce her authority as the official arbiter of Technicolor aesthetics. Her position could well have required strengthening, since Jones had claimed for himself the title of "first color consultant" and predicted "a tremendous influx of stage colorists," and Mamoulian, an independent director, was holding forth on the color's dramatic potential.[11]

Infighting aside, Jones, Mamoulian, and Kalmus all promoted a similar view of color's function. Though Jones and Mamoulian appeared more willing to stylize color for conspicuous dramatic effects, they echoed Kalmus in their views that hue needed to be tied to the emotional tone of the narrative and that it should be carefully harmonized. Despite Jones's busy palette for *La Cucaracha,* he warned, when discussing *Becky Sharp,* that "to think in terms of color . . . does not mean an abundance of color: this cannot be too strongly emphasized."[12] Mamoulian's prescription was identical: "The cinema must not . . . go about color as a newly-rich. Color should not mean gaudiness. Restraint and selectiveness are the essence of art."[13] Moreover, like Kalmus and Jones, Mamoulian drew on broad color associations ("to feel blue, to be green with envy") to establish that color could "increase the power and effectiveness of a scene, situation, or character."[14] If Kalmus was not directly responsible for *Becky Sharp*'s design, the film's colorists still propounded a rhetoric of dramatic control and moderation similar to hers. All three experts offered the same aesthetic responses to the demand that Technicolor demonstrate its worth to feature filmmaking.

Design Principles to Foreground Color

Becky Sharp, the sixth film adaptation of William Makepeace Thackeray's novel *Vanity Fair,* was based also on Langdon Mitchell's stage play.[15] The film follows the exploits of Becky Sharp (Miriam Hopkins), a strong-willed social climber, in England and Europe at the turn of the nineteenth century. Through a series of romantic entanglements involving Joseph Sedley (Nigel Bruce), Rawdon Crawley (Alan Mowbray), and her best friend's husband, George Osborne (G. P. Huntley, Jr.), Becky ascends the social ladder and then plunges back down it. The adaptation's clunky plot is unified in part by the character of Amelia Sedley (Frances Dee), Becky's best friend and moral foil. Throughout the film, Becky exploits Amelia by wooing both her husband and her brother and otherwise taking advantage of her social connections. The final episode, though, finds Becky somewhat reformed when she selflessly clears the way for Amelia's second marriage.

Becky Sharp extends the demonstration mode to handle this feature-length narrative. The film's color centerpiece is the Duchess of Richmond's ball sequence, which takes place just midway through. These two reels stand out for the rigor with which color effects are tested and showcased. In a sense, the ball sequence is a demonstration film unto itself, something like *La Cucaracha* interpolated into a somewhat less-adventurous feature. The sequence well deserves the attention that it has received from scholars and commentators, but before delving into its detail, we should attend to its context, the general principles of *Becky Sharp's* design.

As a whole, the film is somewhat less florid than *La Cucaracha,* but it still showcases color vigorously. In one sense, it follows Kalmus's recommendations. The settings are generally held to a range of cool neutrals and browns, allowing the characters to introduce more assertive colors. Still, the palette is quite wide, and nearly every segment offers boldly contrasting hues or features some manner of color foregrounding. From the perspective of color theory, we might note that variation of hue dominates differences of value and saturation. The emphasis is not on the careful gradations of tones within a narrow group of colors, but on displaying striking splashes against more or less neutral backgrounds.

The designers associate the most prominent colors with the main players, which bespeaks an attempt to link, and subordinate, color to action. The choice of hues, however, and the techniques used to display them point to a countervailing tendency to demonstrate color and keep it conspicuous. In this respect, *Becky Sharp* departs, forcefully, from Kalmus's prescriptions for guarding against intrusive design. The tension between subduing and flaunting color is important for most Technicolor design, but unlike films that follow in the mid-1930s, *Becky Sharp* leans strongly toward display.

We can get a good idea of the film's standard procedure for handling color by taking a close look at the opening sequence. In it, the film stresses color as a mark of difference from black-and-white, and makes clear that color has been choreographed from shot to shot in order to display the technology and organize viewers' attention. Before the action begins, the frame is taken up entirely by a silver-gray curtain, mimicking a black-and-white screen (Figure 3.2). Color is introduced in stages. First, one of Becky's classmates at Miss Pinkerton's Academy for Young Women parts the curtains and peeks through (in medium shot), bringing the flesh tones of her face into the field of gray (Figure 3.3). The moment briefly showcases three-color's improved rendition of skin and facial features, but color is kept low-key. Then, she opens the curtains wide and reveals a group of young women huddled around her. In unison they shout "Amelia," and the camera tracks back and pans left as they rush forward and surround their classmate (Figure 3.4). This action continues the steady revelation of hue. The foremost three students are clad in Smoke (gray slightly tinted blue), Iris (gray slightly tinted lavender), and Gray Sand (beige of very low saturation). As they pass the camera, they reveal

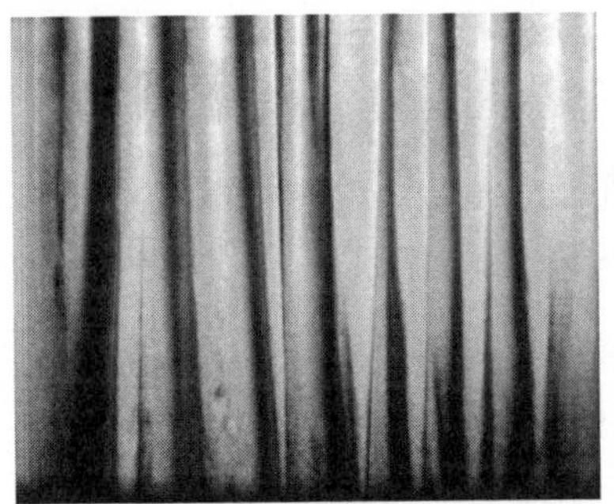

3.2, 3.3, 3.4, and 3.5. The opening of *Becky Sharp:* A curtain mimics black-and-white, parts first to reveal the skin tone of a woman's face, then a group of students, who create a dash of blue as they rush forward.

a fourth student, who is wearing a relatively brilliant Crystal Blue (high-value light blue) dress. She provides a momentary surge of color as she passes, surrounded by other women in various shades of beige and gray (Figure 3.5). Staging and camera movement cooperate to phase color in, teasing the viewer while keeping hue at the forefront of our awareness.

The pan concludes once all the students (thirteen of them) encircle Amelia in a medium long shot. Amelia stands out by virtue of her lustrous brownish red (between Barn Red and Pompeian Red) satin hat, bow, and shawl. These are the film's first reds; her Cream dress offers a more moderate contrast with her classmates' (Color Figure 4). Amelia's close-up finishes the introduction of hue by bringing into frame the green leaves and tiny bright red flowers on a plant that her friends have given her: accents of red, green, and blue complete the palette.

Unlike the opening of *La Cucaracha,* which immediately introduces bold reds, greens, blues, and yellows, the first frames of *Becky Sharp* progressively reveal a more modest range of color. The set has been so largely confined to various shades of gray that the touches of color become conspicuous. It is as though traces of hue have been forced onto a black-and-white set. The first shots of Becky vividly illustrate this aspect of the design. The camera pans right from a high-angle shot of Amelia and her classmates to Becky, sitting across the room beside a single friend. The shot pivots from one area of color (carried by Amelia's bow and her blue-clad classmate) to discover Becky with her Bachelor Button blue hat and neck bows. Between these two points, the camera scans a field of gray, broken only by a deep brown desk set on a matching throw rug. This kind of design fulfills Kalmus's and Mamoulian's prescription that designers avoid an "over-abundance" of color. But the distinction between the background and the touches of color is so pronounced that the hues leap forward. Like other aspects of *Becky Sharp*'s color design, the scheme follows some of Kalmus's basic rules, but in an overt, obvious way. The isolation of strong colors against strict neutrals gives the style a labored appearance. Color has been so cautiously deployed that it appears stylized.

This method of design is obviously intended to use color to steer viewers' attention. For instance, when Becky and Amelia converse, their classmates' costumes form a wash of grays and soft blues. Miss Pinkerton (Elspeth Dudgeon) wears a rather severe black and white dress that singles her out as a point of contrast without interacting with the colors of the two main characters. When Joseph arrives, he is in a generally neutral outfit of grays and browns, but also a Yolk Yellow (green-yellow) checked vest, a new color that helps mark him as a significant figure. In this way, more-active or more-assertive colors guide viewers toward the main characters. The eye can leap from accent to accent without fear of losing the story.

However, the strong distinctions between hues and neutrals also create challenges. Having introduced color highlights, Mamoulian and Jones must now juggle them to avoid distractions. Even the cool colors that Kalmus recommended for background players can, in this environment, grab attention away from the main action. In this scene, the Crystal Blue dresses of two classmates require careful handling. These dresses have clearly marked functions near the start of the scene: they give a burst of color as the students rush forward. The bright blue also supports a bit of comedy. In medium long shot, a student clad in dark blue-gray tries to read Amelia a poem while a student in Crystal Blue desperately tries to muffle the sound of her music box at frame right. The strong color behaves like the unruly music box, yanking our interest from the dreadful poetry (Color Figure 4). Later in the scene, these dresses become a lia-

3.6. The blue dress trespasses into the far left of the frame.

bility. When Amelia greets her brother in long shot, the costumes trespass into the far left of the frame, stealing our attention (Figure 3.6). Miriam Hopkins, though, is spared such competition. Staging and composition ensure that Becky remains the only bearer of strong blue when she is on screen. In handling color details, Mamoulian and Jones attempt to balance foregrounding and restraint. Yet the strict contrast of neutrals and accents creates a game of chromatic cat and mouse in which areas of color can dart around and elude the grasp of narrative interest.

The relatively simple color scheme, with its pronounced contrasts, goes hand in hand with a method of lighting that gives equal weight to all details. Lighting in this sequence is typical of that in much of the film. General illumination is high-key, with directed head and shoulder light helping pick out the main figures. Flat, even lighting into the background ensures the proper registration of color and detail in the rather large set. Because there are none of the pronounced areas of highlight or shadow that might help discriminate among zones of action in a black-and-white film, color control is especially significant. In the main, light serves to accentuate hue and support the choices made in color design.

The strategies of the opening extend to the film as a whole. *Becky Sharp* incessantly plays bright, saturated accents against neutral backgrounds. While sheer repetition might tame this kind of design, making it familiar and therefore unnoticeable, Mamoulian deploys specific techniques of editing, camera work, and staging to underline the accents and sustain the demonstration. Of the film's twenty-one segments, sixteen clearly employ color-foregrounding techniques. Usually he reveals a color, or some property of color, that has been momentarily suppressed. Seven segments open with tracks backward that unveil sources of pronounced hue (bouquets of flowers or colorful props) as the frame widens; camera movement draws attention to the new colors as they enter the field (Figures 3.7 and 3.8). Transitions between scenes also push the play of color to the fore. Dissolves are heavily used in *Becky Sharp* (all together they connect twenty-nine scenes), and they often deliver rather hard chromatic contrasts. When a shot of Amelia and William Dobbin (Colin Tapley), mourning her first husband's death in a gray stone chapel, dissolves to Becky's dinner party, color surges into the frame, announcing three-color's contribution to the image and stressing Becky's callow indifference to Amelia's plight (Figures 3.9 and 3.10).

These methods of suppressing and revealing color will be retained by future Technicolor films because visual flourishes at points between scenes or at the start of a sequence are amenable to the classical style. Yet *Becky Sharp* lays unique stress on such moments. A design of bold color set against fields of neutrals grants individual hues remarkable graphic weight. The films of the restrained mode, discussed in the next chapters, tend not to confer such power on hue, but to concentrate on tonal variations within families of color. Later films with assertive designs (such as *The Adventures of Robin Hood,* discussed in Chapter 6) return to an em-

3.7 and 3.8. The camera tracks back from Becky's hands to reveal yellow roses.

3.9 and 3.10. Color surges during a dissolve from Amelia grieving to Becky celebrating.

phasis on hue, but their more complex palettes and body of conventions militate against the kind of emphasis on isolated accents (like the students in blue dresses) that *Becky Sharp* so readily exploits.

The demonstration mode also distinguished itself from later trends by extending foregrounding devices well beyond transitional passages. The combination of bold accents in virtually monochrome settings helps ensure that as characters enter a scene, a new set of hues will leap forward, prolonging the color parade. Kalmus's rule of emphasis has been interpreted to mean that each major player should carry a conspicuous color. In a scene between Becky and Joseph, she wears high-value Lemon Drop yellow polka dots on a white dress, and he is in an Emerald jacket and Daffodil yellow tie. The shared yellow accents, the brightest and most saturated colors in the scene, echo one another so strongly that they call attention to their alignment. Just when these bold costumes have been displayed fully, Becky's husband, Rawdon, enters, bringing onto the scene his Fiery Red coat, with its Citrus gold cuffs and collar, and his Azure Blue slacks. He completes the scene's palette so that it presents accents from each of the major color groups: blue, yellow, red, and green. The staging of characters creates a near constant pageant before the camera.

Beyond these methods for maintaining color's prominence, *Becky Sharp*'s devotion to color showcasing is most powerfully demonstrated by the specific narrative situations that Mamoulian and Jones arrange to press hue. Even when they are fairly central to a scene's dramatic development, these elaborate contrivances amount to color gimmickry. A most striking example occurs when Becky cuts out a silhouette of Amelia, who poses behind a white sheet. The scene opens on a black-and-white shot of Amelia's shadow thrown on the muslin sheet. A track backward progressively reveals color. First, Becky comes into view on the left, cutting Amelia's silhouette out of black paper. The strong American Beauty red trim on her white dress breaks the chromatic silence. Next, the shot reveals George, standing over Becky's shoulder, in his Fiery Red officer's coat with its deep Imperial Blue and bright gold (near Dandelion) accents (Color Figure 5). When the film cuts to the other side of the muslin to reveal Amelia, in a soft Cloud Pink dress, colors are once again muted. The silhouette screen foregrounds color in several ways. In addition to serving as a reminder of black-and-white, cutting around the screen presents the hard shift from saturated, strong red accents to an environment of pale pastels. Moreover, because it initially withholds the texture and color of Amelia's image, the screen helps build the visual impact of her eventual appearance.

3.11. Passive observers provide color while Becky and Amelia are reduced to silhouette.

As the scene develops, Mamoulian milks the gimmick by having Becky rush behind the screen to give Amelia the cutout while George and Rawdon, also in his red officer's garb, stand in the foreground. The staging flamboyantly inverts the principle that the key characters should carry the strongest colors. Here, the passive observers (George and Rawdon) hold the foreground with vivid accents of red, blue, and yellow, and the two women are reduced to colorless shapes (Figure 3.11). The silhouette screen does offer a nominal dramatic function, since it allows Becky to flirt with George literally in front of his wife, Amelia. But the screen also allows Mamoulian to work a game of hide-and-seek with color, giving the scene the appearance of a technological exhibition. Drama is a mere pretext for formal experimentation.

These devices are part of a more or less continuous manipulation of hue that keeps color near the forefront of graphic interest. Subsequent modes of design, especially in films with broad palettes, such as *The Adventures of Robin Hood,* will present complex varieties of hue and develop means for momentarily emphasizing specific sets of colors. *Becky Sharp,* however, offers generally simple combinations, which result in bold color contrasts, and devices seem forced because their foregrounding functions are so noticeable. In the demonstration mode, color techniques diverted attention to the fact of film style.

In a 1961 interview with David Robinson, Mamoulian recalled developing the color scheme for *Becky Sharp* across the film so that it would correspond to the dramatic climax: "My idea was to build up the colour dramatically. I wanted to start with black, white, grey; then ooze into colour. And I wanted the dramatic climax of the film to coincide with the colour climax, which would be predominantly red, because that is the nature of red."[16] One of the remarkable aspects of *Becky Sharp*'s design, however, is a general lack of just such a chromatic development. Despite Mamoulian's intentions, the high degree of foregrounding tends to interfere with any clear pattern of color scoring. From the first, strong colors are set against neutral backgrounds, and this continues more or less unabated for the entire production.

Only in one brief stretch of the narrative does the design conform to Kalmus's color vocabulary, which held that colors of lower saturation were more serious and refined. In the series of events during which Becky accepts money from her lover, Lord Steyne (Cedric Hardwicke), attempts to present it to her husband, Rawdon, and is eventually abandoned by him, her wardrobe color is depressed to match the dramatic tone. When she collapses on the floor after Rawdon's departure, the composition is relatively muted: Becky is in off-white lace on an Ochre carpet with Oxblood Red and Tapestry Blue details. Even here, though, Becky's Bachelor Button blue hair bow and belt inject jarring hues into the frame. Moreover, this stretch of the film also offers color foregrounding through vivid accents like the yellow roses in Becky's parlor and the bright strawberries on Becky and Steyne's dinner table. So even at its emotional and dramatic turning point, *Becky Sharp* continues the campaign to display color.

Intensified Demonstration: The Duchess of Richmond's Ball

But if the color design does not develop in a meaningful way across the film, Mamoulian and Jones did implement color scoring within a particular scene. Nearly every commentator on *Becky Sharp* singles out the Duchess of Richmond's ball as evidence of the film's dramatic approach to color. The scene must owe a good part of this attention to Mamoulian's promotion of the sequence as the pinnacle of *Becky Sharp*'s design. In his paper "Some Problems in Directing Color Pictures," the ballroom sequence provides the sole example of the proper, dramatic, and emotional use of color:

> You will see how inconspicuously, but with telling effect, the sequence builds to a climax through a series of intercut shots which progress from the coolness and sobriety of colors like gray, blue, green, and pale yellow, to the exciting danger and threat of deep orange and flaming red. The effect is achieved by the selection of dresses and uniforms worn by the characters and the color of backgrounds and lights.[17]

Whenever he discussed color, Mamoulian would return to this scene, most notably in his interview with Anthony Slide and in his article "Colour and Light in Films" for *Film Culture* in 1960. When, as noted above,

Mamoulian told Slide that he intended the "dramatic climax of the film to coincide with the color climax," he was referring not to the end of *Becky Sharp,* but to the Duchess of Richmond's ball, a scene that occurs in reels four and five. The sequence is certainly the film's most spectacular set piece, and so it follows that it should be an arena for the production's most ambitious color design.

Close analysis of the sequence is complicated by the state of the preservation print at the University of California–Los Angeles, which I consulted. Indeed, the history of this sequence is a testament to the fragility of the medium. In 1943, Pioneer Pictures sold *Becky Sharp* to Film Classics, which shortened the film, released it in two-color Cinecolor, and junked portions of the negative.[18] In the mid-1980s, with funds from the National Endowment for the Arts and the American Film Institute, film preservationists Robert Gitt (of the UCLA Film and Television Archive) and Richard Dayton (of YCM Laboratories) set out to reconstruct the film. Gitt and Dayton were faced with an incomplete set of materials. For reel four, which features the start of the ballroom sequence, there were no surviving yellow materials. Reel five, in which Napoleon attacks and the guests flee the ball, was missing important portions of the magenta record.[19] To solve these problems, Gitt and Dayton printed the magenta record of reel four twice in order to simulate yellow, and printed the yellow record in portions of reel five twice to simulate magenta. In the resulting print, colors were compromised at the start and toward the conclusion of the sequence, full three-color occurring only in the middle. Gitt and Dayton described the shifting color with reference to Joseph's jacket: "In the course of the Duchess of Richmond's ball, which takes place during reels four and five, Nigel Bruce's costume changes from dark green to deep blue and then to a light blue, as we go from simulated yellow, to full three-color and then to simulated magenta."[20]

Fortunately, additional preservation materials were retrieved from the Cineteca Nazionale in Rome late in 1984, and they were incorporated into the preservation print. According to *American Film,* that material was used to fine-tune the print's overall color balance and to improve reel nine. My viewings suggest that the color in the Duchess of Richmond's ball may have been evened out somewhat. A noticeable shift does occur at the break between reels four and five: Lady Bareacres's (Billie Burke's) dress changes from medium gray Blue Mist to light Pistachio Green.[21] The end of the sequence, though, does not appear to undergo a radical variation in color. Gitt suggested to me that the sequence is mostly accurate, aside from the loss of purples and greens in a few shots of guests fleeing.[22] Still, given the relatively unstable colors, my description relies on the full three-color portion of the scene (after the start of reel five and before the lighting change that occurs during the attack) for identification of the major colors, and I extrapolate to account for details in the surrounding portions.

Though Mamoulian suggested that he built color across the sequence as a whole, from subtle hues to a chromatic climax, analysis reveals a less unified, more eclectic approach. Indeed, Mamoulian's most systematic color scoring is concentrated in the scenes of guests and soldiers fleeing the ball after the onset of Napoleon's cannon attack, a relatively brief portion of the sequence. Before taking up the variety of experiments and effects presented by the Duchess of Richmond's ball, we might first consider the portion that most closely accords with Mamoulian's conception of dramatically organized color.

The director presented his most detailed discussion of the scene in the 1960 *Film Culture* article, and it is worth quoting at length. After describing the situation, in which news of Napoleon's march stirs a panic at the ball, Mamoulian explains:

> Now, in terms of realism, the officers who heard the news first and had an immediate duty to perform, would certainly leave the building first. Yet, visually, color-wise, it would have been wrong. All British uniforms of the period were red. Were I to show these in the first shots and then follow them with less striking mingled colours of the civilians, I would be decidedly building towards a chromatic anti-climax. So I went against plausibility and reason, and based this montage purely on colour-dynamics, believing that the rising excitement of just the colours themselves would affect the audience more strongly than a realistic procedure. I divided all guests into groups according to the hues of their costumes and photographed them, as they were running away, in separate shots; this, in order of the colours in the spectrum, ranging from cold to warm. This resulted in the officers leaving the building last instead of first. But the colour montage, from purples and dark blues to oranges and reds, achieved its emotional purpose of building up to the climax of the officer's scarlet capes in flight.[23]

Mamoulian posited his manipulation of color on the associations between hue and emotion that he shared with Kalmus and Jones. In its literalness, his idea for the sequence seems on par with Jones's red light in *La Cuca-*

racha. Here, though, the color scoring rests on a more complex organization of hue, developed across a series of shots.

The play of chromatic highlights in this portion of the sequence is accentuated by a dramatic change in lighting. As the terror begins to spread, a gust of wind throws open the ballroom windows and extinguishes the candelabra. In a long shot of the dance floor, Mamoulian eliminates general overhead illumination, darkening much of the frame and leaving hard, bright pools of light. The effect eliminates most of the ambient neutrals, leaving strong hues highlighted against the darkness. Moreover, the combination of hard, directed light and a generally darkened background increases the apparent saturation of these remaining hues.[24] For example, the Daffodil (strong yellow with a touch of orange) accents carried by a woman near the center of the dance floor seem to flare and glow as she moves against the darkness through a pool of light. The shift in lighting helps the filmmakers motivate stylized effects while generating a renewed emphasis on hue. In this environment, Mamoulian's color patterning becomes more conspicuous.

The systematic arrangement of hue that Mamoulian described emerges during a montage of guests rushing through doorways and down stairs. In two very brief series of shots, extras are staged so that color progresses from cool to warm hues. The first series begins with a shot of the ball's musicians, clad in black and white, racing away from the camera and toward a doorway. The composition momentarily depresses color, limiting the palette to blue-gray and black, broken by a single Dark Blue urn perched just inside the door. From here, the sequence rebuilds color. The next shot shows a line of guests rushing though one of the ballroom's great windows, its Porcelain Blue curtains billowing at the left edge of the frame. After a musician and a few soldiers in deep blue or black, there appears a group of women with costume accents in Porcelain Blue, Parrot Green, Medium Blue, and finally Shamrock green and Dandelion Yellow plaid. The last figure to cross the frame is a soldier with a Meadow Green jacket and Fiery Red accents.

The organization of color from cool to warm continues with a cut back to the doorway that reveals a new throng of guests. The foreground is kept dim so that colors flash briefly as the guests reach a pool of light at the threshold. At the front of the group are a woman in Lavender and another in Rich Gold, but they are swiftly overtaken by five women in gowns ranging from Mars Red to Vivid Orange, and a sixth in Prism Violet. Across these three shots, then, Mamoulian has grouped the extras so that they present a chromatic development from near monochrome to cool hues to warm hues.

The next series of shots repeats this pattern. A new group of guests are framed in long shot as they rush leftward down a flight of stairs. Here, the rightmost portion of the frame is kept dark, so colors are highlighted as figures pass through the middle. At the front of the group are gentlemen in black and white, once again forcing the range of color down to a minimum. Following the men, a group of women in lighter colored gowns appear, and they immediately activate the field of light. The foremost woman wears a gown of Coral Blush pink and white, and she is directly followed by a woman in off-white with Red Violet accents, one in Porcelain Blue, and another in reflective Turtledove silver satin. Just before the cut, a woman in a Porcelain Blue gown and one in Pistachio Green enter the light. Mamoulian cuts away to a shot of Joseph and his young servant hiding behind a potted fern. When he returns to the scene on the stairs, the action continues from the point of interruption. A group of women in blue and green clear out of the frame as another group, lead by a woman in Vivid Orange and including others in Fiery Red and Mars Red, enters the light. Again, Mamoulian has arranged the extras in roughly from cool to warm hues (Color Figure 6).

In these six shots, color is carefully organized, though not in as sustained a manner as Mamoulian described. Given the speed of the action, it seems doubtful that the formal pattern would be recognized as such in a single viewing. Rather, the montage gives a general impression of a movement toward red while keeping color accents prominent through the groupings of extras and the lighting design. Further, the sequence presents not a single, uniform development of the palette but the repetition of an effect. Color twice pulses from cool to warm, visually accentuating the tumult. But if the color score is not as obtrusive as in the climax that follows, it is still remarkable for the intricacy of its design. Mamoulian has indeed shaped the montage around "colour-dynamics," and his staging and costuming decisions have been determined by his interest in creating particular chromatic arrangements. True to the demonstration mode, color is given the highest stylistic priority.

As the sequence reaches its climax, however, Mamoulian presents much more overtly stylized color compositions. He shifts between bold blues and reds, culminating in a swell of brilliant, warm color. First, a line of soldiers in Sky Blue capes sweeps down a corridor in two shots. They are framed in a high-angle long shot, and then in a lower medium shot.

Together, the compositions present a spectacular mass of blue streaking across the frame on a strong diagonal (Color Figure 7). A cut to outside the estate's front door continues the emphasis on blue as the soldiers stream out. The interior compositions are then repeated with soldiers in Fiery Red capes charging through the corridor. Outside, two shots present the red-clad officers as they pour from the door. Then, the entire frame is washed in red light as a high-angle shot presents the soldiers running down the drive. A red street lamp in the corner of the frame motivates the colored illumination (Color Figure 8). After a brief shot of soldiers mounting their horses, the street-lamp composition returns, once again bathing the image in red as the soldiers' capes billow in the drive below. Upon reaching this height of intensity, the red light tinting the entire image, the sequence continues to emphasize the red and blue contrast. Four shots of the red-caped soldiers mounting and riding off are followed by a high-angle shot of the front gate as first the blue- and then the red-caped soldiers thunder out. The montage closes with a low-angle shot of the red-caped soldiers storming through the gate.

This sequence of shots most closely approaches the organization of color described by Mamoulian. The development from the pronounced blues to the blaze of red clearly manipulates color for visual climax. Perhaps the most remarkable aspect of this color scoring is its forcefulness. Though Mamoulian suggested that the colors build up "inconspicuously but with telling effect," the climactic juxtaposition of the blue and red capes, sweeping through identical compositions, is jarringly emphatic. As a demonstration of Technicolor's emotional power, the sequence, rather than suggesting that color can complement established techniques, promotes three-color to a position of primacy. In seeking to use color dramatically, Mamoulian made it the dominant element, imposing the pattern of chromatic advancement onto the action.

In his discussion of Technicolor aesthetics, Richard Neupert uses the Duchess of Richmond's ball as an illustration of how clumsily Technicolor designers aligned color with narrative function:

> The suspense that builds as Napoleon's cannon fire nears is paralleled so deliberately by the gathering of more and more red uniforms in the frame that the scene becomes comical. Either a character is the color of the potted plants, or else he is a soldier running around to add some contrasting red to the mise-en-scène. While such overly simplistic color schemes were meant to support the dramatic action, they actually de-

> tracted from it by calling attention to the clumsily fashioned color design (cool harmonious colors for the vulnerable people contrasted with the bloodred uniforms paralleling the rockets' red glare).[25]

This description is not entirely fair to the sequence because it oversimplifies the color relationships. Indeed, the palette in the ball sequence is the most complex and varied of the entire film. Still, Neupert's observation rings true. In trying to give color a clear dramatic function, Mamoulian resorted to a particularly deliberate mode of design. This kind of obvious manipulation would not offer a lasting approach for the use of Technicolor. As in *La Cucaracha,* the emphatic color scoring should be understood as part of a project to demonstrate Technicolor's potential. The sequence presents a clear and obvious illustration that color might serve a narrative function, just as it provided Mamoulian with a striking example that he could cite in promoting his work.

Most commentators on the ball sequence follow Mamoulian's lead and focus on the passage described above. Broadening the analysis somewhat, however, reveals that the scene also employs a less systematic, more flexible model of color scoring. As news of Napoleon's march begins to spread, jarring contrasts of hue broadly punctuate the moment. Here we find the seeds of a long-lasting method for binding color and drama, suggesting that the scene's true influence lay in its less-pronounced color devices.

When the cannon fire first sounds, Mamoulian cuts among the responses of various guests. He cuts from a group of red-coated officers to Wellington, clad in Dark Blue with red and gold accents, to the gambling room crowded with redcoats, to a parlor with large gold table topped by a vase of lilacs and surrounded by women in red, blue-green, and yellow, finally returning to Wellington as he consults with an officer. The brief montage introduces locations to which the sequence will return as panic spreads, and it initiates the pattern of cutting that juxtaposes strong accents. Here the color swells with the intense reds of the gambling room and then diminishes with the shot of the parlor and the return to Wellington.

When the cannon fire continues, Mamoulian repeats the technique with two more flurries of shots. He moves from a master shot of the crowded ballroom, with its extensive range of accents, to a series of individual reactions. Each composition offers a new set of dominant hues. The first features a dancer in a Biscay Bay (medium blue with a touch of green) gown, flanked by women in orange. The second offers accents of

3.12, 3.13, and 3.14. Rapid cutting between strong colors heightens the moment of cannon fire.

Vibrant Orange and Arcadia blue-green. The third presents a dancer in Lemon Drop yellow, and the fourth returns to the woman in blue as she asks her partner, "What was that?" (Figures 3.12, 3.13, and 3.14). The final round of rapid cutting presents different sets of guests as they venture explanations for the rumbling ("cannon," "thunder," "artillery"). This time a shot of the gambling room, with its intense mass of red, closes off the exchange as an officer declares, "No, it must be a thunderstorm." The speed of the cutting, in conjunction with the well-defined accents, generates a rapid barrage of hues, heightening the moment.

In these passages, Mamoulian draws on the scene's diverse palette and channels it toward a general form of color scoring. Particular colors are not associated with particular emotions; rather, the juxtapositions of accents underline the moment with a dynamic graphic play. The red uniforms in the gambling hall augment this pattern, but the sequence does not seem to stress the literal associations that Mamoulian, Jones, and Kalmus were fond of promoting. Nor is the color as deliberately patterned as in the climax. The hues merely contrast; they do not progress. This level of color scoring, the deploying of conspicuous accents for momentary punctual effects, would prove a more durable means of making color expressive.

3.15. Red-clad officers flood into the ballroom.

When Mamoulian does place more weight on red as an expressive element, he quickly reverts to the more general kind of punctual scoring. Staging, rather than editing, supports color when a distinct blast of cannon fire halts the dance, spurring officers, clad in red, to advance into the ballroom. The result is a flood of red as the officers pour into the cooler, less chromatically intense room, an effect amplified by the relative stasis of the other guests (Figure 3.15). Mamoulian's staging coordinates red with the onset of the attack, exploiting what he called "the exciting danger and threat of deep orange and flaming red."[26]

This conspicuous emphasis on red, however, is not long sustained. Nor is the color parceled out in a manner that builds toward a climax. Rather, it works as one bold hue among others. For instance, a shot of the gambling room as the officers rise and rush off left creates a sweeping mass of red. But it is followed by a view of the parlor, with the lilac bouquet in the center, as women rush from right to left. Here the costume colors are less unified, presenting vivid dashes of yellow, orange, and red, as well as blue and green. The scene marshals masses of hue and intense accents to achieve visual dynamism, but this is not the kind of precise progression that one might expect from Mamoulian's description. Color presents a series of jolts, loosely supporting the urgency of the narrative, rather than an extended pattern of development.

When placed in this context, the treatment of the climactic sequence of soldiers rushing to battle appears as one approach among several. Mamoulian tries out different levels of engagement between color and narrative (punctuation, obvious patterning, emotional associations with a particular hue) and several methods for highlighting color as a presence (editing, staging, variations in lighting). *Becky Sharp* does not refine a specific color style so much as vigorously demonstrate Technicolor's various possibilities.

The significance of the ballroom sequence extends well beyond its fiery climax. As a whole, the scene offers *Becky Sharp*'s most spectacularly varied palette. Like *La Cucaracha,* the two-reel sequence presents an experiment in handling the gamut of color. Mamoulian and Jones explore different options for integrating that palette into the flow of the sequence. They alternately showcase it as a source of spectacle and manage it as a background to action.

Of all of *Becky Sharp*'s innovations, the strategy of displaying color through the extension of establishing shots would prove one of its most durable contributions to Technicolor style. In such establishing sequences, as in other transitional passages, style can come forward more forcefully and with less risk of distracting from narrative development. *Becky Sharp* most fully realizes the method in the ball sequence. The film dissolves from a monochrome image of Napoleon's shadow against a gray wall to a breathtaking overhead view of the ballroom (Figures 3.16 and 3.17). A torrent of hue follows the brief reduction to black-and-white. Seven more establishing shots offer the most ornate color compositions in the film. Officers in their Fiery Red coats and gentlemen in black tuxedos dance with women in gowns of deep saturated Meadow Green; lighter Tarragon Green; bright Flame Scarlet; somewhat deeper Chinese Red; Radiant Yellow orange; deep, almost purple, Olympian Blue; lighter, less saturated Cobalt Blue; white; and Turtledove silver. This opening shows off *Becky Sharp*'s largest set, and the space is a field for the play of vivid color. It also introduces a motivation for color foregrounding that subsequent Technicolor films will thoroughly develop.

Once the scene returns to the major characters, the filmmakers both draw on and control this palette to guide and anchor attention. The first shot of Becky provides an example. After briefly framing the Duchess of Richmond in medium long shot, the camera pans and tracks to re-

3.16 and 3.17. Napoleon's silhouette dissolves to reveal a play of vivid color.

3.18. Becky in silvery white surrounded by officers in red.

veal a group of officers gathered in a semicircle farther down the stairs. The strong reds of their uniforms against the Stratosphere blue wall immediately mark them as the center of interest. The camera continues to arc, until it reveals Becky in the center of this semicircle. She wears a silvery White Swan dress with metallic Champaign Beige and Rich Gold spangles. Becky's graphic prominence is guaranteed by the contrast between her relatively neutral outfit and the strong reds of the surrounding officers (Figure 3.18). The costuming choice makes sense in such a chromatically busy environment. Color contrast provided by the group of red coats guides attention within the frame and motivates a trajectory for the camera movement. Like *La Cucaracha, Becky Sharp* employs color more pragmatically in the midst of an ongoing display.

Mamoulian and Jones test another option for handling color during Becky's meeting with Lord Steyne. Here, the filmmakers apparently intend to keep the broad palette boldly on display while staging important action. When Becky and Lord Steyne waltz, the range of color expands. The camera tracks their movements in medium to medium long shot as they pass before dancers and guests costumed in green, orange, yellow, red, blue, and pink. Mamoulian and Jones may well have expected that the contrast between Steyne's predominately black-and-white outfit and Becky's bright off-white dress would hold interest against the ever-changing accents. Placing simply colored costumes against a more assertive background reverses the film's standard method of design, but it still might ensure that the key figures stand out adequately from their surroundings. Certainly such a transposition would well serve later Technicolor projects, as in *Gone with the Wind*'s armory bazaar scene, where Rhett and Scarlett are clad in black before dancers in blue and red.[27]

The effect in *Becky Sharp,* though, is the continual introduction of distinct, vivid, potentially distracting accents behind the central characters. The generally flat illumination contributes to the effect, as does a shot scale that keeps the background figures fairly near the plane of focus. But the method of staging the background extras is most responsible for rendering them conspicuous. A close description helps capture the shot's complexity and specify how color competes for visual interest. Background details are introduced one or two at a time within an otherwise neutral setting. First, Becky and Steyne pass a woman seated against the back wall and clad in a Royal Blue dress. Next to her sits another guest in a Blue Green dress, and beyond her, a table with a spray of Strong Blue flowers. As the camera tracks steadily leftward, these accents emerge and pass out of the frame. When the woman in green passes off frame right, a red-coated officer with a partner in Tigerlily red-orange sweeps through the background. Next, the shot reveals a woman in a Snapdragon yellow gown and, as she moves toward the right, a soldier in Imperial Blue and a woman in Vibrant Orange emerge from the left. Soon the background accents emerge more quickly and mingle. The couple in Vibrant Orange and Imperial Blue circle back to the left as another couple bring in Flame Scarlet accents and cross off right. Swiftly they are followed by a gentleman in a black coat and a woman in a truly horrible gown of Shamrock green and Dandelion yellow plaid (Color Figure 9). After a few similar passing accents, the shot concludes as a soldier in blue and a woman in extremely saturated Geranium red spin through the background.

The background accents are perceptibly choreographed. Rather than isolate the central characters against a generally colorful environment (as the problem is handled in *Gone with the Wind*), Mamoulian stages the action to reveal a series of well-defined and varied dashes of color. Each accent is clearly displayed before being pushed off to make room for the next. Once more, *Becky Sharp*'s general mode of design results in the unusually conspicuous arrangement of color. Every new detail bursts forth against the blue and gray background. Greens and reds, oranges and blues follow one another and mingle as the foreground couple waltzes by. The filmmakers let color upstage the action.

The two reels of the ballroom sequence are a tour de force of experimental techniques for managing color, so it seems fitting that they should also present a more adventurous approach to lighting. Mamoulian and cinematographer Ray Rennahan attempt low-key lighting effects on the balcony set, where William comforts Amelia and where Becky has a rendezvous with Steyne. The scene is a test of how closely Technicolor could approach black-and-white standards. For example, when Amelia and William are framed on the balcony, the composition throws chromatic emphasis on the background while keeping the foreground figures in near silhouette. The foreground is kept dim, a touch of blue light highlighting the balcony's railing and portions of the figures. A key light from the rear right provides just enough illumination to pick out the edges of the characters' shoulders and portions of their faces. The left of each figure falls into darkness. The background, meanwhile, presents a blaze of light and color. Dancers in saturated red move back and forth before and behind the Porcelain Blue curtains and carpeted staircase that frame the dance hall (Color Figure 10). Mamoulian and Rennahan clearly labored to combine the lighting effects with pronounced color. The shot seems to proclaim that Technicolor can borrow the visual vocabulary of black-and-white without backing off the constant display of hue.

Nonetheless, the composition shows the limits of three-color's flexibility with regard to lighting. As discussed in the next chapter, Technicolor stock was not responsive enough to render areas of highlight and graded shadow as precisely as the film available to a black-and-white cinematographer. Though they achieve a low-key look, Rennahan and Mamoulian do not venture nearer to the characters than a medium long shot, and they lose most of the figures' detail and texture. Later in the sequence, when they do offer medium shots and medium close-ups, the filmmakers pour in a good deal more light. Rennahan was able to achieve good facial detail only at the cost of complex modeling and without the convincing approximation of low-key offered by earlier compositions.

The Duchess of Richmond's ball is *Becky Sharp*'s most ambitious sequence. It crystallizes the film's identity as a prototype or, to use Herbert Kalmus's term, "proving-ground" for color production. Chromatically, the scene goes for broke, and it might well stand on its own as a demonstration of the process. This sequence, like *La Cucaracha,* reaches toward a bold conception of filmmaking that grants color a place of stylistic primacy. This is perhaps most obvious during Becky's waltz with Steyne, when the incessant stream of accents challenges the central action. At the same time, though, Mamoulian and Jones introduce more modest uses of color, and they touch on a range of devices that would eventually blend with the classical system. The sequence's establishing shots mark out territory in which color can safely become assertive. Similarly, the most obvious color scoring accompanies action that is somewhat tangential to the main line of narrative. Napoleon's attack forms a spectacular background for Becky's personal manipulation of Rawdon, George, and Steyne. As an occasion for spectacle, this event is relatively open to stylization. Finally, although some of the color scoring is peculiarly elaborate, Mamoulian also tests a more general, flexible kind of punctuation that involves momentarily heightening the play of accents. In its eagerness to try anything, to rush through a series of possibilities, scene is both an intensification of the film's overall project and its centerpiece.[28]

Becky Sharp's Reception

The decidedly mixed critical reception of *Becky Sharp* reflected the film's prototype status. The trade and popular presses viewed the film as a more or less successful experiment in color production and a failed period drama. The *Hollywood Reporter* offered one of the few entirely positive reviews, but still concluded, "Color is the thing to sell."[29] *Variety* better mirrored the consensus in suggesting "the Technicolor values will be the prime appeal, particularly in view of the basic photoplay deficiencies."[30] Slighting the performances, direction, and narrative construction, the paper continued: "The excellence of the color and the shortcomings of the motion picture ingredients would suggest that all technical preparation was motivated in the direction of the technic rather than the script."[31] The trade recognized the film as first and foremost a novelty and a demonstration of three-color.

A common complaint held that the color had been too readily foregrounded, to the detriment of the drama. The *New Yorker* critic pointed to one of the film's more restrained scenes as evidence: "When Rawdon casts Becky from him, you see not her so much as you see the dress she wears and the Aubusson carpet on which she sinks."[32] Though the critic found the color design "a spectacle in beautiful taste," he shrewdly noted that the dramatic material had "the finesse of a lumber camp."[33] It was generally agreed that color would still have to prove itself capable of supporting, rather than dominating, a production. The *Life* review concluded, "It remains a question as to whether or not color can be kept in its place in the creation of a full length film."[34] Andre Sennwald echoed this sentiment in the *New York Times.* He called the film "both incredibly disappointing and incredibly thrilling."[35] *Becky Sharp* succeeded in presenting "an animate procession of cunningly designed canvases," but this technological achievement overwhelmed the story. Sennwald recommended that the "problem is to reduce this new and spectacular element to a position, in relation to the film as a whole, where color will impinge no more violently upon the basic photographic image than sound does today."[36]

Despite the warnings issued by Jones, Mamoulian, and Kalmus that color should not be overemphasized, *Becky Sharp* indulges in a near-constant play of foregrounding and strong juxtapositions of hue. *Variety* recognized that the film's duty to demonstrate three-color had encouraged this forcing of color. In its report on the film's premiere, the trade noted:

> One of the major problems seen in *Becky Sharp* is need for greater selectivity in use of tone and tint for agreeable impression to both the cultivated and the average audience eye. . . . Some of the less happy combinations are considered due to the fact that Technicolor is using *Becky Sharp* as its showcase, incorporating many colors merely to show the range of the process to the trade.[37]

In a similar fashion, Karl Hale used *Becky Sharp* as a negative example in his advice column to amateur filmmakers in *American Cinematographer*. Hale described how the red in an officer's uniform "pulls your eye to that coat and it adheres to it." When Jones and Mamoulian place a vase of red roses in the background, Hale complained, "Your eye is constantly pulled away from the people and to the flowers." Likewise, when Becky, clad in a strong blue dress, plays a scene with William, in uniform, Hale noted, "The interests are constantly clashing. Your eyes are pulled from one character to the other depending upon movement."[38] Like the *Variety* reporter, Hale was responding to basic aspects of the film's design that keep color an assertive element. Both the introduction of colorful decorations into neutral backgrounds and the inclination to costume multiple characters in strong hues are choices that would be largely eliminated from the next round of Technicolor features. *Becky Sharp*'s use of color was understood to be an imperfect introduction to the process, one that demonstrated color's potential but would require revision if color were to be sustained.

Still, *Becky Sharp* prevailed as a promotion for three-color. Aside from the *Life* reviewer, who grumbled that Miriam Hopkins "looks as if she were in the last stages of scarletina," few critics found serious fault with the new process's rendition.[39] Color had won respect, even if the drama had not. Pioneer's bid to impute an aura of legitimacy through Jones's participation paid off in praise from *The New Yorker* critic, who declared: "Thanks certainly to the various sciences concerned, such a man as Robert Edmond Jones has been allowed to employ his skill for our pleasure. . . . What someone else, someone other than Mr. Jones . . . with a weakness for pretty postcards may do with the marvel of the new scientific advance I shudder to think I may some day know."[40] The new process was, for the moment, insulated from the charges of tastelessness that had damaged two-color. Similarly, the Duchess of Richmond's ball received special praise as evidence that color could become, as Sennwald put it, a "constructive dramatic device."[41] The obviousness of Jones and Mamoulian's design served to bring color effects to the attention of reviewers. This may have made color seem distracting, but it also ensured that color would be noticed and evaluated.

Conclusion

Pioneer Pictures' productions, and the discussions of color aesthetics that issued from Kalmus, Jones, and Mamoulian, were vital in introducing three-color Technicolor as a viable new technology. *La Cucaracha* and *Becky Sharp* present experiments in color design, demonstrations of three-color's range, and the various functions that color might perform. The designers argued that three-color could pose a meaningful contribution to film style, and the films conspicuously manipulate color for obvious dramatic or emotional effects. If this approach erred, it was in giving color too high a priority in the hierarchy of film style. In making formal choices, the filmmakers consistently favored alternatives that relied on color. Instead of making color functional *within* the classical system, the demonstration mode showcased color, making it a readily observable, extrusive element. As Jones's vision of forging a new operatic form suggests, it was a case of trying to make Technicolor sing before it could talk.

At the same time, the films are catalogues of color techniques. Because they attempt to run through so many different options, these productions never really elaborate color design in a rich or textured manner. Each color technique is something of a one-off effect. A device may be repeated and varied fairly mechanically, as with the dissolves in *Becky Sharp* or the mood lighting in *La Cucaracha,* but color is not likely to be meaningfully extended or structured into an overarching pattern. The demonstration mode did not encourage the development of palettes across a film, the formation of complex color motifs, or the exploration of different levels of cooperation between color and other elements of style. As we will see, these were tasks taken up by the restrained mode.

Becky Sharp is particularly interesting in that it does reduce the range of color somewhat and channels chromatic emphasis toward points of narrative interest. In most cases the designs are fairly simple, since there is rarely much modulation within a single hue. The film lays out its palette in large blocks of color, unlike the fine, mosaic-like combinations of later assertive designs, typified by *The Adventures of Robin Hood* or, later, *Meet Me in St. Louis.* In its simplicity, the film takes up Natalie Kalmus's suggestion about the "judicious use of neutrals" by confining most of the mise-en-scène to unassertive grays, blues, and other cool hues of low saturation. Yet in playing vivid accents against this background, the design inevitably pushes color to the forefront. *Becky Sharp* attempts to fulfill the rule of emphasis, but does so inelegantly, favoring prominent distinctions of hue rather than middle-range variations of saturation and value.

Similarly, *La Cucaracha* and *Becky Sharp* attempt to forge connections between drama and color by way of a literal color vocabulary. Rhetorically, these moments are visual equivalents of the designer's discussions about the language of color: they draw attention to color's dramatic potential. The mood lighting in *La Cucaracha* and the chromatic organization in the Duchess of Richmond's ball are attempts to show how some established conventions of color meaning could be brought to film; they demonstrate that color was an understood and controllable signifier. In these instances, the filmmakers attempted to attach semantic meanings to color rather than to concentrate on giving it a structural function. Though this kind of color scoring died off when efforts turned to a more thorough integration of color into the classical style, it served notice that Technicolor would try to define its process as integral to the narrative.

We might view Pioneer's first productions as aesthetic dead ends. But these films also introduced techniques that would continue throughout the 1930s. The keying of color to the lead female performer, the exploitation of transitional sequences for color foregrounding, the guiding of attention into depth through the placement of accents, the use of momentary color contrasts to punctuate a dramatic development, and the attempt to incorporate low-key and other monochrome lighting effects are all procedures that developed as major studios adopted three-color. The choice of genres, a musical and a costume picture, was also somewhat prescient, since these formulas offered conventional motivations for stylistic play; they would become perennial standbys for Technicolor. In testing options, these prototypes provided a model for the further exploitation of color. In a comparable fashion, the aesthetic guidelines that Natalie Kalmus offered in "Color Consciousness" would inform most successful color design in the classical era. Her basic principles proved enduring, though flamboyant and deliberate implementations of them, as in *Becky Sharp*, would wane.

Finally, the tendency to exploit color's novelty, to draw attention to it as a formal element, would persist in even the most restrained productions. The demonstration mode of design was not wholly divorced from later Technicolor styles; rather, it represented one end of a spectrum that ran from overt display to the thorough subordination of color. If the films that immediately followed *Becky Sharp* presented a swing of the aesthetic pendulum away from intensive color foregrounding, the more assertive productions toward the end of the 1930s constituted a return. By then, however, filmmakers had built up a range of conventions for handling chromatic display less overtly or obtrusively.

In his comment that color would need to be reduced to a position whereby "it will impinge no more violently . . . than sound does today," Andre Sennwald keenly anticipated the problem faced by Technicolor after *Becky Sharp*. Technicolor had effectively showcased the three-color process, and the demonstration films enticed major studios. But if color were to become a sustained formal option, it needed to conform to the roles accorded to film style within classical cinema. Color would have to cooperate with and recede from the stylistic forefront, and three-color needed to prove flexible enough to meet the demands of regular production. *The Trail of the Lonesome Pine* initiated a mode of design that directly wrestled with this problem by restricting the palette and limiting color foregrounding. As we will see in the next two chapters, the restrained mode constituted a decided effort to assimilate, rather than showcase, three-color Technicolor.

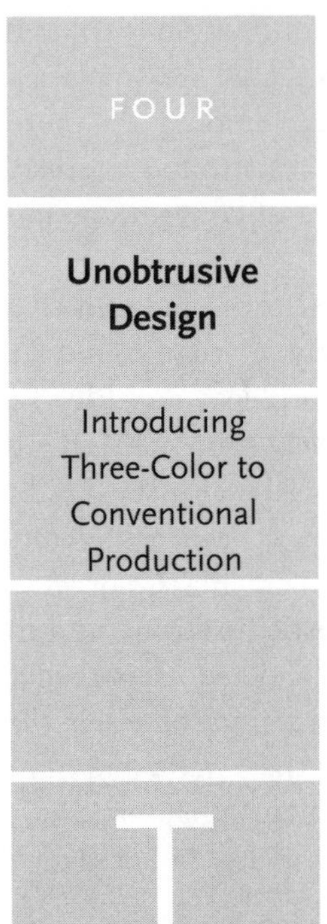

FOUR

Unobtrusive Design

Introducing Three-Color to Conventional Production

Though Technicolor has become synonymous with garishness in our contemporary lexicon, classical Hollywood's approach to three-color was founded on a subdued, restrained mode that flourished between 1936 and 1938. This type of design developed as a direct response to technological, commercial, and aesthetic currents in 1930s cinema. A close look at 1930s designs illustrates how color aesthetics were shaped by a web of institutional pressures and how modes of design eased color's integration into the classical style. The restrained mode is the linchpin to an understanding of Hollywood's use of color.

The Technicolor look and the company's market strategy entered a new phase of development after *Becky Sharp. Variety* concisely sized up the matter: "Color is king in Hollywood. But he sits on an uncertain if not shaky throne."[1] Beginning in 1936, the company turned to the problem of building a regular market with the major studios. In his autobiography, Technicolor founder Herbert Kalmus grouped together films from 1935 through early 1938 as the "first fifteen important feature-length pictures produced in three-color Technicolor."[2] For Kalmus, these features "demonstrated that the Technicolor three-strip process was as successful for features as it had been for cartoons and short subjects." Just as importantly, the films provided a training ground for "a large number of producers and directors and actors and film technicians [who] gained actual experience with the three-color camera."[3] Kalmus's "first fifteen" is an arbitrary number, but films from the period are united by his goals of placing Technicolor features on a firm commercial footing and familiarizing the industry with the new process.

This was a time of cautious experimentation. On the one hand, Technicolor lobbied studios to cast aside the association of color with pure novelty. If the new process were to last, it would have to prove its potential for enhancing drama and story and overcome its short-lived attraction as a gimmick. On the other hand, Technicolor had to convince producers that the increased costs would be justified by adequate product differentiation and larger grosses. In July 1935, *Variety* encapsulated the majors' attitudes as they entered this era of Technicolor: "Despite some nibbling by a few producers, most major producing companies continue to be wary of color for feature pictures. Whether color for features is commercially profitable, and will the public pay more and in larger numbers to see such pictures, has the producers guessing."[4] These were the questions that the designers and technicians at Technicolor set out to address in the years following *Becky Sharp.*

From the start of 1936 through 1938, twenty-four full-color features were processed at the Technicolor plant. Production nearly doubled each year; thirteen features were released in 1938 alone. Though far from staggering, these figures depict an industry slowly and steadily gaining confidence in Technicolor. The additional costs for color production were quite high; Kalmus estimated that in 1937 the use of Technicolor increased production outlay by $150,000 a feature.[5] But Kalmus may have been conservative. Color could cost a good deal more. At the high end, for instance, *Variety* estimated that in *The Goldwyn Follies,* an additional $600,000 in production expense was due to color.[6] Despite such ominous figures, Paramount, United Artists, Warner Bros., Twentieth Century–Fox, RKO, and MGM had begun to release color features with some regularity by 1938.

Perhaps most importantly for winning studio support, Technicolor established a successful box-office record with a number of ambitious releases during the late 1930s. In 1937, the *Hollywood Reporter* exhibitor poll rated *A Star Is Born* as "the best money picture of the year," and *Variety* placed the film as the tenth-best grosser of the season.[7] In 1938, Warner Bros.' *Adventures of Robin Hood* placed fifth on *Variety*'s "Top Grossers" list, and the animated feature *Snow White* took an easy first (Figure 4.1).[8] Re-

4.1. *Snow White,* top grosser of 1938.

leased in January 1939, Twentieth Century–Fox's production of *Jesse James* became the top-grossing picture of that year.[9] Because each of these features was a prestige picture, it is hard to argue that color was a deciding factor in box-office success.[10] Nonetheless, the studios had trusted Technicolor with some of their top productions, and these films had performed well, suggesting that three-color had found a comfortable, though limited, place on the majors' rosters by the end of the decade.

As color found a niche within the industry, there appeared an important shift in color style. Technicolor engineers set their sights on making the technology more flexible so that it could better square with the standards of black-and-white practice. In conjunction, color designers subdued variations of hue in favor of an emphasis on tone and value, qualities more amenable to the dominant black-and-white style. The insistent foregrounding present in *La Cucaracha* and *Becky Sharp* gave way to a less obtrusive look that was judged more easily integrable with narrative. This was the restrained mode of color design.[11]

As an approach to design, the restrained mode was far from monolithic. Indeed, the three case studies in this chapter and the next show how filmmakers could use the style for markedly different ends. *The Trail of the Lonesome Pine* established the style and used color to develop fairly subtle motifs while allowing it to recede to the background. *A Star Is Born* and *The Goldwyn Follies* (both considered in the next chapter) developed the mode to allow for a more overt display of color, dramatic punctuation, and elegant decoration. At the end of the decade, the restrained mode was eclipsed by the complex and assertive designs of films like *The Adventures of Robin Hood* and *The Wizard of Oz.* But even these films built on the methods for integrating and controlling color that had been formed within this extraordinarily important, though nearly forgotten, mode of design.

The Case against Color

The merits of color for motion pictures were a matter of vigorous debate in the late 1930s, and the main point of disagreement was whether Technicolor could easily meld with the aesthetics and practices of conventional production. Few sources lay out the terms of this debate more forcefully than a series of bizarrely antagonistic articles appearing in *American Cinematographer* in 1936. Emphasizing the failings of color processes, unsigned articles entitled "Why All This Hubbub Regarding Color," "Is All This Color Ballyhoo Justifying Itself," and "Just What Is So Mysterious about Color" claimed to have been written on behalf of the American Society of Cinematographers (ASC). The articles set out a unified attack, questioning the value of color for feature films and defending black-and-white's dominance. The author proclaimed: "The multiple-hued films appear mainly to have enhanced appreciation for the superlative artistic and dramatic creations that have been evolved in monochrome."[12]

Among general points about production slowdowns and color's cost, the critic offered several specific aesthetic objections. For one, color should be rejected precisely because conventions for making it compatible with the established style had not been developed, and it ran the risk of dominating other stylistic elements: "[Color] is not at this stage of the game, a controllable quantity in the sense that light-and-shadow is. . . . Story, cast, sets, wardrobe—every item involved—must be whittled down to the narrow capacities of the process."[13] Obtrusive color designs were blamed for "the partial eclipse of drama and story or action." The author complained, "Colors perform strange tricks at the most unexpected times and for no apparent good reason. One may suddenly decide to stand up and cheer, or roll over and play dead. And the perverse little devil usually does it at just the wrong time."[14] Finally, the very use of color was held to encourage a distracting overemphasis on photographic technique: "Any competent Director of Photography, could, if he were so short-sighted, make his black and white so dominant in artistic content as to steal the picture. But he knows better."[15]

Behind many of these assertions was animosity toward Technicolor's emphasis on scientific principle, which seemed to ignore the craft-based know-how of a working cinematographer. "Just What Is So Mysterious about Color" begged the "budding young scientists fresh from campus lecture halls [to] turn over their processes intact to practical studio production men."[16] Citing *Lonesome Pine*, the author noted that "men wise in picture making subdued the color, de-emphasized it . . . not a high tribute to color's professed dramatic content."[17] Since color was apparently incompatible with the goals of effective cinematography, the critic recommended bracketing it off from the main line of production. Color might be best used for interpolated sequences, since "ten to twenty minutes of color comes as a pleasant and enjoyable change," or "an occasional musical or spectacle fantasy" could capitalize on it as a curiosity.[18] As a major addition to film style, though, color intruded unacceptably without offering any requisite advances in narrative or artistic substance.

At its most basic, the argument assumed that the Technicolor Corporation valued proper color rendition at the expense of practical and artistic cinematography. As an example, the critic related the following: "In one specific instance, the cinematographer worked in a light key much lower than demanded by laboratory conceived charts and results were surprisingly eloquent. But the colorists continue to pump in their terrific light, in abject devotion to their elaborate chartings."[19] The *American Cinematographer* articles blame Technicolor engineers for an inflexibility that was out of keeping with both the day-to-day demands of studio practice and the visual range thought necessary to serve film drama. The tension between the scientist and the "cameraman" was played out in a debate about film aesthetics.[20]

These were by far the most outspoken arguments against color in the professional press, and they could not honestly claim to represent the ASC's dominant attitude. Yet this criticism clearly enunciated the objections that color had to overcome. During the late 1930s, Technicolor's designers and engineers labored to prove that color need not mean the abandonment of long-standing ideals of well-crafted cinematography.

Constraints on Cinematography

Technicolor engineers had to prove that their system could complement rather than dominate standard production practices. Key areas of research and development included lighting, makeup, and processing. In each domain, technicians and filmmakers worked to help three-color better accord with norms of black-and-white.

The most salient imposition on regular studio practices was three-color Technicolor's illumination requirements. Ultimately, the process's famous appetite for light was the prime technological factor in the Technicolor look of the 1930s. At the base of the Technicolor system was a set of film stocks with a collective speed equivalent to around sixteen ASA.[21] However, a good deal of light was lost within the camera. The magenta filter on the top layer of the bipack had a factor (a measurement of the amount of light lost when it passes through a filter) of approximately five. The green filter placed before the single strip of negative that registered green light had a factor of around six.[22] This meant that together the filters accounted for a loss of light equivalent to at least two f-stops. These and other variables reduced the effective speed of the Technicolor system to around four ASA.[23] Technicolor speed would remain near this level until the production of *Gone with the Wind* (1939), when engineers introduced a new set of stocks and filters.

By comparison, in 1935, Kodak introduced Super X black-and-white stock, with an ASA of forty, followed in 1938 by Plus X, with a speed reportedly equivalent to eighty ASA.[24] Obviously there was a significant gap between the lighting requirements for Technicolor and those for standard black-and-white. In 1936, the Society of Motion Picture Engineers' studio lighting committee reported that average black-and-white set illumination ranged from 250 to 400 foot-candles, whereas Technicolor levels ranged from 800 to 1,000 foot-candles.[25] Throughout the 1930s, engineers toiled to reduce these lighting levels, and they underplayed the disparity between monochrome and color requirements.

In addition to increased intensity of illumination, Technicolor required light with a color temperature equivalent to that of sunlight in order to register hues properly.[26] To attain the required illumination and color temperature, producers turned to arc lights, which hadn't been in general use since the 1920s.[27] After the transition to sound, studios relied predominantly on much quieter and cooler incandescent lighting. In 1935, the Mole-Richardson Company was commissioned to design improved and silent arc lamps.[28] Early on, though, Technicolor filmmakers had to rely on updated equipment from the silent era. Recalling his experience shooting *The Trail of the Lonesome Pine* with these lights, Technicolor cinematographer William H. Greene emphasized their shortcomings:

> The only possible course was to lay a good foundation of general lighting . . . and to build up key and modeling light as best one could with the obsolescent Sun-Arcs and rotaries which were all we had to use for such service. Under such circumstances it was necessary to use more light and more lamps than were truly desirable. This inevitably limited the range of effects which could safely be attempted.[29]

As we saw in *Becky Sharp,* the initial set of lighting tools imposed constraints on spotlighting and modeling, making the manipulation of fine highlights and shadows difficult, even impossible.

By the end of 1936, Mole-Richardson introduced high-intensity arc lights, which represented a substantial improvement.[30] In general, they offered lighter and more compact units that could provide precise control of light.[31] At the spring 1937 meeting of the Society of Motion Picture Engineers, C. W. Handley reported that Technicolor had managed to reduce average illumination "by more than forty percent," in part because of more efficient equipment.[32] This reduction would bring Technicolor illumination requirements into a range of around 460 to 580 foot-candles, still substantially greater than those for black-and-white.[33] Nevertheless, the new research in lighting had significantly decreased the number of lights required on a Technicolor set. Handley estimated that with improved equipment, the ballroom set for *Becky Sharp* could have been illuminated with only 167 units, while in 1935 the production had required an astonishing 384 lamps.[34] The trend was clearly toward lighting designs that used fewer, more powerful units.

Differences in color temperature between lights were routinely neutralized through the addition of gels. High-intensity arcs would be fitted with light, straw-colored filters to compensate for an excess of blue in their output; incandescents could be fitted with light blue filters to correct their yellowish light. The variations in color were also exploited for effect lighting: uncorrected incandescent lights simulated the warm yellow of lamplight, and unfiltered high-intensity arcs produced steel blue moonlight.[35] Although minor improvements continued, by late 1936 the basic arc units and schemes for their use were in place.

The impact of these lighting requirements on cinematographic style is difficult to measure. Technicolor cameramen and representatives were at pains to underplay the gap between monochrome and color lighting styles. As William H. Greene rather slyly noted, "Several outstanding black-and-white cinematographers have stated that they would not be afraid to take their monochrome cameras on to a modern Technicolor set and stake their reputations on getting a thoroughly satisfactory black-and-white shot."[36] Of course, a more daring test would be to place a Technicolor camera on a monochrome set. To be fair, Greene was suggesting that respected techniques of black-and-white cinematography could be achieved in Technicolor. Other accounts indicate that the lighting styles were by no means commensurate. As late as 1944, Ronald Neame wrote of his experience shooting *This Happy Breed:* "Lighting for Technicolor is rather like drawing with a piece of charcoal after having got used to a very fine pencil."[37]

One consequence of heavy reliance on large, high-intensity arc units was a loss of the flexibility afforded in monochrome by smaller, softer incandescents. After the introduction of faster stock in 1939, Ray Rennahan, Technicolor's chief cinematographer, commented on the newfound flexibility of "handier units . . . especially in lighting people." He noted that the newly usable incandescents allowed "precise lighting of faces in close-ups, exactly as they would be used in black-and-white."[38]

As was typical of Technicolor propaganda, Rennahan's acknowledgment of previous limitations appeared only after new developments could purportedly solve them. Only after the new stock appeared did technical writers admit there had been a loss of flexibility before 1939. Color cinematographers were especially handicapped when it came to the complicated shadow and modeling effects, which were valued in glamorizing close-up work. The problem: in order to reach required illumination, light from high-intensity arcs had to be kept hard and undiffused. In late 1939, cinematographer Ernest Haller explained, "The only lighting units on a Technicolor set that have used much diffusion have been the [large general-illumination lights known as] broadsides."[39] For Haller, it was only after the introduction of faster film stock that color could approach monochrome technique: "Now, with the faster film, we can soften our modeling light just about any way we wish." He concluded that the additional versatility would be especially valuable in close-ups, since it "enables a cinematographer to use all the little tricks of precision lighting he has used in monochrome to glamorize his stars. I am sure that color is going to be more flattering than ever to the women."[40] Before 1939, the relative inflexibility of available spotlighting blocked Technicolor's attainment of monochrome ideals.

At the same time, three-color mandated a more consciously measured use of light. This is most clearly illustrated by Technicolor's requirement of exposure-meter readings on the set. While black-and-white lighting was routinely balanced by eye, Technicolor insisted on foot-candle meters to determine light levels.[41] The rule was governed by the Technicolor lab's desire for well-exposed negatives that would properly register color values. In his brief history of film lighting, Charles Handley described the situation:

> The cinematographer still does much of his light balancing by visual means, but he also reads the incident light in various areas and when

> he goes beyond the latitude of the system in order to obtain a certain dramatic effect he has been forewarned.[42]

A more careful balance of light, coupled with the need for higher illumination, meant the more accurate direction and placement of lights. Ray Rennahan explained that the new arc units offered better control of the beam, but this also meant that "there is less 'spilled light' to rely on for general lighting. Our lighting must be done more accurately."[43] Where excess light could be counted on to take care of some background and general illumination on a black-and-white set, Technicolor required that each area be carefully brought up to acceptable, measured levels.

The restricted latitude of three-strip also meant that highlights and shadows required more attention than in monochrome shooting. Greene offered the most lucid discussion of the problem in a 1937 article for *International Photographer:*

> Many of your most capable monochrome artists key their lighting essentially to their shadow illumination, following the old adage to "expose for the shadows, and let the highlights take care of themselves." You cannot do this in color. There, the thing to be watched is the highlights. If they get too much light, the color is simply washed out, and you have an unpleasant glare of white light on the screen. If, on the other hand, you build your lighting with a watchful eye on the highlights, and let the shadows graduate naturally down from them, your scene will be much more satisfactory.[44]

Greene suggested that Technicolor lighting narrowed the range between dark and light, encouraging a somewhat flatter look. James Wong Howe recommended solving this problem by diffusing and softening bright areas so that lighting served "merely to suggest a highlight."[45] This care with highlights was matched by a similar need to soften shadows, since dark areas fell more quickly into blackness.[46]

Given these constraints, filmmakers endorsed two different general approaches to Technicolor lighting. One view saw color as providing a means of separating planes, and thus encouraged flatter lighting that would strongly register hues, the approach on display in *Becky Sharp.* Peter Mole, in a review of his company's arc lighting equipment, explained:

> In general, a rather flatter lighting balance than would be used for black-and-white seems to produce the best results in color. This is to be expected; in monochrome photography, the only possible method of sepa-

> rating objects and planes is through contrast of light and shade, while in a natural-color scene, much of this can be achieved by natural color contrasts.[47]

James Wong Howe, writing of his experience on Selznick International's *Adventures of Tom Sawyer* in 1937, offered a more nuanced description of how this approach might work. Howe advocated soft modeling from floor-level arcs, "with a bare minimum of fill-in and backlighting from units above." Backlight and rim light, standard for black-and-white cinematography, were "seldom necessary in color, for we have inherent color differences to serve the same process."[48] Softer, more even light with fewer highlights allowed hue to stand in for cues that stronger lighting contrast provided in black-and-white.

An alternative solution was proposed by Technicolor's own cinematographers. In general, these craftsmen stressed the similarities to black-and-white lighting, arguing strongly against flatter illumination. In 1935, Ray Rennahan noted, "I get the best results in color if I light with a trifle more brilliance and contrast, with a stronger separation of planes, than I'd do in black and white. Color photography does not lend itself well to overly flat or soft illuminations."[49] Like William H. Greene, Rennahan minimized the distance between standard practice and the special requirements of color.

Rennahan's intent was to stress a creative freedom in color lighting equivalent to that offered by monochrome. A flat lighting aesthetic, by placing more emphasis on the role of color at the cost of varied illumination, would encroach on the cinematographer's traditional arena of creativity for establishing mood, stylizing the image, and exhibiting virtuosity. Therefore, Technicolor was presented as a complement to standard practice, as when Technicolor cinematographer William Skall wrote: "Lighting for natural-color cinematography should not be a problem; any color process must inevitably require more light than is usual in monochrome, but aside from this one requirement, the principal difference I see between the two is that in color you have far greater possibilities."[50]

Throughout the thirties, efforts were made to eliminate the necessity of flatter illumination. By June 1937, Rennahan claimed that the process was more responsive and that he now lit "almost exactly as I would for monochrome. The highlights do not have to be watched as closely as they did a little while back, and the shadow detail is also more easily preserved."[51] Ultimately, the nature and real benefit of these improvements remained unclear, and Rennahan's claims might be read as part of Technicolor's promotional efforts. Even as Technicolor's cinematographers aimed at erasing the gap between color and monochrome aesthetics, there were technological factors that could not be ignored. With a four ASA system, color lighting could never achieve parity with black-and-white, despite the aim of achieving equivalent effects at higher illumination. Throughout the thirties, color cinematographers had to work within narrower latitudes and with less flexibility than their counterparts shooting in monochrome.

The quest for strong shadows and high contrast had to be balanced against Technicolor's desire for a fully exposed negative, but Technicolor cinematographers were also at pains to prove that light could still serve the dramatic and pictorial functions common to black-and-white. The best example of how important monochrome aesthetics were for defining Technicolor lighting is the case of colored lighting. Colored lights, which had been exploited in *La Cucaracha* and *Becky Sharp* to show off three-strip's potential, were now strongly discouraged because they departed from black-and-white schemes. Simulated moonlight or lamplight was acceptable, but William H. Greene echoed a general opinion when he stated, "Pictorialism and mood can both be served best by an uncolored use of good dramatic lighting such as we would expect in a fine black-and-white production."[52] Color would not replace the expressive possibilities of light and shadow.

In fact, conspicuous dramatic lighting was a marked trend in late-1930s Technicolor. Scenes that required effects lighting encouraged cinematographers to experiment with the process's limits, reducing illumination "right down to black and white standards."[53] Productions in this period, beginning with *The Garden of Allah* (1936), often incorporated isolated instances of low-key effect lighting and silhouette composition. As the next chapter will demonstrate, Greene's work on *A Star Is Born* provides an excellent illustration of how Technicolor cinematographers sought to retain the expressive power of light.

Another production technology that required significant alteration for use with Technicolor was makeup. Successful reproduction of flesh tones was central to establishing the superiority of Technicolor. In a 1955 lecture given to the Technicolor Control Department on the subject of color separation, Russell Conant offered a striking explanation why flesh tones were considered of supreme importance:

> It is rare that anyone in a motion picture theater audience has ever seen any of the original scenes of a picture photographed. . . .

> The person in the audience can only compare the color reproduction with some mental impression of what he thinks people and objects should look like. As long as the rendition is not contrary to expectations based on memory and experience, the performance can be satisfying and pleasing.
>
> While this situation usually provides some range of acceptance in rendition of objects, it doesn't mean that anything goes. . . . Moreover, every person in the theater audience has a pretty good idea of what human flesh looks like. They know with generally good agreement whether the reproduction is good, just passably fair, or definitely bad in this respect.
>
> For this reason, particular emphasis is put on the adjustment and control of a process so that it will render consistently pleasing flesh tones. Beyond this, the rendition of other colors and tones must be reasonable and satisfying. This provides some tolerable latitude in the adjustment of a process which is fortunate.[54]

Conant was speaking after twenty years of refinement of three-color, but the reproduction of flesh tones remained the area in which color fidelity was most valued. In the 1930s, the formulation of new makeup offered the first and most fundamental step in ensuring proper skin color.

Through 1936 and 1937, Max Factor developed special makeup for the three-color process. In June 1936, *International Photographer* indicated that a new type of makeup had been employed on *Lonesome Pine, The Dancing Pirate,* and *The Garden of Allah.* Reportedly, the makeup was more reflective, allowing a substantial reduction in illumination.[55] One year later, the same publication reported that further improvements would allow films to avoid the "apparently jaundiced skins being projected" in *The Dancing Pirate, Ramona* (1936), *The Garden of Allah,* and *A Star Is Born.* The latest improvements would be first employed on *Vogues of 1938.*[56] The makeup line was refined throughout the 1930s, and claims of perfection should be viewed with some suspicion.

Max Factor provided a more detailed explanation of the new developments in an interview with *American Cinematographer.* Factor described the new "T-D" series as "scientific duplications of natural skin-tones, subdued to fit the limitations of the color camera."[57] The new series used a thinner liquid foundation that held pigment in colloidal suspension, rather than the heavier greasepaint paste used in black-and-white.[58] All hues were formulated to "give the camera a makeup which it will interpret as a perfect reproduction of that natural tone."[59] Apparently, this involved toning down the white components to avoid glare, deepening the pinks and reds, and carefully controlling blue and yellow.[60] Factor emphasized an important difference from black-and-white when he noted that "modeling makeup," which simulates highlight or shadow, "thereby simplifying the cinematographer's task," could not be replicated in color.[61] Flesh tones were one area where color rendition was more important than the tonal contrast of monochrome cinematography. A certain degree of flexibility of mise-en-scène was lost.

Attempts to describe the unique rendition of skin tones offered by Technicolor have been rather vague. In his technological history of dye-transfer, Richard Haines refers to the "Technicolor tan," which he attributes to makeup and "bastard-amber gels on the lights." He also notes that skin tones were "very saturated" in the thirties and forties.[62] Though it is not clear that colored lighting was utilized in the way he suggests, skin tones in Technicolor do have greater density than in contemporary color cinematography. Certainly the T-D makeup contributed to the apparently saturated skin tones, and perhaps this was by design. Technicolor makeup was part of an aesthetic system that valued "pleasing tones" and sought to foreground flesh tones as a point of difference from black-and-white.

A final technological issue directly related to the Technicolor look, but far less documented than lighting, was processing. Although various commentators referred to improvements in processing throughout the midthirties, they provided little significant detail. Technicolor engineers were secretive when it came to the fine points of laboratory work. In general, they aimed to increase the responsiveness of the system and allow the lab to work with a less dense negative. Film stock was hypersensitized at the Technicolor plant, probably through flashing, which increased sensitivity but lowered contrast.[63] Similarly, matrix stock would also be flashed to help offset its high-contrast characteristics, which tended to wash out highlights.[64] When Rennahan declared that highlights and shadows were more easily handled in 1937, the improvement was probably due to some combination of these sensitizing techniques. Problems with contrast, shadow quality, and, perhaps, sharpness continued to be addressed through the use of a silver halftone image printed from the green negative record.[65]

Another point of gradual improvement during this period involved mordants, the chemicals that hardened the blank's emulsion, helping it absorb more dye and prevent blurring. The stock used for blank was a fine-grained release stock, which had to be soaked in a chrome-alum bath for the mordant to be added.[66] As former Technicolor engineer Richard Goldberg notes, metallic mordants are fairly poor, and Technicolor continued research into improving the system until the late 1950s, when premordanted blank became available.[67] It is likely that improvements in mordants throughout the Technicolor era led to increased saturation and dye contrast.

In the end, inefficient mordants and the use of a halftone silver image limited the saturation of color, and may partially explain the relatively muted look of many Technicolor prints from the 1930s, compared with the more saturated look of those from the '40s and '50s. Such factors are probably secondary, though, to an aesthetic that urged restraint in color design. The vivid displays in *La Cucaracha* and early interpolated sequences, such as the final sequence of *The Little Colonel* (1935), attest that the technology could provide assertive color if that were a major goal.

The Aesthetics of Restraint

Assertive and brilliant color, however, does not appear to have been the main goal during the late 1930s. Instead, as engineers worked to bring their system up to black-and-white's standards, there was a coincident effort by Technicolor designers to limit and control the palettes placed before the camera. The extension of three-color to full features altered its status as a device. Because color was on screen for the duration of an entire film, it could no longer function as a singular effect—as in a sequence interpolated into a black-and-white film—or as the sole purpose of a short subject. Color, like lighting, became a fact of mise-en-scène, and its novelty was partially tamed by its ubiquity. *Variety* noted of *Ramona:* "After the first few hundred feet the natural colors become pleasant rather than distinctive, with the story finally asserting itself and coming to the fore."[68] And the trade went on to praise the color design, which receded from attention: "The fact that the color angle becomes less noticeable as the picture unwinds, and never interferes with the telling or reception of the story, is evidence that color has finally found its place in film production."

In their published comments, color designers began to downplay arguments, like those offered around the release of *Becky Sharp,* suggesting a near moment-by-moment coordination between hue and dramatic intention. Instead, commentators offered more modest claims about color's abilities, developing some of Natalie Kalmus's suggestions and emphasizing restraint and the avoidance of high contrast. For example, *American*

Cinematographer helped specify and elaborate on her general observations about color harmony when it published a talk given by Gilbert Betancourt to the ASC in 1937. A "former designer and color coordinator," and not a Technicolor employee, Betancourt offered as his prescriptions in "Present Color Trend Is Toward Subdued Hues" as a general aid to the society. He reaffirmed that bright and aggressive color designs lacked taste. He framed his aesthetic as part of a natural evolution: "History tells us that man first used color some one hundred and sixty centuries B.C. During these many centuries he has gone from the savage's bright hues and contrasting color combinations to the present trend toward true color harmony in a refined form and subdued or pastel hues."[69]

Good taste dictated that the primitivism of bright, high-contrast schemes be avoided. Like Kalmus, Betancourt backed up his definition of good taste with reference to nature, which harmonizes cool colors with the moderate use of warm, bright hues. Additionally, he specified the exact types of harmony and palette that were acceptable. After explaining the basic relationships of hue on a standard color wheel, Betancourt suggested: "While contrasting or complementary color combinations will continue being used for advertising, traffic signs, and posters, the trend of good taste is toward the more subdued types of harmony such as the analogous [closely related hues], the split complementary [the combination of a hue with those that surround its direct opposite on the wheel], or even monochromatic [various shades and tints of a single hue]."[70]

Successful designs would moderate contrast by avoiding the juxtaposition of directly opposed hues. Betancourt emphasized gradations of closely related colors, encouraging a tightly harmonized look. Although a scheme based on split complementaries could involve some high contrast, such as the combination of violet, yellow, and green, Betancourt headed off the most assertive color schemes by urging designers to rely on pastels and to limit warm colors.

If the argument against Technicolor held that the firm's scientists were bent on forcing color forward at the expense of drama and traditional production practices, this aesthetic countered the objection by seeking to check obvious chromatic play. Bold designs were not to be completely discouraged, but they should appear only briefly. Betancourt recommended: "The color contrast in any arrangement of hues should vary as an inverse function of time . . . if a particular color scheme is to be viewed for a long period of time it should be more subdued than if intended only for a short period."[71] This concession allowed for brief flourishes of color that might renew spectators' awareness of it, as long as the design quickly reverted to one based on subtlety. Indeed, this became a defining strategy of the restrained mode, a style that encouraged the keying of color contrast to specific, transitory moments of narrative.

Writings by cinematographers indicated some of the ways that this aesthetic was taken up in actual production. James Wong Howe, in his discussion of *The Adventures of Tom Sawyer,* echoed the importance of subduing and controlling color. Howe was one of the few non-Technicolor cinematographers to write of his experiences with the process during this period. He claimed that he benefited from working on a picture originally planned for black-and-white, since he thereby avoided "temptations to insert color here and there simply for the sake of color rather than because it should naturally be there."[72] To underscore the importance of detecting distracting background colors while shooting, Howe compared controlling hue to managing highlights in monochrome: "In natural color cinematography we must learn to place background color in the same category as such highlights. A splash of red or blue in the background of a color shot can distract audience attention in exactly the same way as strong highlight in monochrome."[73] The experienced cinematographer could adjust his methods for monitoring compositions to account for color. Again, the drive to subdue color suited a profession that validated generally unobtrusive work. Howe warned that "color consciousness should not be exaggerated," reflecting the prevailing disposition against color foregrounding and the more general desire of cinematographers to avoid inessential ornamentation.[74] In this sense, the restrained mode complemented the professional ethos of the working cameraman.

As noted with reference to lighting, Technicolor's cinematographers were quick to point out that color offered greater expressive opportunities than black-and-white. Yet this potential also implied a greater need for control, as William H. Greene noted: "Color is vastly more revealing, not alone of the actors, but of the cinematographer. It shows much more quickly whether or not the cameraman is thoroughly in harmony with the mood of the action."[75] Presumably, this is because of color's purported emotional content. Citing the courtroom scene in *A Star Is Born,* Greene explained that the film, as a "swift moving modern comedy-drama," did not always permit him to "indulge in striking light-effects" that might help emphasize dramatic tone. Greene had to keep his lighting higher-key, but still concluded, "In color . . . there is a certain advantage in that the dull gray set, photographed in color, and lit drably, gives a much stronger feeling of dull courtroom drabness than would be possible in monochrome."[76] Color helped convey the scene's emotional atmosphere without the need to resort to the additional ornamentation of complex lighting. Greene saw that limiting the set to a monochrome design enabled color to offer a less overt means of serving the drama. In comparison to Jones's or Mamoulian's equations of specific colors with specific effects, Greene's view of color's dramatic power appears much better suited to the cinematographer's inclination toward quiet virtuosity.

The aim of all this emphasis on subdued and controlled color schemes was to integrate three-color with the stylistic conventions already in place. Herbert Aller summarized the situation plainly in *International Photographer* when he applauded the Technicolor cinematographers of the 1930s who "carried with them the inalienable thought that the audience when leaving the theater must not say the story lagged for the sake of color."[77] At the same time, the goal was not the complete effacement of color. The question whether color could significantly contribute to box office remained central to Technicolor's marketability. For film style, this meant that color needed to offer a significant addition to, and a means of differentiation from, standard black-and-white. Ultimately, an aesthetic that prescribed restraint in color design while claiming that color increased cinematography's dramatic range could serve the purpose. Color foregrounding was not altogether dismissed, however. As the analyses that follow will demonstrate, the display of color became strongly tied to well-established motivations for spectacle. Moreover, variations from the subdued palette took on punctuating functions similar to lighting or music. For the time being, though, highly assertive and stylized color was discouraged.

A Measured Response: Color in *The Trail of the Lonesome Pine*

The Trail of the Lonesome Pine was the first thoroughgoing attempt to employ three-color Technicolor in a film produced through mainstream commercial channels. It was also the first truly successful three-color feature. Based on the popular John Fox Jr. novel, which had already been filmed three times, the Paramount release relied upon a well-tested property, and was bolstered by the box-office draw of Sylvia Sidney and the then-developing stars Henry Fonda and Fred MacMurray (Figure 4.2).[78] Paramount supported the film with unprecedented full-page color advertisements in the nation's leading newspapers.[79] The tactic worked, and the feature performed strongly in key cities. In July 1936, *Variety* reported that the film had grossed $1,500,000 domestically against a cost of $625,000, "with an additional cost of $250,000 for color prints."[80] The

4.2. Sylvia Sidney and Fred MacMurray pose between takes on *The Trail of the Lonesome Pine.* Courtesy of the Academy of Motion Picture Arts and Sciences.

1937 *International Motion Picture Almanac* lists *Lonesome Pine* among the five highest-grossing films of 1936 and suggests that it had earned $1,600,000.[81] The film was the most successful Technicolor feature of the year, and it served as the model for a brief cycle of color outdoor dramas, particularly Twentieth Century–Fox's *Ramona* (1936), and Warner Bros.' *God's Country and the Woman* (1937), *Valley of the Giants* (1938), and *Gold Is Where You Find It* (1938).

In contrast to their response to *Becky Sharp,* critics perceived the film as properly integrating the new technology into a solid dramatic context. *Variety* threw this issue into sharp relief:

What *Becky Sharp*'s significance was supposed to portray is actually promulgated by *Lonesome Pine.* It is evidence that color can be utilized as a forceful complement to cinematic entertainment providing the basic story ingredients are sturdy. *Pine* doesn't permit the color appeal to subjugate the primary phase of any film entertainment.[82]

In a similar vein, the *American Cinematographer* critic quoted producer Walter Wanger: "The goal we set at the start of production and never deviated from, was to hew to the story line and let color fall where it may."[83] Even Paramount's publicity posed color as an embellishment of otherwise marketable material. Text on the poster trumpeted: "In black and white this Paramount picture would be a triumph . . . in natural color it marks the start of a new era."[84] Against the perception that color was overemphasized in *Becky Sharp, Lonesome Pine* was promoted and recognized as bridling three-color, using it to enhance time-honored marks of quality. Within this context, *Lonesome Pine* appears as a key film in the history of Technicolor.

Set in the Blue Ridge hills of Virginia, the film centers on a romantic triangle between coal-company engineer Jack Hale (Fred MacMurray), country girl June Tolliver (Sylvia Sidney), and her fiancé and cousin, Dave Tolliver (Henry Fonda). The romantic entanglement is complicated by a feud between June's family and the Falins. After the Falins inadvertently kill June's little brother, Buddy (George "Spanky" McFarland), Dave sacrifices his life to end the violence between the families. His death brings peace to the mountains, and presumably clears the way for June's betrothal to Jack.

Lonesome Pine is the landmark film in the restrained mode. Despite Wanger's claim that the production team "let colors fall where they may," the film's persistent avoidance of bright and saturated hues underscores an extraordinary attention to color. Obvious color cues from the original novel are largely avoided in the film. The book opens with Jack catching sight of a "crimson flash" when June crosses his path in the forest.[85] In the film her costume is an unassuming, nearly black, blue color (Majolica Blue), which blends into the woodland shadows.[86] William H. Greene described the production's efforts to subdue color: "Whereas in many productions in times past, everything colorful that could be thought of was put before the camera, in this film people and places were photographed just as they really are."[87] Greene added, "Even red and black checkered shirts, which might well be found in the mountains, were not allowed because the effect might suggest that they had been added to bring out more color." Color was eased into the background so that "the audience will not be conscious of the fact that they are looking at color. They will only see men and women going about the business of life looking real."

Toward this end, the restrained mode settled on a narrow range of dominant hues and deployed limited departures from that range to fulfill fairly specific functions. To gauge the film's inventiveness, an analysis of *Lonesome Pine* must begin not with moments of brilliant or striking color, but with the schemes that enable color to recede from attention. For it is against these tightly harmonized designs that measured deviations can create spectacle, punctuate action, and develop emotional motifs.

Where *Becky Sharp* splashed highlights against neutral backgrounds, *Lonesome Pine* eschews the accents and varies the neutrals to create a more complex texture. Mise-en-scène in *Lonesome Pine,* dominated by cabin interiors and woodland, is generally rendered in shades and tones of brown and gray. When other hues are present, they often possess a pronounced gray undertone. Because differences of hue are deemphasized, tonal qualities, distinctions between dark and light, have greater power in *Lonesome Pine.* In interiors at least, manipulation of light, rather than color, proves the primary tool for rendering expressive touches.

But this does not mean that the restrained mode favored simple or monotonous designs. Consider, for example, the first shot of Dave in the Tolliver cabin, the film's main interior set. A medium long shot shows him glancing out the window above his bed, where he is convalescing after a shootout with the Falins.[88] The dominant impression is of gray and brown, carried mainly by the wood tones of the cabin wall and the Slate-colored shirt draped around Dave's shoulders. However, a patchwork quilt covering his bed varies and deepens the palette. Here, large areas of deep brown and Slate are mixed with panels of flat Rose Shadow and light Gray Sand beige, stitched together with knots of oxblood yarn. A single patch of light blue-gray and another of slightly brighter red add variety without disrupting the gray-brown cast of the shot. The quilt also coordinates with other elements of set decoration, like the gray curtains with oxblood trim that cover the window above Dave's bed. *Lonesome Pine*'s design combines details of flat, unsaturated colors to create a varied but neutralized background for action. Hard color contrasts are rejected in favor of a mixture of neutrals (gray and beige) with analogous hues (red-rose and brown) of roughly constant saturation and subtly graduated brightness. The various colors converge because of their low saturation, and they contribute tightly harmonized texture and visual interest to the shot without departing from a subdued palette. This is a substantial development beyond the "color against neutral" design that typifies *Becky Sharp.*

The restrained design had important implications for the debate about lighting in Technicolor. As hue recedes from attention, tonal gradations must step forward to suggest volume and define space. Thus, in addition to the general high-key illumination, figure lighting (especially facial and top lighting) rather than color delineates planes and characters. Throughout the film, William H. Greene blends moderate top and edge lighting with bright overall illumination in a compromise between the heavy edging of monochrome cinematography and the flat light common in *Becky Sharp.* For example, in the shot of Dave looking out the window, a strong key light, motivated by the window, provides a highlight along the side of his face. This provides a clear edge of light that helps separate his facial features from the well-lit background. In a fashion that recalls James Wong Howe's advice, Greene does not attempt the bravura edge lighting of black-and-white, but depends on less conspicuous key lighting along shoulders and faces. If the demonstration mode leaned on color to direct attention around the frame, the restrained design reduced color's responsibilities and modified high-key black-and-white lighting techniques. In combination with a muted mise-en-scène, light provides texture and emphasis from shot to shot.

Nearly all of *Lonesome Pine*'s eight interior sets feature a similarly restrained approach to color and light. Minor differences distinguish the locations. For example, the Falin cabin is flat gray, and Jack's tent features a light brown and tan mise-en-scène, which contrasts with the Tolliver's darker brown and gray scheme. Within each of these sets, small details of slightly contrasting hues add visual interest, but the ultimate effect is the convergence and recession of color. When exterior settings are used for simple conversation scenes, they follow the same conventions. The palette is somewhat broadened by elements like green foliage and blue sky, but a bright and saturated mise-en-scène is generally avoided in favor of a neutral background to the action. Though Greene uses edge lighting somewhat more than in interiors to separate figures from their surroundings, reflectors and overhead scrims direct and diffuse sunlight for unobtrusive, even illumination. *Lonesome Pine*'s basic design encourages the viewer to overlook color or at least to accept it as something more than a gimmick. But the real power of restraint was twofold. First, the recession of color encouraged cinematographers to experiment with expressive lighting. Second, and more crucially, careful deviations from the dominant look could become prominent and functional.

Giving Light Its Due

One motive for the early assertion that color was expressively equivalent to lighting was that, as we have noted, illumination requirements made dramatic lighting difficult, even impossible. If lighting, the cinematographer's means of achieving distinction, was to be handicapped, then color was pitched as a more than adequate compensation. This argument was never entirely successful, and the restrained mode admitted the importance of expressive lighting conventions. A neutral palette keeps color from usurping light's established domain. This was an especially important choice when expressive color and light were almost mutually exclusive. Technological hurdles prevented the complex mixture of saturated color and high-contrast lighting from being achieved until very late in the decade.[89] So, with color in the background, in a few sequences William H. Greene attempted shadow and contrast effects to underscore emotional tone.

The clearest example occurs when Dave teases June about a secret she keeps in her bedroom closet. Dave remains innocently romantic throughout, but the viewer realizes that June has fallen in love with Jack. She has hidden Jack's pen, a token of his affection, in her closet. Greene underlines the emotional discord by casting the love scene in comparatively strong shadow. Color remains well within the dominant palette: Dave is clad entirely in gray, June in her black-blue skirt and blouse. The brown and gray tones of the set are varied only briefly by the orange glow from a fireplace in the extreme background and by a flat rose blanket draped on the headboard of June's bed. This palette provides a neutral backdrop for the play of shadow and highlight.

As the scene starts, the characters move into and out of the light in an intricate play of contrast. Both figures are silhouetted as Jack playfully chases June into her bedroom. When June moves into a well-lit background and leaps over her bed, Dave hesitates in the shadowed foreground before following her to the closet door. The two-shot of Dave and June at the closet develops the expressive lighting scheme. A cast shadow of a window frame on the rear wall contributes texture to the composition. As Dave presses June to the closet door, shadowing, presumably from the window pattern, covers his nose and eyes. June receives fairly even key and edge light until Dave embraces and kisses her, pulling her somewhat into shadow. The overall illumination is just below medium-key, but even this limited shadowing accentuates the tone of romantic conflict. When the sequence enters a standard shot–reverse-shot pattern, the illumination evens out, but significant shadowing returns after Dave departs and June enters her closet. She opens the door and is enveloped in darkness. The final shot reveals June's secret by framing her from within the closet and tilting down to a close-up of Jack's pen sitting in a small basket. Heavy shadows on the closet door cover June as she enters and moves through pools of light. The silver pen and straw basket are illuminated against a nearly pitch background.

This lighting approximates the low-key effects that marked artistic sensitivity in black-and-white cinematography. Greene limits his experiment by bracketing an evenly illuminated conversation with brief instances of high-contrast lighting. Still, the irony of the situation is gently enhanced by staging a love scene in shadow. Despite the limitations on Technicolor lighting, this sequence attempts to fit color within well-established paradigms of expressive cinematography. The restrained approach offered a style that helped bring color in line with craft practice. In *Lonesome Pine,* expressive lighting is rather fleeting and tentative, yet it points toward the bold experimentation with chiaroscuro that Greene will take up in *A Star Is Born.*

The Power of Variation

The greatest advance of the restrained mode was to make clear that against a tight palette, small variations become significant. A finely tuned design can draw attention to, and get use from, relatively minute and precise changes in color. The most common function of these measured departures is momentary narrative punctuation, as a brief scene between June and Jack in segment seven illustrates. As Jack packs and prepares to leave his small forest camp, June appears and informs him that her father has agreed to sign his contract. The exchange is set in a small wooded clearing where muted green and light brown foliage, brown wood, and gray-brown boulders dominate the color scheme. The scene opens with a panning shot that moves from a medium composition of Jack glancing off right to a long shot of June standing before a small group of boulders. Light and color are delicately managed to emphasize her appearance. The pan briefly introduces a brightly lit patch of gold-brown brush just to the left of June as she returns Jack's gaze. Though the hue remains within the palette's brown dominants, lighting lends the patch of gold an intense saturation that far surpasses any other element in the frame. Color and light punctuate June's arrival. Once the action is underway, the striking color is carefully blocked from view. This is really a variation on the revelation of color within a scene that we see so often in *Becky Sharp.* Now, however, the punctuating color is closely tied to its surroundings: the accent emerges organically from the background.

In inaugurating the restrained mode, *Lonesome Pine* offers this standard scheme for making color punctual, and then develops and expands it. The technique is elaborated into a bravura moment of tactful emphasis when June confronts Jack after her little brother is killed in a bombing at his construction site. The scene takes place in Jack's Gap Town engineering office, a set featuring the familiar shades of brown and gray with several flat gray-green Mistletoe accents carried by details such as a hanging lamp, a desk blotter, and a small metal box. Previously, these details helped vary the neutral background without strong contrast, like Dave's quilt described above. When June arrives, however, the accents briefly leap forward because of their close coordination with her costume.

As she enters the scene, a medium shot of the office door isolates her against a brown wall and bookcase with a few oxblood books. Immediately, a cut backward reframes the scene in long shot that places the other characters in the midground and June at the center rear. The reestablishing shot allows Jack to notice and then react to her arrival. The composition also strikingly arranges the green accents to echo June's wardrobe. The lighter green desk blotter at the foreground center of the frame, the hanging lamp toward the top of the left rear wall, and the metal box sitting on a table right of center frame suddenly converge around June's green and brown costume. The correspondence of costume and set briefly activates colors that had been unobtrusively planted within the decor. In the next medium long shot, which frames June and Jack, the green box has been cheated so that it appears at the bottom-left edge of the frame. Since the interior is limited to brown and gray hues, the systematic placement of even a slightly divergent color creates an arresting effect.

The set's overall color scheme reiterates June's Stone Green hat, skirt, and tailored coat, which she wears over a brown blouse. This is an excellent example of how Technicolor sets often harmonize with the costumes of the female lead. But the precision of the green accents across both shots, and their absence from any subsequent composition in the scene, reveals a more specific function. In punctuating June's arrival, the accents provide a brief visual flourish that coincides with a shift in the scene's development. June's appearance is crucial: it sets up her most significant confrontation with Jack, one in which he finally proclaims his love. Color has been keyed to emphasize a passing moment, operating like a brief shift in music, which might underscore a turning point in the story. The tech-

4.3. June visits Jack in his office. Publicity still courtesy of the Academy of Motion Picture Arts and Sciences.

nique is astonishingly subtle. With its texture of closely related hues, the restrained palette became a sensitive instrument for amplifying minute color correspondences.

Lonesome Pine also builds upon this principle of measured variation to give color more-complex functions. Color patterns and motifs that accrue meaning across a film stand out more readily within a restrained design. In Technicolor design, the female star's wardrobe conventionally offers a key source of color, making it a good candidate for patterning. For example, June's costumes and surroundings become more colorful as she falls in love with Jack: as she becomes engrossed with the city engineer, she sheds her backwoods tomboy style to embrace one of sophisticated femininity. Through the first twenty-four segments, June appears in the nearly black Majolica Blue knit skirt and short-sleeved blouse. When she travels to Gap Town to impress Jack, she adds a cape and a white lace collar to the dress (Figure 4.3). June finally discards the outfit when, hoping that a city education will ignite Jack's desire, she leaves town for Louisville. As she boards the train, June wears a gray plaid dress with a gray cape and a straw hat. The costume change introduces variation without departing from the palette. A black and red-brown band on June's hat provides the most striking color in her ensemble. Unlike Miriam Hopkins's invariably brash costumes in *Becky Sharp,* June's change of attire is keyed to character development without being conspicuous.

Moreover, once flagged as significant, the pattern of changes in costume color becomes charged with narrative meaning. We can understand the green and brown outfit that June wears after her brother's death as part of this general motif. The suit marks June's attempt to emulate Jack's idea of sophistication, and its coordination with his office literally helps her fit his décor. When she angrily rejects Jack after he refuses to seek vengeance for Buddy, June rips open her coat and throws off her hat. She exclaims: "This is what you wanted me to be, ain't it? Pretty, nice words, hollow words? Well, I don't want it!" June refuses Jack's colors when she tears at her clothes, but this is wholly redundant, since the dialogue and action emphasize her emotional retreat. Because it doesn't depend on assertive hues, and because color reinforces rather than carries the moment, the manipulation is well integrated. In *Lonesome Pine,* rather limited shifts in color can develop patterns and support the story without recourse to the literal equations of the demonstration mode.

Twilight on the Trail: Building Motifs

The restrained mode had a propensity for color patterns, and these were used in *Lonesome Pine* to forge a more abstract pictorial motif. In the pattern of saturated red-orange accents that weaves across the film color becomes a supple register of emotion. Red-orange forms a chromatic motif, a systematic repetition of color that carries dramatic resonances. Meaning accrues around the color as it is repeated, rather than being imposed as part of an external color vocabulary. In *Lonesome Pine,* the motif is built through a series of transitional or atmospheric passages that depict the beauty of the natural setting. These sequences are tied together by the character of Tater (Fuzzy Knight), a local vagrant who sings as he wanders through the landscape. Tater provides a convenient device for showcasing the production's original songs "Twilight on the Trail" and "A Melody from the Sky." His songs develop musical motifs that comment on the action and help set the film's tone. Tater's sequences are also highly pictorial: they dwell on details of nature, introducing graphic patterns in which color plays a central role. Both the visual and musical motifs coalesce near the end of the film during Buddy's funeral, when they poignantly underpin an emotional climax.

In the atmospheric sequences, color is muted and then reintroduced. *Lonesome Pine* establishes the pattern almost immediately. In the first segment following the prologue, shots of June, looking into the distance from atop a hill, alternate with images of Tater singing "Twilight on the Trail." The sequence is an overture of motifs, including the eponymous lonesome pine under which June stands and the song itself, which will return during her brother's funeral. Visually, the scene introduces the suppression and revelation of color, and it signals the design's emphasis on tone rather than hue. For example, the first shot of Tater frames him climbing a slope, backlit by a silver and light blue-gray cloudscape. Two tree trunks frame the scene with vertical silhouettes, and the lower fore- and midground are filled with muted green foliage. Gradations of light and dark dominate any contrasts of hue, suggesting that a Technicolor film can beautify a landscape using monochrome techniques. The sequence closes with a burst of relatively vivid color. As Tater's song slowly fades, a high-angle pan of the lake ends by framing the Tolliver cabin. The blue sky and greenery reflected in the lake fill the frame, contrasting with the burnished orange foliage of a tree that appears briefly in the foreground. These more assertive natural colors provide a momentary splash before the thoroughly restrained palette of the next scene.

Having introduced the pattern, Tater's subsequent song sequences repeat the technique to build associations. His second song, a brief rendition of "Poor Me," accompanies a similar suppression and revelation of hue. The scene begins with a nearly monochrome shot of Tater, clad entirely in brown, approaching the camera down an incline, strongly backlit by sunlight. Tree trunks and boulders are partially silhouetted to provide brown and gray accents. The camera pans left to reframe Tater in a long-shot profile as he pauses before a brilliant orange sumac tree caught by the sunlight. The burst of orange arrests the camera movement. Tater finishes his song, and the camera resumes its pan, removing the orange accent and settling on Jack's camp. Simple camera work introduces and removes the splash of orange, providing a fleeting graphic punctuation before the scene begins. Moreover, this second instance of color foregrounding reinforces the pattern that links Tater's singing with natural tranquility.

In Tater's third song, his rendition of "A Melody from the Sky," the film develops the pattern, drawing on it to underscore story events. The scene takes place immediately after Dave has confronted June about the secret in her closet. Tater's love song and the color highlights that accompany it echo Dave's romantic giddiness. A high-angle pan follows Tater and Buddy walking along the lakeshore, passing beneath orange leaves lit brilliantly by the sun. The lake, reflecting the deep blue sky and the tree line on the opposite shore, dominates this composition. When they reach the Tolliver cabin, Tater and Buddy meet Dave, who joins in whistling the melody. The sequence is redolent with irony, coming as it does directly after the shot of June in reverie over Jack's pen. Dave's joy appears especially naïve given our new knowledge of June's closeted affection. Graphic contrast between the comparatively low-key shot of June and the explosion of color that accompanies Tater's panorama underlines this hard shift in dramatic tone. Bringing Tater and Buddy together for this pastoral sequence also helps set up the emotional payoff of Tater singing at Buddy's funeral.

More immediately, the lush scenery and color return in a strongly altered context one scene later, after Dave discovers June's true feelings. The last shot of the "Melody from the Sky" sequence frames the deep blue lake and orange foliage after Tater, still singing, has exited. This composition lingers, gaining an expressive charge. A scene later, as Dave walks dejectedly toward the previously romantic lake, the repeated framing and the complementary contrast of orange set against blue emphasize the changed mood. Pictorial strategies developed around Tater's songs gain dramatic resonance as they are reiterated in contrasting situations.

The emotional use of color peaks during Buddy's funeral. In fine melodramatic fashion, the sequence pulls together several motifs associated with June's little brother and juxtaposes them with images of his grieving family. Shots of Buddy's toy crane; Corsey (Otto Fries), Buddy's engineer friend; and the family dog (a particularly cruel touch) combine with Tater's broken reprisal of "Twilight on the Trail" to recall earlier, happier sequences. Color and compositional motifs echo throughout the scene. The funeral is preceded by the most striking shot in the film, a brief view from above a bank of clouds gathered around a distant mountain peak and reflecting bright orange sunlight. The image marks an ellipsis between the scene of Dave hollowing Buddy's coffin from a great log and the funeral. It offers a brief caesura before the intensely emotional funeral, and it reactivates the orange motif. Natalie Kalmus's analogy between color and a musical score seems apt, the orange hue functioning like a familiar refrain played in an emotionally shifting setting.

The funeral sequence repeats familiar pictorial patterns. Extreme long shots of the funeral party present subdued colors. Mist covering the background veils the forest in a gray cast, neutralizing hues and accentuating shadows and rays of sunlight. This tactic recalls Tater's first rendition of "Twilight on the Trail." Yet at the center of the gathering, a pile of orange leaves and foliage covers Buddy's funeral bier. Editing foregrounds the orange-red accent by framing June's parents, and then the preacher from behind the casket. The scene's final shot reintroduces the leaves as a brilliantly lit foreground element while the Tolliver dog, apparently crippled with sorrow, crawls toward the gathering from under a fence. The camera reframes to a heavily edge-lit medium shot of June. She notices the dog and breaks into tears. The orange foliage rather practically reminds the viewer of the coffin's location and marks the season. More importantly, the repeated framing around the leaf pile exploits hue to reinforce emotional effect.

Like the more identifiable and concrete motif of Tater's song, the orange accents highlight the emotional distance traveled since the film's start. One would be hard pressed to affix a precise meaning to the color scheme. Unlike Mamoulian's or Jones's use of red for danger or rage, this orange is not bound to a particular or literal significance. Instead, it forms a visual pattern across the film, reemerging, like the melody of "Twilight on the Trail," at this climax. In a sense, the scene is transitional. It offers an emotionally sharp pause between June's confrontation with Jack, and Dave's scene of self-sacrifice. The scene is open to a kind of stylization, an accretion of motifs, as the pace of the action slackens and the characters enact their ritual of loss. At the same time, the sequence is the film's high point for the alignment of color and narrative. Through repetition, color has been delicately spun into the dramatic fabric of the scene. Color sustains the film's emotional texture.

Chromatic Display

All of these strategies for color recession, punctuation, and underscoring help make the case that Technicolor, by taking a supporting rather than starring role, was integrable with the classical style. But color's added expense required that it also serve as a mark of differentiation, a noticeable and saleable part of the film. Toward this end, *Lonesome Pine* motivates color foregrounding in two limited ways. First, spectacular views of the mountain setting and mass action work as attractions. Second, and in only one extraordinary instance, the love story between June and Jack occasions a striking departure from the otherwise somber palette.

A major attraction of *Lonesome Pine* lay in the presentation of spectacular landscapes in "natural color." One Brooklyn exhibitor forced pine extract through the air conditioner and advertised the showing as "so real-

4.4. Shooting on location for *The Trail of the Lonesome Pine.* Courtesy of the Academy of Motion Picture Arts and Sciences.

istic you'll smell the odor of the pine," illustrating how important natural settings were to the selling of the film.[90] William H. Greene emphasized the point when he boasted that the film "is made up largely of exteriors, vast sweeps which thrill you with their beauty. Shot with a color process that gives you the ultimate in natural color reproductions, these exterior scenes will give the public what it long has been wanting—naturalness."[91] *Becky Sharp* had been produced entirely on a sound stage, but *Lonesome Pine* promised the arresting views, "vast sweeps," afforded by an outdoor picture (Figure 4.4). The film regularly foregrounds scenic elements by elaborating establishing shots and inserting pictorial ellipses between scenes.

Even so, in most of the exterior footage, restraint prevails. True to Greene's professed avoidance of introducing striking hues into the landscape, scenes of mass action emphasize tone rather than hue. For example, the montage of the progress made by Jack's work crew is organized according to movement within the frame rather than by contrast of color. As trees fall, cranes swing, and men drive cattle, the only vivid hues are glimpses of blue sky above the brown and green tones of the work site. Workers are clad almost entirely in brown and gray, the few men in subdued blue shirts adding variation.

The same principles govern more strictly atmospheric sequences. For instance, an elliptical montage covers the passage of winter in four scenic images: Gap Town and the Tolliver cabin covered in snow, the cabin after a thaw, and a low-angle view of pine trees silhouetted against the pale blue sky with a cloud catching soft orange sunlight. Color progresses from near monochrome in the snowy winter through the soft gradations of gray and brown during the thaw, and culminates in the vivid pastels of the sky and cloud. The brief ellipsis becomes an occasion for pictorial emphasis: it adds texture to the film and gently heightens color without venturing outside the tight palette.

Lonesome Pine excels at developing the potentials of a restrained palette for subtle punctuation, patterning, and natural spectacle, but in one instance the film overtly stylizes color, calls attention to it, and engages in a surprising level of formal play. During a telephone love scene between June, now in her room at a Louisville boarding school, and Jack, who is in his makeshift field office, the frame erupts with stunning pastels. Here the designers exploit the love scene, a conventional occasion for glamour, to display Technicolor with a force reminiscent of the demonstration mode. Consider the first shot of June in her new, hyperfeminine bedroom. She is framed in long shot: a lace curtain hangs in the far-right foreground while she reclines in Pink Mist pajamas on off-white bedding tinted a very light pink. Beyond her is a set of frilly light pink curtains against a wall covered in blue-green paper with a pink floral pattern. The pink and green hues, and the ornamentation of curtains and flowers, startlingly depart from the film's rugged mise-en-scène.

More surprisingly, the overt color unexpectedly spills over into Jack's field office. As the couple flirts, Jack begins playing with a set of colored pencils that sits before a black-and-white glamour photo of Sylvia Sidney on his desk. A series of insert shots show Jack using a blue pencil to rearrange red, blue, and green pencils in front of her portrait. As Jack compliments June's eyes and asks if she has a dimple, he arranges the pencils in a V shape to frame the portrait and points to her chin with the blue pencil. In striking violation of Greene's prescription, color has been forced into the scene. The final image presents June's reflection in a mirror that recalls the frame of Jack's photo. Contrast between the monochrome photo and June's full-color reflection refreshes Technicolor's impact. Jack makes do with black-and-white, but the viewer is granted a carefully coordinated composition that flaunts soft pastels and flesh tones unavailable in the photo. In response to Jack's query, she touches her chin and smiles.

Though jarring, the momentary expansion of the palette is bound to some of the film's broad strategies. The sequence is part of the pattern that connects color to June's feminization and Jack's attraction to her. This is the same motivation for the other comparatively minute changes in costume color, but here it launches an especially assertive design. Similarly, true to the dominant style, color design still relies on the careful arrangement of a few hues (pinks and blues) and avoids deep and saturated color. In the spirit of Gilbert Betancourt's recommendations, the narrow range of pastels limits color intensity and ensures easy harmony. Tints of pink create texture much as varied tones of brown do in other settings. The sequence is an important exception to the primary design, but it also provides a model for incorporating chromatic play into the restrained style. The strategy of keeping the color change more or less motivated and relying on "tasteful" coordinated pastels would be developed and nuanced in *A Star Is Born, Nothing Sacred, The Goldwyn Follies,* and other productions in the restrained mode. In its own way, the restrained mode exhibited the general tension of Technicolor aesthetics: the antagonism between supporting the story unobtrusively while showcasing Technicolor as an added attraction.

Conclusion

Adhering to a narrow coordinated palette opened new the possibilities for tying hue to story. Like lighting or music, color offered an additional register through which to establish motifs, set mood, and highlight narrative development.In 1936 there were relatively few established conventions for integrating color, unlike those other components, into the narrative flow. The restrained mode may seem like an exceedingly careful and measured response to color, yet it provided both a means of controlling the distracting potential of color and a relatively simple method for correlating chromatic shifts with the narrative. Repetitions of color stood out within the finely modulated palette, and because deviations were so perceptible, they were ready elements for punctuating dramatic turning points and for underscoring changes in dramatic tone. Moreover, building color associations within the film, rather than imposing external codes, became a turning point in developing color's expressive functions.

The style seemed well suited to goals of unobtrusiveness and dramatic enhancement, and reaching those goals helped negate the perception of

Technicolor as a short-lived novelty. Yet, as demonstrated by the sequence of the Louisville telephone conversation, color remained a novel mark of difference, an element that could occasionally be emphasized, as if to announce its unique contribution to the image. The mode of restraint and motivated divergence was tempered by a lingering drive to renew the novelty of the process. The two films analyzed in the next chapter illustrate just how thoroughly restraint and display could be interrelated.

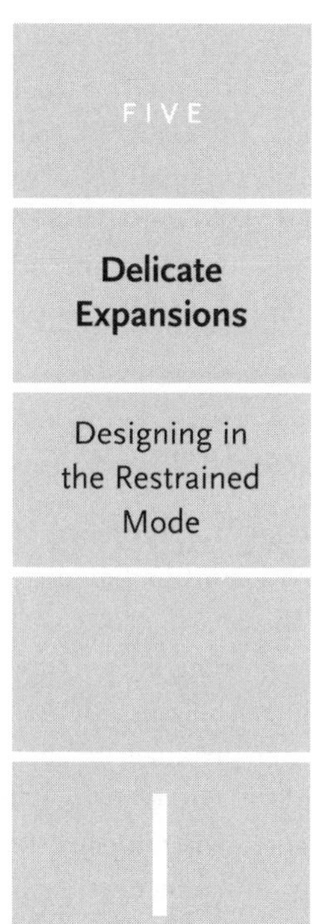

FIVE

Delicate Expansions

Designing in the Restrained Mode

In initiating the restrained mode, *The Trail of the Lonesome Pine* presented the style in its most austere form. During the mid to late 1930s, producers extended and deepened the mode, stretching it to accommodate different genres and dramatic situations. These films laid the foundation for subsequent Technicolor color design, making color functional without overemphasizing it. Working with narrow palettes and tight harmonies in films like *Ramona, God's Country and the Woman, Vogues of 1938, Dodge City, Nothing Sacred,* and *Jesse James,* filmmakers successfully forged a viable system for integrating color into feature films. When designers expanded the Technicolor palette toward the end of the 1930s, they developed practices that were born in the restrained mode. Because this aesthetic was so crucial to Hollywood's adoption of Technicolor, this chapter explores how it expanded to support a wider range of films.

A Star Is Born and *The Goldwyn Follies* stand out as exemplars of restraint because they downplay strong juxtapositions of hue in favor of saturation and value, but they also exploit opportunities for color foregrounding and scoring. These productions strike a tactful balance between function and display; they approach color delicately, ensuring that it both blends with other elements of style and is able to recede. In *A Star Is Born,* color withdraws to the background during sequences of truly daring chiaroscuro. Elsewhere it surges forward, building a thematic association between Hollywood artifice and garish design. *The Goldwyn Follies* brings restraint to the musical genre. Working within a small set of coordinating colors, the film achieves a highly polished, determined look. Together, these films suggest how, after *Lonesome Pine,* designers broadened the options for working with color while remaining within the province of restraint.

A Star Is Born: Color for Modern Comedy and Drama

Any history of Technicolor must acknowledge the influence of Selznick International Pictures, formed in 1935, with David O. Selznick as president and John Hay Whitney as chairman of the board. Along with his considerable finances, Whitney brought the remaining six-picture contract with Technicolor initially intended for Pioneer.[1] Selznick demonstrated a stronger commitment to color than any other producer of the 1930s. Of the ten films he produced between 1936 and the end of 1939, half were in color. At the forefront of Technicolor's efforts to win widespread support, *A Star Is Born* garnered critical praise and box-office success. Against a cost of $1,221,382, the United Artists release returned a healthy $2,550,000.[2] It remained the only of Selznick International's productions to earn a place on *Film Daily*'s list of ten highest grossers during the decade (*Gone with the Wind,* released in December 1939, wouldn't surpass *A Star Is Born* in earnings until 1940).[3]

The film was billed as "the first modern picture in Technicolor," and though *Lonesome Pine* was also set during the 1930s, *A Star Is Born* was the first movie to bring three-color to swank, high-style urban settings (Figure 5.1).[4] The film also broadened Technicolor's territory with its mix of comedy and melodrama. The narrative follows an arc similar to that of *What Price Hollywood?* which Selznick had produced at RKO in 1932. The first half is a Cinderella story that follows Midwestern farm girl Esther Blodgett (Janet Gaynor) as she rockets to fame as a Hollywood star under the name Vicki Lester. The second half shifts the focus to Esther's husband, Norman Maine (Fredric March), a failing actor futilely struggling with alcoholism. When Esther elects to abandon her career to care for Norman, he takes his life to spare her the burden. The film ends with Esther's triumphant return to the screen as she famously announces to a radio reporter: "This is Mrs. Norman Maine." The Cinderella story showcases Hollywood glitz, but Maine's disintegration demands subtle under-

5.1. Title card for *A Star Is Born.*

scoring, a mixture that made the film an excellent vehicle for color. *A Star Is Born* offered the opportunity to see three-color exercised in genres that would largely be displaced by musicals, adventures, and period prestige productions in the 1940s.

A Star Is Born negotiates between the restrained mode and a bolder, more decorative approach. It has a more dynamic color design than *Lonesome Pine,* and it strategically shifts between subdued and assertive color arrangements. Like its predecessor, the film keeps color in the wings so that it can be brought out more forcefully at key moments. Sets based on actual locations, like the Central Casting office, were created with less color contrast than the originals.[5] To a greater extent than in *Lonesome Pine,* though, the shifts in color are keyed to changes in narrative tone. Besides using the restrained mode somewhat more flexibly, the film also explores more deeply the expressive possibilities of black-and-white, or tonal, techniques.

"Good Dramatic Lighting": Emulating Low-Key Effects

One of the most striking aspects of *A Star Is Born* is not color but the surprising amount of low-key and chiaroscuro cinematography that William H. Greene manages. This was a vital component of the restrained look as practiced by Selznick International. The production illustrates Greene's contention that "good dramatic lighting" could best convey mood and pictorialism. In contrast to *Lonesome Pine* and *Becky Sharp,* Selznick's production boasts extended sequences of true high-contrast lighting for dramatic effect. The low-key sequences caused some concern for Selznick and Whitney: preview response cards indicated that audiences found the first portion of the film, especially scenes in Esther's bedroom and in the train station, as well as the first love scene, too dark.[6] Still, the film's look was praised in the trade press, and Greene's efforts earned him an honorary award for best color cinematography at the 1938 Academy Awards.

Greene's experiments were emblematic of a time when color was still seeking its place in the classical style. By the mid-1940s, when the obvious emulation of black-and-white techniques seemed less important, Technicolor cinematographers moved away from forceful low-key.[7] During the late 1930s and early 1940s, though, color low-key was fairly widespread, and interesting examples can be found in major studio productions like Fox's *Jesse James* (1939) and Paramount's *Shepherd of the Hills* (1941). Selznick International, though, specialized in pushing Technicolor's low-key limits, vigorously pursuing black-and-white standards. The studio's line of experimentation culminated with the breakthrough lighting effects of *Gone with the Wind* at the decade's end, but *A Star Is Born* was an important proving ground for effects lighting.

In several extraordinary sequences, *A Star Is Born* makes the most of color's recession to bring lighting forward. Greene's achievements are all the more impressive given the hard arc lights and slow system speed with which he had to work. Effects that may have seemed unremarkable in black-and-white were hard won in Technicolor. The moments of chiaroscuro can appear somewhat stilted or overwrought because the unforgiving Technicolor shadows demanded rigid compositions; a slight movement could cause an actor to fall off into darkness. Thus, the effects tended to be more obtrusive than they might have been in black-and-white. Yet the effort was apparently worth the semblance of tonal control that it offered.

Greene's commitment to chiaroscuro is powerfully displayed when Norman and Esther first kiss, in the courtyard of her boardinghouse. The lovers' first kiss offers a conventional place for the cinematographer to stylize an image. Rather than use color to glamorize the moment, Greene treats the shot with some extremely careful modeling. Norman turns his back toward the camera and maneuvers Esther so that she is framed over his shoulder in medium close-up (Figure 5.2). The image is exceptionally dark. His head and shoulder form a shady mass on the right side of the frame and cast a sharply defined shadow across half of Esther's face. The shadow area is actually translucent, allowing an eye light to be reflected back through the darkness. When Norman bends forward to kiss her, his shadow briefly fills the frame, leaving only Esther's eye lights remaining—a meticulous lighting balance (Figure 5.3). Norman pulls back, and

5.2 and 5.3. Conspicuous low-key lighting for the first kiss.

her face reemerges into the light. Greene's method boldly mimics monochrome cinematography, expunging hue in favor of light and shadow. The choice directly confronted complaints that Technicolor might limit the cinematographer's art.

Greene's lighting is similarly conspicuous in key scenes across the film. At times the low-key effects function simply to depress the palette so that color may surge forward when brighter illumination returns. For instance, Esther's farewell to her grandmother (Mary Robson) is staged on a barely illuminated train platform, but it prepares the way for a vivid "California, Here I Come" montage. Elsewhere, the key of light is aptly tied to the drama. While the demonstration films prioritized color for handling expressive tasks, *A Star Is Born,* typical of a restrained drama, accommodates black-and-white conventions. This is never more apparent than in the scenes surrounding Norman's death.

While recovering from his latest lapse, Norman overhears Esther's plans to leave Hollywood, and he silently resolves to drown himself. His unspoken decision must be communicated visually. After a brief shot of the partially opened bedroom door, the camera dollies in to a close-up of Norman lying in bed. In a nearly pitch-black frame, a single shaft of light illuminates his eyes and forehead. The close-up is repeated three times as Norman reacts to Esther's conversation in the next room (Figure 5.4). This really daring use of low-key strips the image of color and isolates Norman's eyes, emphasizing the moment when, upon hearing Esther's plans, he closes them (Figure 5.5). Later in the scene, vertical and horizontal shadows cross Norman's figure when he emerges from the bedroom (Figure 5.6). Then, after his final embrace with Esther, he steps toward the beach and shadows pass over his face and body (Figure 5.7).

The scene bears comparison with the equivalent moment in *What Price*

Hollywood? In that case, cinematographer Charles Rosher's pronounced shadow work helps stylize and communicate the washed-up Hollywood director's (Lowell Sherman's) unspoken decision to shoot himself. In what might be termed a proto-noir sequence, strong vertical and horizontal bands form a grid of shadows covering the set (Figure 5.8). When the character stumbles through the room and discovers a gun, a key light placed near the ground throws his looming shadow across the background. Greene's treatment of the scene feels like a reference to Rosher's, an attempt to prove that similar effects could be done better with the addition of color. Whether or not Greene was responding to an implicit challenge posed by the earlier film, the scene illustrates how important conventions of monochrome cinematography were to the Technicolor style. For dramatic underscoring, the virtuoso deployment of highlight and shadow was equally, perhaps even more, important than color. *A Star Is Born* impressively extends the path opened by the closet love scene in *Lonesome Pine,* solidifying a defining trait of the restrained mode.

5.4 and 5.5. Chiaroscuro as Norman reacts to Esther's conversation.

5.6 and 5.7. Norman moves through shadow as he contemplates suicide.

5.8. The suicide scene in *What Price Hollywood?*

Of course, chiaroscuro and even mid-key shadow effects also interact with color. Though it establishes the mood for Norman's suicide, for example, the lighting carries a double function. In suppressing color, it clears the way for a bravura reemphasis of hue when Norman approaches the sunset. The brilliant orange sunset is first glimpsed through the beach doors from Norman's point of view while he embraces Esther, and it figures prominently as he walks out to sea. The color, limited in intensity by the rear projection process, is nonetheless made dazzling by contrast with the cool and drab tones of neighboring shots. Light and color work together for dramatic emphasis, although their relationship is one of simple opposition. By stressing tonal qualities, the restrained mode thus laid the groundwork for a thorough integration of color into the cinematographer's repertoire.

Restraint and Departure: Color Design in *A Star Is Born*

As expected, color in its own right is also pressed into expressive service, and in this area too *A Star Is Born* sought to integrate it with established techniques. Color for *A Star Is Born* was planned by Lansing C. Holden, a one-time director (*She* [1935]) and art director who had worked with Selznick on *The Garden of Allah* (1936). Holden received screen credit as color designer, and he worked in a capacity that mirrored, perhaps replaced, that of the Technicolor Corporation's color consultant.[8] Indeed, there was apparently some enmity between Natalie Kalmus and Selznick's production team. When several preview cards complained that *A Star Is Born* would have been preferable in black-and-white, John Hay Whitney deduced that "the sender of all three cards was one and the same person, who probably knows Mrs. Kalmus."[9] But if Holden competed with Kalmus and the Color Advisory Service, his ideas about color were nonetheless strongly in the spirit of her prescriptions in "Color Consciousness." Holden described the duties of a color designer thus: "His function is to supervise sets, costumes and properties; he must plot the color scheme as a whole and for each individual scene; he must assure the most dramatic and harmonious use of color in the same way that a musical director supervises the score of a picture."[10] Although he was no friend of Natalie Kalmus's department, Holden shared with it widespread assumptions about proper color aesthetics.

Holden's essay "Designing for Color," published in the 1937 anthology *We Make the Movies,* provides insight into *A Star Is Born.* His comments follow the general tenor of the debate about color's proper role. Suitable color design, Holden argued, should abandon novelty for dramatic emphasis:

> Since colors which may seem natural to the eye often appear too brilliant and artificial when confined to a small screen, it is best to avoid colors which are too brilliant or harsh. The color designer should keep them subdued and soft in tone. In the early color pictures, the problem of recording colors was more important than their control. But now that the technical aspects have improved so greatly, we can turn our attention to the use of color in enhancing the moods and dramatic structure of the motion picture.[11]

Like Gilbert Betancourt, Holden essentially followed Kalmus's suggestions, spinning them in the direction of low-contrast restraint. Like Kalmus, he stipulated that "the center of interest must be the center of color," that background "should be kept a cool, neutral color" to set off the performer's face, and that sets must be "designed to set off the costumes of the principals."[12]

Yet he also offered a warning, one directed at Kalmus's equations of color and emotion. Citing the ballroom scene in *Becky Sharp,* he conceded:

> Color can undoubtedly be used to assist the mood of the story and to arouse emotion. But audiences should not be conscious of these various effects any more than they should be conscious of incidental music in a dramatic scene. The danger in using color for emotion is that it looks like a trick.[13]

For Holden, even where color design could clearly embellish the mood of a scene, it should be unnoticeable to the spectator. Like music, color should support narrative without necessarily commanding attention.

C1. *La Cucaracha*: Complementary colors guide viewers' attention.

C2. *La Cucaracha*: Choreography is organized around color contrast.

C3. *La Cucaracha*: Red light expresses Pancho's rage.

C4. *Becky Sharp*: Amelia completes the introduction of hue.

C5. *Becky Sharp*: Mamoulian's color gimmickry in the silhouette scene.

C6. *Becky Sharp*: Guests in red and orange follow those in blue and green.

C7. *Becky Sharp*: Soldiers' capes create a spectacular mass of blue.

C8. *Becky Sharp*: At the height of the sequence, the frame is washed in red.

C9. *Becky Sharp*: Background accents compete for visual interest during Becky's waltz.

C10. *Becky Sharp*: Low-key lighting during the ball.

C11. *A Star Is Born*: Texture rather than color dominates Norman's bachelor apartment.

C12. *A Star Is Born*: Red and green accents at the Ambassador Hotel swimming pool.

C13. *A Star Is Born*: Coordination between orange and blue accents and costumes during Esther's studio makeover.

C14. *A Star Is Born*: The fan magazine glows like a beacon of Hollywood's allure.

C15. *Robin Hood*: Costumes create a forceful display of hues across the frame.

C16. *Robin Hood*: Costumes balance interrelated accents while dancers create swirling color just beyond focus.

C17. *Robin Hood*: Set and costume colors guide the eye through the frame.

C18. *Robin Hood*: The primary triad punctuates Sir Guy's introduction.

C19 and **C20.** *Robin Hood*: Precise harmonies signal Robin and Marian's unspoken allegiance.

C21. *Robin Hood*: At the end of the second establishing shot, varied colors draw our attention into depth.

C22. *Robin Hood*: Marian's costume harmonizes with her surroundings while the bishop's purple flags our attention.

C23. *Robin Hood*: The purple accent separates Marian from the background and harmonizes with her costume.

C24. *GWTW*: Cold white highlights convey Wilkerson's intrusion into candlelit Tara.

C25. *GWTW*: Color temperature elegantly separates planes and guides the eye.

C26 and **C27.** *GWTW*: As Melanie's health fails, she moves from warm to cold light.

C28. *GWTW*: Scarlett's dress forms an inky mass against the crimson and black stairs.

C29. *GWTW*: The unprecedented play of highlight and shadow in a Technicolor close-up.

C30. *GWTW*: Scarlett's cool image is sandwiched between warm accents at fore and rear.

C31. *GWTW*: The kiss gives remarkable force to shifts of color, yet Scarlett's highlights are the only proper flesh tones in the frame.

Original Photography

3 Strip Technicolor

C32. *The Aviator:* The top image shows the film as shot, the bottom image shows the effect of the three-color look-up table. Courtesy of Miramax Films and Technicolor.

In certain respects, *A Star Is Born* evinces the unobtrusive harmonies recommended by Holden, Betancourt, and others. As in *Lonesome Pine*, texture is accomplished through tonal gradations within a limited set of hues, lit to ensure variation in the background while avoiding sharp color contrast. Now, instead of rustic cabin interiors, the restrained style often connotes fashionable minimalism. Lyle Wheeler's sets tend to be rendered in either neutral blue-gray or a mixture of brown, gray, and beige-gold tones. Much of the mise-en-scène squares with Holden's claim that he and Selznick felt "color should not be noticeable, that it should not get in the way of the story; we tried to lose the gaudiness."[14] Yet the sets themselves are often so stylized that they demand attention, and if the palette is tight, surface textures and design details become especially prominent.

Norman Maine's bachelor apartment offers an extraordinary illustration of how the film balances a few related colors with a rich set of textures. Limited color contrast accentuates the set's high style. Featured in only one scene, when Norman drunkenly phones Oliver Niles (his producer, played by Adolphe Menjou) and then Esther to arrange her screen test, the set's strong lines and massive curving wall immediately lend the impression of modern luxury. A detailed description gives some sense of the incredible variation of texture within the set's neutral design. At the left, Norman's bed, with a vertically striped mauve-brown (Ash Rose and Mauvewood) headboard built into a curved blond-beige paneled section of wall, is covered with a tan (near Desert Dust) blanket. Dressers in blond-beige flank either side of the bed, and a glossy brownish Red Earth vase sits on a shelf behind the headboard (Figure 5.9). The center of the room is dominated by a large window with diagonally striped cream (between Ecru and Dawn) and Almond brown outer curtains, flat grayish Pearl Blue inner curtains, and Beige wooden blinds. Along the far right wall, from background forward, sit a large, nearly black, Madder Brown easy chair; a highly polished caramel brown dresser with a circular mirror; and, toward the foreground, a horizontally striped Cream Pearl and flat Camel brown easy chair with a caramel brown end table-dresser. A matching striped easy chair and end table are placed in the center foreground. Other set dressings, including lamps, a few chairs, and small objets d'art are rendered in varying shades of brown, black, and beige. This mixture of tan and gray walls with brown and caramel accents provides a neutralized background for Norman's antics (Color Figure 11).

But if the colors are fairly uniform, other elements secure remarkable

5.9. The left half of Norman's bachelor apartment.

detail and visual interest. Texture and variation is achieved through contrasting patterns, such as the varied stripes on the bed, chairs, and curtains. Similarly, the varied finishes of set materials—highly polished surfaces set against flat fabrics and walls—lend an impression of complexity within the narrow range of color. Though the lighting scheme is high-key, directed pools of intense spot illumination, motivated by onscreen lamps, pick out specific furniture pieces and contrasting patterns. This lighting also emphasizes depth by striking the cool blue-gray draperies, which offset the tan window blinds at the rear, creating a graphic spike to accent the background. In black-and-white this set would have had the same deco flair; it would have lost none of its sophisticated elegance. For Wheeler and Holden, color becomes a subtle addition to techniques for creating texture through a play of tone and pattern.

Other sets tend to follow the same principles: Wheeler's architecture is heightened by overtly limited and stylized color design. The repression of color contrast also serves practical goals. It helps ensure that the performers will function as the "color center" of the compositions, and relegates the chore of providing background variation and texture to structure and lighting, whose level of detailed variation keeps the sets from succumbing to the high-contrast "color against neutral" look that plagued *Becky Sharp.* Characters are also often clad in shades of gray, brown, black, and white, so tonal contrasts and gentle back lighting separate players from backgrounds. As in *Lonesome Pine,* the restrained palette helps ensure that traditional cues for guiding attention are not displaced by color.

Unlike *Lonesome Pine,* though, *A Star Is Born* features a dynamic palette that is more open to color foregrounding, and these fluctuations are more clearly tied to narrative developments. Holden proposed a rather general correlation between narrative and color, and in doing so he suggested a motivation for more assertive color:

> In general color may be used like music to heighten the emotional impact of a scene. If the scheme of a picture is restrained so that there is little color in early scenes, which are played mostly in shadow, then even moderately bright colors will give the effect of greater brilliance in the climax. This problem had to be solved in David O. Selznick's *A Star is Born,* in which in the early scenes the costumes, sets, extras and bit players were designed in subdued colors, so that as the story of the young girl who wanted to be an actress moved from the North Dakota farmhouse to the rooming house in Hollywood, and then to her first screen test, the contrast between the low and high key scenes became more marked, and once her success was established the color reached its highest level.[15]

He may overstate the film's consistency in keying color to narrative, but his design does innovate by moving between restraint and assertion for spectacular and narrative effects.

Once again, the tension between integrating and displaying color technology seems pertinent. In reference to *A Star Is Born, Variety* posed the problem in this manner: "It is a fact that after a short period of several minutes at the beginning, audiences will rarely be conscious of the color tones. They are there, however, and it would be interesting to know whether the picture would be equally potent in black and white."[16] If color ceased to be noticeable, how would it justify its expense as a visible mark of difference from black-and-white? To answer this problem, Holden's color score exploits rudimentary narrative motivations for limited but striking color designs. Through the first half, the film alternates between restraint and the brief flashes of color that accompany Esther's climb to fame. Visually arresting color is largely associated with Hollywood's promise of wealth and glamour. In a surprisingly intricate development, such color supports the film's reflexive commentary about movie artifice.

The pattern begins even before the story is underway, in a credit sequence that instantly draws attention to color. Brilliant neon red credits roll over an animated skyline of Los Angeles, complete with flashing red and vivid turquoise lights. In a rather pointed display of Technicolor's range, the film cuts to the yellow cover of *A Star Is Born*'s shooting script, completing a red-yellow-blue triad. Opening with a splash alerts viewers to the power of color, but it also associates assertive design with the location and business of Hollywood. Color play is quickly suspended as the script opens to the first page and the frame is filled with black print on an

5.10 and 5.11. The low-key lighting of Esther's departure contrasts with a daytime panorama of Hollywood.

off-white page. The transition literally embodies the principle that color should recede as narrative gets underway. The recession of hue continues throughout the scenes in North Dakota, where it appears that Esther has grown up in a world of strict restraint and low-key lighting.

Esther's arrival in Hollywood occasions a brief but tremendous expansion of the palette. Set to the tune of "California, Here I Come," a rapid montage of Hollywood settings fires volleys of color across the screen. The barrage of hue is made more brilliant by its contrast with the near monochrome, low-key train-station scene that precedes it (Figure 5.10). The montage opens with a title card over a daytime panorama taken from the Hollywood hills, introducing high-key light and a soft but vivid blue sky (Figure 5.11). Subsequent compositions are even more intent on stressing color contrast. A shot of the Ambassador Hotel swimming pool juxtaposes red and green accents with vivid blue pool water and a peach and gray awning at the rear. When the shot reveals a studio's camera equipment at the pool's edge, it drives home the association of high color with Hollywood artifice (Color Figure 12). Hollywood, as the introductory title describes it, is a "Metropolis of Make-Believe."

Thematic connections, at this point, are secondary to sheer chromatic indulgence. The next three shots continue the trend, featuring, in particularly saturated hues, a blue bus, a yellow train, and a silver airplane, each approaching the camera and emblazoned with the words "City of Los Angeles." The montage finally meets back up with the central narrative at Grauman's Chinese Theater. Color contrast swiftly recedes as the image moves from Grauman's red awning, framed against the sky, to Esther—and the introduction of brown and tan tones into the sunny exterior. The first medium long shot of Esther in Hollywood wrenches the palette back to the hues of restraint. She wears a two-tone black dress and carries a tan and brown (Caramel brown and Topaz) suitcase. Behind her pass a pedestrian clad in a brown overcoat and a city bus, also deep brown. Brilliant top lighting catches Esther's red hair, which fairly glows. The resources of color, briefly displayed in the brash montage, are once again moored to character-centered narrative.

The key of color broadly follows shifts in the narrative's mood. The bold montage parallels the giddiness of Esther's long-awaited escape from her small town, and the palette contracts as she begins her struggle. The musical score also parallels the development. A folksy rendition of "Auld Lang Syne" poignantly accompanies the train-station scene, and it is followed by a brash jazz fanfare at the start of the Hollywood montage. Then, a speedy full-orchestra version of "California, Here I Come" climaxes with the shots of Grauman's, slows down, and is more gently carried by strings as the film returns to Esther's quiet colors. Whereas color in *Lonesome Pine* served particular narrative functions as a specific punctuating contrast or a developed motif, here, like the music, it more generally bolsters the prevailing emotional tone.

The association of high color with both Hollywood artifice and the upward sweep of Esther's career is cemented during another montage, which depicts her immersion in studio culture. The sequence culminates in the studio beauty salon, where color and artifice align. The scene realizes Holden's suggestions to Selznick that the set feature "spots of color in make-up paraphernalia" and "girls in background in yellow, orange, and blue."[17] Esther is seated with her back to the camera, and a small table with colorful glass jars sits in the foreground. The jars are Vibrant Orange and Horizon Blue complementaries. This punch of color is heightened by the presence of two extras, also clad in Vibrant Orange and Horizon Blue. In one of its boldest compositions, the film draws attention to color by exaggerating the rules of harmony and coordination between setting and costume and combining them with powerful contrast (Color Figure 13).

The reflexivity becomes more pointed when the film cuts around to a close-up of Esther as studio makeup artists manipulate her face. They pile on bloodred lipstick to achieve "the Crawford smear" and bleach-white powder for a "Dietrich" flesh tone. In a particularly biting commentary on studio artifice, the image mocks Hollywood glamour even as it distorts Lansing Holden's axiom that the actor's face must provide the color center of a scene. The film is especially ambitious in aligning color and theme while also exploiting opportunities for straightforward visual display. Restraint, the film demonstrates, need not mean the complete expunging of color.

A Star Is Born was also the first restrained film to make thorough use of a loophole in the generally somber aesthetic advocated by Kalmus, Betancourt, Holden, and others. In their discussions, they offered room for forthright color display if it could be roughly coordinated with the mood or tone of the narrative and if its duration was in inverse proportion to its visual power. Montage sequences, like establishing shots, were logical vehicles for this kind of color foregrounding. The condition of brevity would be met, and strong color could quickly establish tone, helping clarify extremely compressed episodes. In a film as restrained as *A Star Is Born,* these brief flourishes had the added benefit of developing conspicuous patterns and accruing significance.

A Star Is Born develops the restrained mode's potential for weaving chromatic motifs, though thematic associations of particular colors are rather nebulous. As in *Lonesome Pine,* red-orange accents, because they are so generally avoided in the restrained mode, are ready candidates for catching attention and gathering meaning. Like the autumnal oranges in *Lonesome Pine,* the chromatic motif in *A Star Is Born* is repeated in shifting contexts, forming a pattern that can bolster the dramatic weight of an episode without being obvious or symbolic. The approach follows Lansing Holden's proposition: "It is not so much the colors that evoke certain emotions but the way in which they are used which determines their emotional effect."[18] However, the color pattern here is more difficult to trace than in *Lonesome Pine,* since it does not benefit from being linked to a more commonly recognized motif like Tater's song.

As noted earlier, red-orange first appears in the opening credits, but it quickly becomes bound to Esther's dreams of Hollywood. During the first scene, set in the drab farmhouse interior, Esther's fan magazine generates a red highlight. In a long shot that frames the entire living room area, the magazine appears on an end table at the foreground left. The only red accent in the room, it receives directed spotlighting from above, making it glow like a beacon of Hollywood's allure (Color Figure 14). When Aunt Mattie (Clara Blandick) decries the magazine's intrusion into the family's quiet and sensible home life, she helps tie the splash of color to its narrative meaning.[19] The magazine coordinates with Esther's muted red scarf, linking her to an object that seems out of place in the subdued domestic set. Color helps define the character's motives.

The connection between high color and the lure of Hollywood solidifies during the "California, Here I Come" and studio-makeover montages, and it still carries a thematic potential that is activated during Norman's suicide. Here, the careful color restriction during Norman's final con-

5.12 and 5.13. Colors alternate in Norman's final farewell to Esther.

5.14. The setting sun, a conventional stand-in for Norman's death.

versation with Esther is contrasted with the orange-red sunset that he catches sight of through the window. The juxtaposition is emphasized by alternations between Norman standing in front of the doorway, sun behind him, and his final glance at Esther, clad in the deep green velvet dress (Figures 5.12 and 5.13). The setting sun, sinking on the horizon as he swims out to sea, stands in, rather conventionally, for Norman's death (Figure 5.14).[20] At the same time, the return of the luminous red-orange hue recalls Esther's dreams of a Hollywood career, fitting nicely with the film's explicit thematic contrast of rising and falling stars.[21] The sunset's conventional association with death and closure is reinforced by the color association. That the chromatic motif is built into a more traditional cultural reference helps obviate the danger noted by Holden, that the emotional use of color "looks like a trick." Color is redundant when used with other systems of meaning. Technicolor's place in the classical mode tends to be one that duplicates and enhances extant devices.

A Star Is Born responded to the challenges posed to Technicolor during the 1930s in a particularly rich and influential manner. William H. Greene's low-key lighting and extreme shadow brought color into contact with cinematography's traditional reliance on tonal contrast. Although successful integration partly meant bending color to fit codes of unobtrusiveness, *A Star Is Born* also set out vigorously to showcase Technicolor. The chromatic play was broadly tied to narrative concerns, and it found expression in areas traditionally open to ornamentation in monochrome cinematography. The film was a benchmark for color design in the mid-1930s. It built on techniques introduced by *Becky Sharp* and *Lonesome Pine* and cleared the way for the more intricate work of films like *The Adventures of Robin Hood* and *Gone with the Wind.*

The Goldwyn Follies: A Restrained Musical

Released in February 1938, Samuel Goldwyn's production *The Goldwyn Follies* would become United Artist's top-grossing film of the year.[22] Goldwyn first used three-color for the final number in his Eddie Cantor vehicle *Kid Millions* (1934), and he chose a musical format for his first full Technicolor feature. The film was only the second feature-length live-action musical in three-strip, the previous being Pioneer's poorly received (and lost) *Dancing Pirate* (1936). *Goldwyn Follies* used the backstage format to weave acts by radio and stage performers into a loose story line, a model that had proved successful for Paramount's similar film, *The Big Broadcast* (1932). The result was an episodic narrative for which subtle color motifs would have been out of place. Rather, *Goldwyn Follies* brought Technicolor to a genre plainly built around the spectacular display of lavish production values. The film is a standout in Technicolor design because it strove for the spectacular within the limits of the dominant "tasteful" color aesthetic.

Variety identified Technicolor as the key selling point for an otherwise generic production. Minus Hollywood star power, the film relied on radio and stage talent combined with the attraction of color. As the trade paper noted, "Lacking the flash and glitter provided by Technicolor, 'The Goldwyn Follies' would just be another extravaganza. The rainbow dressing gives it the punch of importance."[23] The "flash and glitter" of color design appears carefully regulated, favoring restrained harmony over bold contrast. Restraint doesn't simply help color recede: it creates the film's high-style gloss and production polish. *Goldwyn Follies* provides a fascinating contrast with the assertive, sometimes garish look of the popular Fox musicals of the 1940s. Even the film's biggest production numbers, which might easily justify bold, colorful designs, are held to the dominant style. Nonetheless, *Goldwyn Follies* manages to stylize color by gently expanding the restrained palette to include pastels and by coordinating costumes and sets.

Goldwyn Follies' paper-thin premise, as scripted by Ben Hecht, is little more than a framework for the song, dance, and comedy sketches. Film producer Oliver Merlin (Adolphe Menjou again), fearing his films have lost touch with the American public, hires "country girl" Hazel Dawes (Andrea Leeds) to advise him on his latest production, *The Forgotten Dance.* While steering the production toward popular tastes, Hazel falls in love with Danny Beecher (Kenny Baker, from radio's *Jack Benny Show*), an aspiring tenor. Comedy and musical performers audition and rehearse for the film-within-a-film, setting up the variety of numbers.

Throughout, color provides a subdued background for the performances. Although the studio's cinematographer was Gregg Toland, whose penchant for low-key is well known, the film generally adheres to Technicolor cameraman Ray Rennahan's professed affinity for conventional lighting "with a trifle more brilliance and contrast." Illumination is usually high-key, with additional top lighting outlining the main players' heads and shoulders. Once again, Gilbert Betancourt's suggestion that good taste should engage monochromatic and analogous harmonies, and avoid extreme contrast, rules the day. Large areas of heavily saturated color are almost entirely avoided. Splashes of bright, warm colors occasionally provide decorative accents, but these tend to be fleeting and carefully managed so as to recede during important action. As in other restrained films, lighting and understated chromatic distinctions, rather than strong color contrast, provide the central means for separating players from settings.

A Tightly Coordinated Look

The most pronounced trait of *Goldwyn Follies'* color design is its persistent coordination. The film's "polished" look is largely attributable to color harmonies between costumes and sets. Costumes nudge color forward within a relatively narrow palette. The principal male actors are usually clad in brown or gray suits that inconspicuously mesh with the neutral sets. Broadly comic characters' outfits are designed with somewhat more latitude, but their contributions to the central narrative are minimal. It is the women's wardrobes that furnish the linchpin of coordination. In what will become standard Technicolor practice, they help negotiate the terrain between tasteful design and spectacular display by repeating and echoing colors to create a perceptibly harmonized look.

Color in the women's costumes is broadly linked to character, a point commented on by Marion Squire in her *Variety* column, "The Girl's Eye View." Squire notes, "The most interesting thing about the picture is the color treatment," and "Omar Kiam does a good job of handling wardrobe colors."[24] Hazel Dawes's wardrobe stresses "girlish simplicity," and Olga Samara's (Vera Zorina's) colors are "more sophisticated." In fact, costume colors and their harmonies with the mise-en-scène are roughly keyed to character traits. This is by no means unusual in Technicolor design, but the musical, with its broadly drawn characters, makes the technique more prominent. The "girlish" Hazel, for example, routinely wears soft, low-saturated shades closely aligned with the sets' dominant neutrals. Against this unobtrusive simplicity, pampered Hollywood star Samara's wardrobe tends toward the ornate, providing either a sharper contrast with her surroundings or a conspicuous matching to the set.

Whereas the colors of the costumes are generally conditioned by character traits, the mise-en-scène highlights tasteful correspondences between the leading women and their surroundings. This tactic certainly follows Natalie Kalmus's recommendations for harmonious composition, yet it can also call attention to the system of coordination. Consider a pedestrian scene in Hazel's Hollywood home, as she unpacks her bags and explains her new job to her chaperone, Glory Wood (Ella Logan). The characters are clad in near red-green complementaries: Hazel in a flat yellowish green (between Beechnut and Tidal Foam) dress and Burgundy belt, Glory in a flat Cranberry dress.[25]

In the first shot, Hazel unpacks a pair of Meadow Green shoes and places them on her steamer trunk in the foreground. Against the neutral set, they form a conspicuous highlight in analogous harmony with her dress. The green hues strengthen the connection between actress and set. The detail also helps tighten the harmony between Hazel and Glory. When Glory stands near the green shoes, she gains a point of coordination with Hazel. Likewise, Hazel's Burgundy belt picks up Glory's dress. These accents unify the color scheme across alternating shots by injecting minor complements into each woman's immediate surroundings. In edging beyond strict restraint, the filmmakers make a concerted effort to ensure balance and harmony and to temper hard contrasts. *Goldwyn Follies'* design regularly works toward such a determined, coordinated look, predicting the "catalogue" aesthetic of later melodramas like *Blossoms in the Dust* (1941) and *Leave Her to Heaven* (1945). The film offers a kind of *House and Garden* view of well-appointed interiors and perfectly matched costumes.

The dressing of room of Olga Samara, true to her character, intensifies this kind of coordination, making it eye-catching. The set is based heavily on pastels, with beige walls and cream-colored trim, and dressed with extremely light tints of blue, pink, green, and yellow. Layered curtains of soft Silver Peony pink and very light Starlight Blue set off the far wall. Samara's costumes on this set match either the pink or blue curtain, making the room an extension of her wardrobe. Other details contribute to a strong impression of coordination. For instance, when Samara embraces Oliver at her dressing-room door, a soft pink lamp on a small brown table at the extreme right background precisely echoes the combination of her pink gown and his brown suit. Once again, the restraint makes such harmonies emphatic. *Lonesome Pine* or *A Star Is Born* might draw on such instances to underscore narrative turning points, but in *Goldwyn Follies* they are decorative reminders of virtuoso art direction. Likewise, in the scene's final shot she reclines against a soft pink chaise and Murmur green pillow demanding of her maid: "Fill my bath with whipped cream." The nearly exact match between gown and chaise, and the complementary pillow, makes Samara's coordination more obvious than Hazel's; it befits the caricature of stardom she represents. Still, Samara's look merely intensifies the film's internal norms; coordinated design suffuses the production.

Reserved and Tasteful Production Numbers

In narrative sequences, the art direction is chiefly interesting for coordinating color without resorting to obtrusive contrast or especially saturated hues. The most exceptional aspect of *Goldwyn Follies*' design, however, lays in its adherence to the same strategies for production numbers. The associations of these sequences with high art (opera and ballet) likely encouraged an explicitly tasteful approach to color. Both of Leona Jerome's (Helen Jepson's) opera performances are executed on flat gray sets that follow the conventions noted above for coordinating color. More remarkably, the two most lavishly produced numbers, Balanchine's dances for Zorina, also remain within an extraordinarily narrow palette. These production numbers testify to the dominance of the restrained mode during the 1930s, and they remind us that stylization need not rely on an assertive palette. A closer look reveals just how spectacular restraint can be.

Zorina's first dance is the "Romeo and Juliet Ballet," in which classically inclined Capulets compete with jazz-dancing Montagues as Hazel and Oliver spy from a soundstage balcony. After the traditional conclusion, with Zorina and her partner languidly collapsing into each other's arms,

Hazel pertly suggests the dance would play better with an upbeat ending. Oliver orders changes, and, Shakespeare be damned, the sequence closes with a very brief finale as the jazz and ballet dancers come together around the joyously united Romeo and Juliet. The ballet number delicately manages color, subduing it at the start and then strategically reintroducing and varying it. Yet, even at its most assertive, the design remains strikingly subdued.

The dance begins as an Aqua Gray proscenium curtain parts to reveal a theatrical town square with the Montague and Capulet hotels at left and right. As with the curtain that opens *Becky Sharp,* its parting reveals not a rich combination of vivid color, but a carefully crafted composition of gray, beige, and a few pastels. Suppression allows the gradual reemphasis of color. Accompanied by a crowing rooster and musical cues that suggest the onset of morning, a flurry of shots depict the town's awakening. Each presents a glamour shot of a dancer or model as she poses in a negligee at her hotel window. Minimal variations from shot to shot, such as a change in lipstick or nail polish, drive attention toward minute details of flesh tone and costume color. Again, the comparison with the opening of *Becky Sharp* seems appropriate: both sequences emphasize skin tones as the source of color interest by introducing them into a nearly monochrome mise-en-scène. Whereas *Becky Sharp* moves swiftly toward the display of vivid costumes, the ballet prolongs the process of revelation, slowly building the palette.

This design choice seems the ideal complement to Gregg Toland's conventional glamour cinematography. The sequence is, frankly, about putting women on display, and lighting rather than color takes the lead in objectifying them. Toland uses diffused modeling light, soft back illumination, and slight soft focus in the medium close-ups—standard black-and-white techniques for beautifying the image. Color is a subtle addition to standard techniques.

Color expands only slightly as the actual dance develops, but it does move forward as a formal element. The tap-dancing Montagues are clad in grayish Niagara Blue tap pants and matte, deep Pink Flambé blouses. This blue-pink contrast provides the most dynamic combination of the sequence, although both hues are flattened by a gray cast. Ballerinas who represent the hotel Capulet, on the other hand, wear white tutus with black diamond patterns. When isolated from the Montagues, the Capulets create nearly black-and-white compositions. Choreography repeatedly separates and intermixes the two sets of dancers, highlighting the color contrast to underscore the clans' rivalry. These color patterns follow musical shifts between classical and jazz motifs, weaving them together as the dancers mingle. Cutting between the tap dancers and ballerinas removes and reintroduces color. When the ballerinas join the ranks of tap dancers in long shot, the injection of black and white into a formation of blue and red creates a brief pictorial climax. Unlike the emphasis on assertive colors in 1940s musicals, the binary opposition of hue and neutral in the restrained mode generates a play of color without departing from a tight palette.[26]

Once the choruses retreat, Romeo and Juliet (Zorina) perform their pas de deux. The dancers first emerge clothed in the dominant mise-en-scène colors: Zorina in a white dress with a very soft blue-green tint, her dance partner in gray pants and a white shirt with brown stripes. He leads her to the main stage, and as they hold a pose, the film dissolves to present a change of costume. An in-place dissolve is a particularly obtrusive form of editing, but, remarkably, the transition offers no spectacular shift in color. Zorina's neutral dress is exchanged for a soft grayish blue dance outfit (between Porcelain Blue and Cyan) with a pearl and white lace headpiece. He is clad in a deep red-brown (near Oxblood) fez and leotard accented with a white collar. Far from dazzling the viewer, these colors simply separate the dancers from the background and provide harmony between the two. Restraint reaches a crescendo in a single close-up of Zorina glancing at her partner after they kiss. Isolated in soft focus against a luminous gray background, the lace and pearls of her headpiece seem to glow. The composition reduces color to a monochrome range except for flesh tones. This is not glorious Technicolor, but a continuation of sedate tastefulness and a heightening of black-and-white aesthetics. Color contracts, just as mass dancing gave way to a more serious display of balletic art.

After Oliver orders the change of ending, the dance reaches its finale, condensing and repeating the overall movement of rising and falling color contrast. Yet at its most adventurous, the palette offers desaturated shades of blue and pink in neutral and pastel surroundings. Color is decidedly orchestrated, but understated. The minimal design grants pictorial weight to subdued variation, and in this way the restrained mode lends style to the production number. It is an exceptionally rare approach to a big dance sequence, but probably only because so few musicals were produced during these years of restraint.

Balanchine's second number, the "Water Nymph Ballet," is *Goldwyn Follies*' most ambitious musical sequence, and it is here that the restrained mode is most stunning. The dance is staged almost entirely in tints of blue and gold-yellow, color forming a central element of display. Set designer Richard Day's stylized Greek amphitheater is built around an extraordinarily narrow palette. A vivid Cyan blue backdrop detailed with a few white clouds hangs above a half circle of white columns. A white statue of a horse stands at center rear, and a circular reflecting pool holds the foreground. At either side of the stage, as if anchored to an off-screen proscenium arch, hang soft Porcelain Blue theatrical curtains with two gold stripes running along their bottom edges. Hue is limited to gold, white, and two shades of blue. The strength of this simple contrast instantly alerts the viewer that color will be a vital source of visual pleasure for the dance.

Balanchine orchestrates color across four distinct phases. The number opens as a chorus of ballerinas clad in light Crystal Blue lace with copper Pale Gold spangles dance with a chorus of men in black tuxedos while one solitary "boy" (as Hazel describes him) stares longingly into the pool. The gold accents prepare the way for Zorina's arrival in the second phase. After all the dancers clear the set, she rises from the center of the pool in a gold lamé one-piece bathing costume and performs a brief solo on and around the water (Figure 5.15). Wearing a gold headpiece, she slowly emerges in medium shot, the reflection from the pool doubling her image. Her arrival boldly introduces gold into the blue and white field, but it also adheres to norms of coordination and the centering of color interest. The third phase ratchets up the contrast: the chorus of ballerinas reenter to dress Zorina in a light Yellow Cream ball gown with gold lamé spangles. The dance plays out various combinations of blue and yellow as Zorina pairs off with the boy, playfully eluding his embrace. When finally they kiss, the ballet enters its fourth phase, and a tremendous windstorm separates the couple, eventually tearing away Zorina's gown. Alone, she returns to the pool and descends beneath its inky surface.

The yellow-blue contrast builds during the first three phases, but it is the fourth that brings color most forcibly forward. Balanchine's color goes beyond simply accentuating the performers' movements—it becomes the source of movement. The onset of the windstorm is signaled by a brief cutaway to a billowing curtain that packs the frame with a mass of blue. Immediately, Zorina arches backward, her bright yellow dress filling the center frame and contrasting with both the background and the previous composition. The chorus now carries Crystal Blue lace veils that are picked up by the wind (Figure 5.16). Zorina is outfitted with a yellow veil that creates streaks of color as she dashes across the frame. Costumes thus allow relatively few dancers to generate large areas of color, and these masses of color overtake the dancers' movements as the source of visual

5.15. Vera Zorina rises from the pool, introducing gold into her blue and white surroundings. Publicity still courtesy of the Academy of Motion Picture Arts and Sciences.

interest. The wind ceases once it strips Zorina of her Yellow Cream gown, and she returns to her more subdued gold lamé one-piece. The change in palette, aided by a shift to slightly lower-key lighting, parallels the shift in the musical score to a tranquil theme. Color is aggressively keyed to the dance's development, and at its height, it actually takes over for the dance.

Goldwyn Follies' production numbers are outstanding for their color experimentation within the confines of restraint. Certain design choices work well within the system's technological limits. The nitrate print I consulted was marked by a pronounced gray undertone that tended to flatten color. The use of sequins, reflective spangles, and lamé on costumes provide dazzle, helping the fabric stand out and creating texture that compensates for relatively low saturation. Simple, well-defined designs constructed around a few hues help make color more predictable and controllable, and can provide striking compositions without drawing attention to process limitations.

However, technology can only partly explain this approach to color. The ballets consciously venture spectacular designs while adhering to the

5.16. Dancers carry blue veils that are picked up by the wind. Publicity still courtesy of the Academy of Motion Picture Arts and Sciences.

ideals of harmony and restraint deemed proper for sophisticated or cultured performance. Style is achieved not by broadening but by further paring down the range of colors available in these sequences. This may be an odd choice when compared with the brashness of musical numbers in the 1940s and 1950s. True to the restrained mode, however, Balanchine maintains chromatic texture and variety through the gradations of analogous and monochromatic harmonies and through noncomplementary contrasts (yellow and blue, or blue and pink). Subdued, harmonious, yet obviously stylized, the color in these sequences well serves Technicolor's efforts to establish three-color's artistic potential while simultaneously guarding against criticism that the color is garish and artificial.

Narrow palettes and subdued harmonies predominate, but as in each of our restrained films, *Goldwyn Follies* provides brief but significant departures, specters of the demonstration mode. Comedic performances, such as the Ritz Brothers' mercifully short appearances, and a single love scene, between Hazel and Danny, occasion the return to color showcasing. When Danny sings "Love Walked Right In" to Hazel during a date at the beach, against a backdrop of colorful umbrellas, *Goldwyn Follies* offers an equivalent of the Louisville phone call in *Trail of the Lonesome Pine.* Such isolated sequences of higher contrast and a more varied palette are de rigueur in the restrained mode. They are not so much lapses as limited reminders of color as a mark of difference. What seems unusual about *Goldwyn Follies* is that rather than heightening color in one of the larger, more expansive production numbers, the film uses adventurous design in a relatively small sequence. Though not obliterated, demonstration has been cordoned off, relegated to providing a brief respite from restraint. *Goldwyn Follies* is not unique in the functions it assigns color; indeed, it breaks little ground. Rather, the film is remarkable for concentrating such effort on achieving decorative effects within the confines of Technicolor's 1930s aesthetic of restraint.

Conclusion

In 1938, Robert Edmund Jones lamented the current trend in color design:

> The color pictures now being made in the studios are not color pictures at all, in any real sense, but colored pictures. Their tones are agreeably subdued in order that they may not clash with one another and the individual "shots" often contain delightful pastel harmonies. But there is very little color in these films and almost no color composition as artists know it. Black-and-white thinking still dominates the screen.[27]

Jones, committed as ever to the emotional language of color, was frustrated by an approach that consigned hue to a secondary, supporting role: "Just as color was about to become a dramatic agent of real value to the screen, Hollywood," instead of refining the experiments of *La Cucaracha* and *Becky Sharp* in overtly and aggressively organizing hue, "took hold of [color], subdued it, 'rarefied' it . . . thwarted it, stunted it and is now trying to ignore it."[28]

Jones's criticism highlighted the shift in style that took place in three-color productions after 1935. One would be hard pressed to find a more direct statement of how unobtrusiveness had come to dominate the field from *Lonesome Pine* onward. We now see that this shift involved a concerted compromise between the demands of the Technicolor lab and the sensibilities of working cinematographers, as well as between color showcasing and the reigning monochrome aesthetics. This restraint was a key step in aligning the possibilities of three-color with the conditions of

Hollywood's well-established standards of style and craft practice. Jones's complaint that studios simply ignored color, however, failed to account for the strategies, founded upon restraint, for integrating it into a system that could vitally support and underscore narrative. In the late 1930s, the functions of three-color may have become redundant with those of other stylistic parameters, such as lighting or music, but they nonetheless attested to a careful and precise attention to color design and deployment. Restraint, of course, did not mean indifference.

The analyses in this chapter and the last have detailed how the restrained mode helped negotiate a place for Technicolor within the classical style. In each film, subdued designs ensured that color cooperated with traditional methods for directing attention and buttressing drama, and conventional opportunities for overt stylization helped showcase color or renew its impact. Our three samples tracked major trends of the era. Other films also employed the strategies represented in these features, offering variations that appeared firmly rooted in the restrained mode as we have seen it in action.

Films from the outdoor cycle, such as *Ramona, God's Country and the Woman,* and *Valley of the Giants,* follow the precedent of *Lonesome Pine* quite closely. Extended establishing shots and atmospheric sequences provide the dominant means for showcasing color within palettes dominated by brown, gray, tan, and gold. Specific tactics of Wanger's production are repeated as well. For example, *God's Country and the Woman* features panoramas of woodland that exploit back lighting and mist to reduce color to near monochrome, one of several pictorial techniques lifted from *Lonesome Pine.* Similarly, when the tough female lumber-camp owner, Jo Barton (Beverly Roberts), falls in love with her competitor, Steve Russett (George Brent), her formerly brown and tan wardrobe shifts to one based on light blue, and pastel accents begin to appear in her surroundings. Although its design lacks the complexity of *Lonesome Pine*'s, the film deploys the same devices toward equivalent ends.[29]

Other films from the period develop devices that we have seen only once or twice in our three examples. For example, the soft-focus close-ups that invoke codes of monochrome glamour cinematography and showcase the color rendition of flesh tones in *Goldwyn Follies* find heavier use in films like *The Garden of Allah* (1936) and *Wings of the Morning* (1937). In the latter film, close-ups of Annabella, the lead actress, feature pastel backgrounds, adding color to the traditional techniques of lighting and focus. To illustrate: when she is framed before a fireplace, shallow focus renders it as an orange-yellow haze that harmonizes with red accents on her dress and her burnt rose lipstick. Such compositions point forward toward the more heavily stylized color cinematography of the forties even as they attempt to emulate focus and lighting techniques of thirties black-and-white styles. The effect is pushed to its extreme in *The Garden of Allah,* in a close-up of Marlene Dietrich framed against the amber glow of lamplight, which contrasts with her blue eyes. The orange wash creates an arresting, glamorous image as she is warned: "You've come to a land of fire, and I think that you are made of fire!" On the continuum that runs between restraint and assertion, these moments fall nearer the demonstration mode. But the function of color—to further ornament images that are conventionally open to stylization—falls well within the trends set out by our analyses. As we will see, *GWTW* most fully exploits techniques for blending complex facial lighting and color effects.

In a more general sense, the emphasis on coordination and harmony that lends *Goldwyn Follies* the finish of a carefully planned production without clearly building chromatic motifs appears to be an option suited to comedy. *The Divorce of Lady X* (1938), *Nothing Sacred* (1937), and *Vogues of 1938* employ this strategy. *Vogues* is especially noteworthy for using the restrained mode both as a marker of high style and in counterpoint to more adventurous musical and fashion-show numbers that showcase colored costumes in a manner that recalls the demonstration mode. These films, which employ color primarily for decorative ends, do not tend to avail themselves of the restrained mode's strength for keying color to narrative developments.

Between 1936 and 1939, under the watchful eye of the Technicolor Corporation, producers cautiously explored the three-color process. The restrained mode presented a distinctive response to color. It avoided simple novelty by restricting palettes to encourage subdued combinations, and by finding methods for tying color to expressive tasks. But as Jones noted, the restrained mode also turned away from the overt color scoring that would have placed the element at the center of stylistic systems. The possibility never was entirely abandoned; *Lonesome Pine, A Star Is Born,* and *Goldwyn Follies* each sought out acceptable motivations and methods for foregrounding color as a novel element, as well as strategies for allowing color to punctuate drama. Such tasks were pursued, however, within the broader project of integrating color into a formally unobtrusive system.

The films analyzed here found ways of working within the limits of restraint, helping develop conventions for making color serve the functions that classical Hollywood assigned to film style. In doing so, films in the restrained mode laid the groundwork for the more chromatically ambitious productions that followed. Beginning with *The Adventures of Robin Hood* and followed quickly by *The Wizard of Oz,* color productions began testing the limits of restraint, eventually developing a group of fairly well-defined color styles. The restrained mode, so central to gaining a place for color in the classical cinema, ultimately became one among several stylistic options as three-color production stabilized and spread.

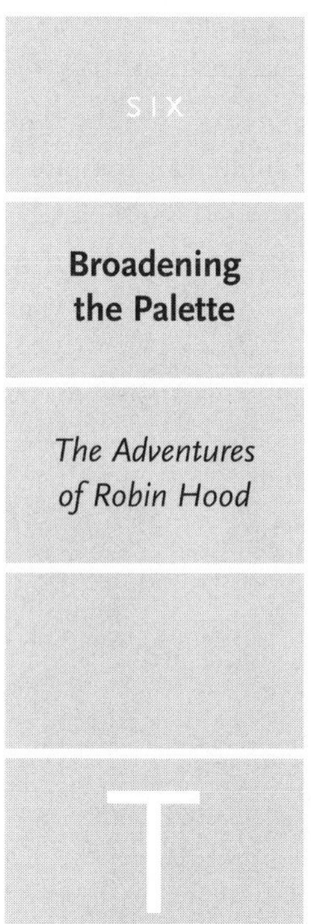

SIX

Broadening the Palette

The Adventures of Robin Hood

T*he Adventures Robin Hood* is a turning point in Technicolor design. For the first time in a three-color feature, the palette is opened wide and intricately organized. Far from returning to demonstration, *Robin Hood*'s assertive design modulates color to effectively direct attention and underscore drama. Indeed, the film draws on the methods forged in the restrained mode and brings them to a system in which hue, rather than tone, is the dominant variable. In so promoting hue, this assertive mode of design limits the power of subtle variations to punctuate, underscore, or ornament. When color is "always on," it may cease to be a meaningful element. *Robin Hood* addresses this problem, and clears a path for films that follow, by varying the function of color across the film. At different stages of the narrative, the color design emphasizes different kinds of tasks, all the while favoring a wide mix of hues. Though restraint would continue to inform an important trend in design, *Robin Hood* laid the foundation for a new way of thinking about color.

With an open palette, the design generates more complex harmonies and contrasts than did previous three-color features; red and green, as well as blue and orange-gold complementaries, figure prominently. Still, *Robin Hood* effectively ties color to drama. It relies on conventions of coordination and narrative subordination while increasing the opportunities to display vivid and complex schemes. At different narrative stages *Robin Hood* takes advantage of restraint, relying on minimal correspondences and changes to underline actions and themes. At other points, bold contrasts and strong color punctuate story material, making the chromatic commentary more obvious. Overall, the production displays a more flexible but no less controlled approach to color design than the films analyzed thus far.

The goals of this chapter are to specify *Robin Hood*'s innovations by setting it in relation to films of the demonstration and restrained modes, but also to confront the way color can guide our experience of film moment by moment. We will first consider basic principles of the color design: its emphasis on variety, and the key techniques by which *Robin Hood* foregrounds and underlines that variety. As the main source of the palette's complexity, costume design emerges as a central point of analysis. With these general characteristics as background, we can explore the functions assigned to color, noting how they are influenced by the design's devotion to assertive display. Finally, through a detailed close analysis of the banquet at Nottingham, we will endeavor to capture and specify the rich and intricate play of color in this film and to help elucidate in a new way how color shapes our encounter with cinema. Encouraged by the density of *Robin Hood*'s color design, this chapter, more than any other, engages with the weave of the film's stylistic fabric.

The Adventures of Robin Hood, released in May 1938, was three-color Technicolor's inaugural historical adventure film. The project was a follow-up to Warner's successful Errol Flynn and Olivia de Havilland vehicle, *Captain Blood* (1935), and it was the studio's most ambitious Technicolor production to date. Warner's had previously produced two rather inconsequential George Brent vehicles in three-color. The outdoor picture *God's Country and the Woman* (1937) was followed by *Gold Is Where You Find It* (1938), set in the aftermath of the California gold rush. *Variety* pegged *God's Country* as a "B-picture" that would find success outside of the major cities, sweeping "through the nabes [neighborhood theaters], especially the hinterlands."[1] *Gold Is Where You Find It,* according to the trade paper, was clearly meant to repeat this success, while attempting to gain support in "key first runs" by virtue of a somewhat higher budget.[2] Warner Bros. entered three-color production rather unspectacularly.

While both of these pictures made a modest profit, neither approached *Robin Hood* in scale or popularity. Made for a negative cost of nearly $2,000,000, the film was, to that date, the studio's most expensive picture by a healthy margin.[3] *Robin Hood* ranked as the year's sixth-biggest moneymaker in *Variety*'s annual list of top-grossing productions.[4] The film became the most successful live-action three-color production yet, solidifying Flynn's position atop Warner's roster of stars and helping Michael Curtiz tie with Henry King as 1938's top-grossing director.[5]

Along with *Gone with the Wind* and *The Wizard of Oz, Robin Hood* is also one of the best-remembered early three-color productions, in part because it brought Technicolor to a genre that would become a staple of 1940s and '50s color production. Like these other films, it also helped develop Technicolor style by placing color more boldly in the service of spectacle. The stylistic development is more a feature of color design than of any technological change. Although research continued to yield improvements in film speed and lighting, the technological background for *Robin Hood* is much the same as that for *Goldwyn Follies,* released three months earlier. Unlike *Gone with the Wind, Robin Hood* shares in the basic conditions that had encouraged restraint.

To a great extent, *Robin Hood*'s assertive design stems from the adventure genre's basic structure, which strings together a series of large production scenes that offer clear opportunities for showcasing color. Certainly, color was accounted for at an early stage of production. In May 1937, a memo from Walter MacEwen instructed screenwriter Norman Reilly Raine to "keep color in mind when rewriting the script." The story editor explained: "When we originally started on Robin Hood it was not contemplated as a Technicolor production. But now . . . Mr. Warner wants to be sure that every advantage is taken of the color medium."[6] The final shooting script contains nineteen specific references to color, many of which were retained in production. The film as written was predisposed to spectacular color.

The story opens with the news that King Richard (Ian Hunter) has been captured by Leopold of Austria. Richard's brother, Prince John (Claude Rains), swiftly lays plans with Sir Guy of Gisbourne (Basil Rathbone) to seize power and wage a campaign of taxation and terror against the Saxon citizenry. Robin Hood (Flynn) organizes against Prince John, openly challenging him during a banquet at Sir Guy's Nottingham castle. Robin soon falls in love with Maid Marian (Olivia de Havilland), King Richard's ward, with whom Sir Guy is also smitten. Prince John and Sir Guy capture Robin at an archery tournament, using, as bait, a golden arrow to be presented by Marian. With Marian's help, Robin escapes execution and flees to Sherwood Forest. Joining forces with the recently returned King Richard, Robin and his men infiltrate Prince John's coronation and attack. In the climactic duel, Robin defeats Sir Guy, frees Marian, and captures Prince

John and his men. In gratitude, King Richard grants equal rights to Saxons and Normans, makes Robin the Earl of Nottingham, and gives him Marian's hand in marriage. Typical of the adventure film, selfless acts are handsomely rewarded.

The film alternates brief stretches of exposition with scenes of action and pageantry. The large "production numbers" involve masses of actors and ornate settings and deliver spectacular color. The banquet at Nottingham Castle, the banquet at Robin's camp in Sherwood Forest, the archery tournament, and Prince John's interrupted coronation motivate the film's most elaborate color schemes. However, even routine scenes integrate a generally bolder palette than we have encountered.

Emphasizing Variety

Robin Hood's most noteworthy design aspect is its insistence on color variation. Whereas the default designs of the restrained mode tended toward a rather narrow array of browns, grays, and earth tones, *Robin Hood* consistently builds up palettes that mix green, red, pink, blue, and yellow. How this commitment to variety permeates the film is apparent in those scenes and sequences that do not foreground color as a source of spectacle or dramatic emphasis. For example, consider the range of color supplied by the ragtag assembly of dispossessed Saxons that Robin shows Marian in the forest. As Robin describes the plight of the "poor devils," the camera tracks past a series of color accents. First, a young child in a blue-gray shirt and dull olive green hat provides a fairly subdued point of variation. Then color picks up as the camera passes by an old woman with a Melon orange vest and Shell Pink cowl. In the background, a woman with bright Porcelain Blue accents on her skirt draws attention while, in the foreground, the camera discovers a man in a Hot Coral red hat. Next to him sits a hunched figure with a vivid Lincoln green scarf. Robin is briefly halted by an old woman in a Pastel Lilac cowl, and the shot concludes after it quickly passes over a succession of purple and blue accents. The huddled masses, in Robin's forest, are fashionably colorful. Hues are somewhat less saturated, and the accents more dispersed, than in the opulent displays of Prince John and his royal cronies, but the film's tendency to pack compositions with diverse colors does not abate.

Far more than films in the restrained mode, *Robin Hood* prods the spectator to recognize color. At times this variety helps draw attention to small details of the mise-en-scène, like the blue stitching on an extra's brown outfit as Robin passes him during the archery tournament, or the

6.1. A fruit bowl with red peppers carries color.

light blue bridle on Will Scarlett's (Patric Knowles's) horse after he brings Much (Herbert Mundin) to Robin and King Richard. Color accentuates the texture and details of a rich production design. At other times, props inject splashes of color without in themselves appearing particularly distinctive. For example, the various table settings in the banquet scenes provide dashes of red or yellow at the margins of the frame. Here, the rather weird contents of the fruit baskets—red and yellow gelatin at the Nottingham banquet, red chili peppers during the forest feast—are meant to go unnoticed; the props serve as simple vehicles for chroma (Figure 6.1). In either case, the near-constant play of assorted colors attests to the producers' efforts to keep hue vital and perceptible.

Adapting techniques from both the demonstration films and the restrained mode, *Robin Hood* develops three strategies for drawing attention to this color design. By alternating scenes of high and low color, extending establishing shots to showcase colorful sets and costumed extras, and selectively suppressing and revealing hues within sequences, the film refreshes color as a point of interest. We have already seen these methods, but *Robin Hood* stands out for foregrounding color more regularly and for employing these devices to serve such a decidedly varied palette. It is worth briefly considering how the assertive mode of design takes up these three routines.

The contraction and expansion of the palette from scene to scene is the film's most notable tool for renewing our awareness of color. Momentary reductions help amplify the normally rich design. This is really a reversal of the tactic used in *A Star Is Born,* where a reduced palette was briefly expanded at key points. Indeed, it harks back to *Becky Sharp,* though, as we will see, the effect is less obtrusive and the color designs are more complex. The first instance occurs just before Robin's introduction. Two brief vignettes illustrating Prince John's tax-collection methods are rendered in subdued gray and brown tones. For example, at a blacksmith's forge, a Saxon landowner is being chained as a slave. The scene is dominated by browns, the forge's flame and the slave's reddish brown (Mineral Red) collar providing accents. A priest in a soft Starlight Blue robe protests and is pushed off by a soldier. The scene mixes a restrained blend of neutrals and subdued, limited reds and blues.

The brief repression helps accentuate the burst of color brought by our introduction to Sherwood Forest. First, amid lush green foliage, Sir Guy and his company gallop through the forest, bringing with them the vivid reds, blues, and yellows of their capes and flags. Next, color erupts in the frame with bright green grass and blue sky as Robin and Will Scarlett charge in at full speed from a rolling meadow. The heroes leap over an obstacle, delivering streaks of red and green. Two cuts deliver a medium long shot and then a medium close shot of Robin and Will, green and red, framed against the blue sky.

The movement from carefully subdued neutrals and accents to strident red and green complementaries adds punch to Robin's entrance. In a film that deals heavily in complex combinations of bold colors, the confrontation between Robin and Sir Guy, which mixes red, blue, and green, benefits from its contrast with the previous sequences. Color has been effectively scored, like Erich Korngold's music, which moves from a stern, foreboding theme during the tax-collection scenes to a stirring crescendo with the arrival of Robin and Will. Contracting and expanding the palette in this manner recalls Mamoulian's transitions in *Becky Sharp.* But here the effect is less severe and more gracefully integrated into the flow of the sequence. Robin's appearance answers the threat posed by Prince John's henchmen, and sound and color augment the moment.

Robin Hood also elaborates the well-developed tactic of extending establishing shots to motivate parades of vivid color. As we will see in our analysis of the banquet at Nottingham, this strategy repeats that of the panoramas in *Trail of the Lonesome Pine* or the establishing shots in *Goldwyn Follies,* but with greater breadth of color and a more precise choreography of hue. Again, the nearest precedent might be found in *Becky Sharp.* The opening of the Duchess of Richmond's ball, with its organization of strong contrasts and display of chromatic plenitude, presents a schema that *Robin Hood* repeats and revises. For example, four establishing shots open the archery tournament, reveling in an exceptional array of red, green, blue, and gold. In a tactic that informs the whole film, spectacle is generated by creatively displaying color rather than by simply demonstrating its variety. The four shots don't inundate the frame all at once, as in the Duchess of Richmond's ball, but reveal the palette in de-

6.2 and 6.3. Color is suppressed and revealed in the climactic duel.

grees, through staging and camera movement. *Robin Hood* expands on an inherited convention to showcase designs of unprecedented complexity.

Bold maneuvers, acceptable in transitions and the openings of scenes, might be judged distracting in the thick of the drama. *Robin Hood*'s third strategy for drawing attention to color involves manipulating the palette on a small scale, often in the midst of action. Once again, a basic version of this tactic had been exercised in *Becky Sharp,* in which Mamoulian revealed accents through camera movement. And as we saw in *Lonesome Pine,* the restrained mode could capitalize on small variations, drawing attention to discrete dashes of color (like the green accents in the Gap Town office). *Robin Hood* has to modify the procedure because the continual variety of color raises a problem for cueing attention. The graphic power of a fresh hue depends either on its intensity or on the simplicity of the palette in the surrounding mise-en-scène.

One way *Robin Hood* resolves this issue is to momentarily remove hues so that they gain prominence when they reappear. This method, less striking in *A Star Is Born* and *Trail of the Lonesome Pine,* seems a logical option for a film with a decidedly complex color scheme. It can refresh the visual impact of color without forcing more color into the frame. The procedure famously adds punch to the climactic duel between Robin and Sir Guy. As they fight, the characters slip beyond the view of the camera so that only their shadows remain on screen (Figure 6.2). After a brief view of these battling silhouettes, Robin, in his green and brown outfit, and Sir Guy, in Flame Scarlet, reemerge, bringing complementaries back onto the scene (Figure 6.3). In the midst of an ongoing action, suppression and revelation renew color's power.

Like the other routines for color foregrounding in *Robin Hood,* this one falls somewhere between the subtlety of the restrained mode and the obviousness of demonstration. The removal of hue is nearly complete (a few candles relieve the play of gray and black with their flames), and the returning color features a bold juxtaposition of complementaries. In its degree of graphic change, the suppression resembles that in the silhouette scene between Amelia and Becky in *Becky Sharp.* In *Robin Hood,* though, the motivation for the effect is not so contrived or overwrought. The technique has become a simple yet forceful embellishment of ongoing action rather than the scene's centerpiece. With each of these three devices, *Robin Hood* returns to the territory of demonstration, but with the greater precision and integration taught by years of restraint.

Costume Color

Clearly, *Robin Hood* exhibits a dynamic color design and exploits a host of devices to foreground it. One thing that the above examples should suggest is the importance of costumes to generating the diverse and assertive range (Figure 6.4). Characters' clothing provides the central means for introducing and varying color, and it offers the film's strongest juxtapositions. Generic motivation is important here. One trait shared by most of the films in this book is that the female leads are granted the greatest range of costume color; they provide the chromatic center of a given scene's palette. Except in *Becky Sharp,* male players have been restricted to a set of grays, browns, and limited accents. As a historical adventure film, *Robin Hood* is granted a great deal more room for color among its male leads. This is especially true of the villains, whose regal pretensions make them prone to opulence. Sir Guy, for example, has seven major costume changes, only two fewer than Maid Marian. Moreover, color accents in his outfits range from saturated Flame Scarlet and Rich Gold to Sky Blue and Ultramarine Green. Even Robin, who usually sports the hallmark Lincoln green and Leather Brown, contributes some vivid Crimson details.[7] And

6.4. Opulent costumes support the broad palette.

as the film expands the field of men's wardrobe, it retains the breadth of feminine costuming.

Warner Bros.' advertising makes readily apparent the importance of costume to *Robin Hood*'s visual design and production values. As part of a seven-page spread run in *Film Daily* prior to the film's release, a publicity writer provided this description of Milo Anderson's designs:

> One simply must see "The Adventures of Robin Hood" to even fairly comprehend the exceptional beauty and variety of its costumes. Executed by Milo Anderson, they represent one of the strongest factors in the production's value from the angle of eye-pleasantry . . . via color, photography and story suspense. Elaborate but never overdone. . . . Striking, but consistently blended in harmony. . . . Modernized, but always in period taste . . . the "Robin Hood" costumes by Milo Anderson will long be remembered as a distinctive achievement.[8]

Buried within the advertiser's aggrandizement is a fairly apt account of the demands placed on costume design in this film. As a source of visual appeal, the costumes deliver varied and striking color. At the same time, like any other vehicle for color, they are bound to codes of harmony and to the support of the narrative, or "story suspense." Most of all, as the ad copy attests, the costumes are conspicuous, meant to be noticed as a mark of quality and expense.

Robin Hood's costumes radically juxtapose strong complementaries. Red and green contrast is especially prominent, presented in scenes that feature Robin and either Will Scarlett or Sir Guy. But it also emerges in the juxtapositions of Robin and Marian during the forest banquet; she wears a brownish Chili Red velvet cape to contrast with his Lincoln green hood and tights. The scheme also shows up in individual costumes, most significantly in Robin's green cape, which features a Cardinal Red lining. This is a distinct break from the restrained mode, which so carefully avoids mixing strong complementaries. As noted in the introduction, various color theorists have suggested that complementaries tend to "attract" one another, since together they complete the spectrum.[9] Whereas the restrained mode saw this as a liability, *Robin Hood*'s costumes exploit it for decorative and narrative ends.[10]

To a degree, these costumes are mandated by tradition. Robin Hood must wear green, and Will Scarlett, red. But from this starting point the film exploits complementaries with unprecedented force. The color scheme can be drawn into underlining story conflicts, as we will see in our close analysis of the banquet scene. But generally, as when Will and Robin first meet Little John (Alan Hale), the decision to use these mixtures must stem from the impulse to foreground color variety. After Little John upends Robin during their famous staff fight, they join Will at the bank of the stream, and their costumes are fully displayed. Will, in red, and Robin, in green, are united with Little John in a red hat, Pastel Yellow tights, and a Sky Blue shirt. Red, green, yellow, and blue are arranged across the frame like hues on a color chart (Color Figure 15).

Whereas the designers of *Goldwyn Follies* and *A Star Is Born* were content to rest with easy harmonies between the women's colors and the men's neutrals, Anderson uses the costumes for *Robin Hood* as a rich exercise in coordination and contrast. In the forest banquet, for instance, we have noted that Marian's Chili Red velvet cape contrasts with Robin's Lincoln green outfit, but the juxtaposition is subdued by the cape's deep brownish undertone. Other accents push the costumes' color relationship in the direction of both coordination and contrast. The clasps on Marian's cape feature large, deep emerald stones that pick up Robin's greens. On the other hand, Marian's faint lavender veil offers significant contrast in both hue and value. The intent is clearly to harmonize the costumes through an intricate play of accents, leaving large areas of each outfit (Marian's shimmering silver dress, Robin's Leather Brown vest) more or less neutral (Color Figure 16). *Robin Hood* balances an array of interrelated accents.

Relationships among costumes are further complicated by set dressing and extras. Consider, for instance, Sir Guy's introduction at the film's opening. A dissolve brings on-screen a long shot of Prince John's room in Nottingham castle. The composition is immediately remarkable for featuring relatively strong contrasts of red, blue, and gold. The shot, a slight high-angle, frames the room, showing Prince John, seated at left, picking at a plate of fruit. Across from him, a red velvet curtain runs down the right edge of the frame. This curtain is the foremost in a series of color accents arranged diagonally into the depth of the shot. The second accent is a midground table, covered in a red velvet cloth with gold trim. An overhead spot picks the table out from the general illumination; the cloth shimmers, aided by reflections from a gold goblet and fruit bowl. Gold fringe along the edge of the tablecloth makes the piece a strong chromatic magnet (Color Figure 17).

The primary function of the red is to set off Sir Guy's rich blue cape as he stands just left of the table, his back to the camera. Sir Guy is the third station in the diagonal of color accents. His vivid blue costume, juxtaposed with the systematic placement of red, makes Sir Guy the color center of the frame. Color leads the eye through the set, defining key areas of the space. The diagonal is completed by another red accent, this time carried on the sleeves of a guard leaning in semishadow against the back wall. Sir Guy's cape is set like a blue sapphire in a band of rubies; the surrounding highlights contribute to its radiance. With this early shot, *Robin Hood* establishes color as a commanding force.

The bravura moment of color choreography is yet to come. The film cuts in toward the table as Sir Guy spins around to face Prince John. As the cut brings the red plane of the tabletop forward, Sir Guy's movement causes his cape to flare, amplifying the red-blue contrast of the previous shot. In the same instant, the gold lining of his cape flashes, and the yellow emblem on the front of his black vest blazes into view. The gold tones on the costume coordinate with the tableware and the tablecloth fringe, and a yellow apple in the fruit bowl serves to match Sir Guy's emblem (Color Figure 18). This powerful combination inaugurates the film's basic triad of red, blue, and yellow, the pigment primaries. As he turns and completes the triad, Sir Guy helps strike what Johannes Itten would call a "color chord." Colors lock together and reinforce one another. The strong contrast makes this first medium long shot of Sir Guy arresting; the repetition of gold and yellow helps connect red and blue areas without subduing the contrast. One would be hard pressed to find a more elegant maneuvering of color mise-en-scène in the 1930s. The moment harnesses all the flash of *Becky Sharp* to a fully integrated use of staging and cutting.

Elsewhere, the interactions of costume and setting are more decorative, but they point toward a general quality of Robin Hood's design. Less concerned about emulating standard monochrome techniques, the filmmakers willingly exploit color as a means to stylize the image. In the forest banquet, for instance, the backgrounds become an active source of color. The initial two-shot of Robin and Marian is staged before a crowd of frolicking outlaws dressed in garments captured from Sir Guy. They generate a constant swirl of orange, green, and blue just beyond the plane of focus. As the revelers move about, coordinating and contrasting accents emerge and retreat, creating a constantly evolving set of color relationships (Color Figure 16). The shallow-focus close-up of Marian is particularly adventurous; background colors are abstracted as unfocused red and gold capes whirl by behind her. At the same time, the compositions avoid the pitfalls of Mamoulian's attempt to blend action and color. Because the colors are so densely packed and in such rapid motion, individual hues never achieve the prominence they enjoy in *Becky Sharp. Robin Hood* is more confident in its use of color: the palette is more complex, and the filmmakers are less concerned with so deliberately staging and motivating the background accents.

Functions of Color

Since color is brought forward so vigorously by the film's design, one might expect color to serve more-ostentatious functions here than in the restrained mode. One influential view of Technicolor is that it encouraged garish and painfully obvious color symbolism. However, this film is actually less effective at drawing on color to build chromatic motifs than either *Lonesome Pine* or *A Star Is Born.* The heavy variation of color means that it is more difficult to thematize specific sets of hues. Instead of giving color symbolic duties, *Robin Hood* shifts its function across the narrative. Some stretches of the film favor spectacular flash, while others more closely tie color to drama. This militates against building motifs over the course of the film, but it enables the assertive design to flexibly serve tasks like punctuation and underscoring. The concept of function provides a key to analyzing this outstandingly intricate design, and it can help us correct an important historical misunderstanding about the way color served narrative under Technicolor's reign.

Robin Hood's design adheres to a large-scale pattern of four phases, with different kinds of color functions favored in each. In the first fourteen segments, until Robin's sentencing after the archery tournament, color is paraded and renewed, but not allowed to recede for an extended period. Early on the film favors methods that emphasize color variety, and thus local changes in dramatic tone are less likely to trigger marked changes in color design. For example, the scene in which Prince John angrily orders Robin's death and the seizure of Saxon wealth immediately precedes the playful scene of Robin and Will meeting Little John. Both scenes feature vivid green, red, blue, and yellow-gold accents despite their dramatic contrast. Color functions decoratively.

Within the environment of this first phase, very broad manipulations of color connect to narrative. For instance, the banquet at Nottingham and the banquet at Robin's forest camp parallel each other because each presents a high point of design; color is more forcefully exhibited as a source of spectacle. During Robin's feast, his men steal the vivid vestments of Sir Guy's company, forcing the royalty into brown and gray rags. The regimented unfolding of color that marks the opening of Sir Guy's

Nottingham banquet is parodied by a chaotic play of highlights during the forest party. That Robin's men have become the source of color reinforces the plot turn in which they, briefly, seize power from their oppressors. Both color and authority change hands; Robin's success has stripped the Norman rulers of their color. In fact, though, color design within this phase of the film must overcome a good deal of interference to achieve significant color scoring. Two scenes of strong decorative color can parallel each other, but in general, foregrounding techniques dominate and dampen subtle variations.

However, in the second phase, consisting of the next eleven segments, variations in color parallel narrative developments more closely. After the brilliant display at the archery tournament, colors are somewhat muted when Robin is sentenced to death, then nearly eliminated as he is chained in the dungeon. The standard array of varied accents returns for Robin's escape and the surrounding sequences. Then, when Sir Guy discovers Marian's complicity and she is sentenced to death, color design once again takes a turn toward more somber tones. The fortunes of the protagonists alter more rapidly in this portion of the film, and color design is more sensitive to dramatic change.

The broad pattern enters a brief third phase in the four swift expository segments that follow Marian's sentencing. Bess (Una O'Connor) warns Much of Prince John's murderous plans, and Much intercepts the royal assassin. As Robin meets King Richard (disguised as an abbot), Will rescues Much, and they race to spread news of Richard's return. During this busy stretch of events, color reverts to relatively undistinguished neutrals and accents. The variation in hue is not truly restrained, since eye-catching highlights continue to surface from scene to scene, but the techniques for renewing an awareness of color are withheld. The rapid flow of action limits opportunities for color showcasing, and this helps set up the last phase of high-profile color design.

When Richard dramatically reveals his identity, color display returns, and it continues through the end of the film. Prince John's interrupted coronation and the climactic battle bring together the boldest costumes from throughout the film and employ nearly all of the favored methods for foregrounding color. The opening and concluding portions of *Robin Hood* tend toward decorative designs and color showcasing. Together they frame two middle portions in which color more readily echoes dramatic tone and then recedes briefly. This structure stems partly from a general principle that favors bold and vivid display during action and spectacle sequences, which are concentrated toward the film's start and conclusion.

By shifting the ways color functions across the film, *Robin Hood*'s design manages to integrate lessons learned from the restrained mode with bombastic, spectacular display.

During the second phase, moment-by-moment manipulations of color underscore narrative developments. Here, the film's debt to the restrained mode is most marked. Following Robin's capture at the archery tournament, for instance, Robin and Marian are clothed in similar tones of deep brownish red. Together, they contrast with Sir Guy and members of his tribunal, who wear rich greens, blues, yellows, and reds. Robin and Marian are chromatically united, sharing a common point of contrast. The play of coordination and contrast is as skillfully developed as in any of the restrained films, and far from the garish or heavy-handed style often attributed to Technicolor.

The purpose of the trial's design is made particularly clear by a series of shots as Sir Guy reads his decree. In medium shot, Sir Guy's flaming costume consumes the frame. His bright Marigold yellow hood with satin Blue Turquoise lining sets off a Fiery Red robe, a blinding version of the primary triad. Editing presents an eye-line match of Marian, and then a brief shot of Robin, as Sir Guy declares, "There may be some who will regret that a man of your peculiar talents should be cut off so early in life." At the end of the sentence, framing returns to Sir Guy, sandwiching the two subdued, coordinated images of Robin and Marian.

Their harmonies are precise. She wears a black dress with a sheer, very deep Eggplant purple cowl topped by a crown with a subtle gold border. Two figures behind her provide a few accents. On the left, a man in a bluish Quarry gray tunic with soft Starlight Blue details establishes a receding but textured foil to Marian's warmer hues. The figure on the right is more heavily shadowed, but a hint of green comes through, and a large, highly polished silver-gray necklace creates a strong achromatic highlight (Color Figure 19). The scheme in Robin's close-up is even sparer, but it offers strong affinities with Marian's. He wears a Deep Red Brown hood (which appears nearly Oxblood Red in the highlights) over a brownish Nutmeg gray shirt. Their outfits share red as a dominant, and that hue is toned down to the point of near neutrality, almost eliminating contrast. The bright silver-gray highlight of Robin's neck iron echoes the necklace in Marian's shot, and a slight hint of soft blue in his far-left background picks up the blue accents behind her, shoring up the somber harmony with surprising exactness (Color Figure 20).

In the second phase of the film, these colors communicate character relationships. Marian had previously favored costumes that incorporated elements of Sir Guy's and Prince John's extravagant schemes while also offering points of coordination with Robin. Here, that coordination has thoroughly won out, signaling her allegiance to the outlaw. Of course, color is not solely responsible for making the point. Earlier scenes established her growing sympathy for Robin's cause, and Sir Guy's knowing glance shows that he has detected her change of heart. Still, color has been precisely scored to the plot point. Since Robin and Marian will not openly declare their love for several scenes, these indirect signs of affection carry some weight. Moreover, the kind of accord developed between them, based on the understated modulation of dark hues and achromatic accents, was dictated by the mood of the event. The shooting script describes Marian as "emotionless" and explains that she "gives no sign" when Sir Guy shoots her the glance. Robin and Marian's reticent hues convey their silent, melancholy attachment.

Such careful contrast and coordination is a legacy of the restrained mode. But while the second phase of the narrative can well accommodate that kind of scoring, punctual accents rule the day in the more florid phases. Punctuation, when it is carried by sudden bursts of color, thrives in the open palette, especially when bold costumes streak across the frame. We have already noted the green and red highlights that help underline Robin and Will's first appearance in Sherwood Forest. Similarly, when Robin's men leap out to surround King Richard, who is disguised as an abbot, their movement across the foreground creates a rush of bright reds and greens. Bursts of color accentuate brief moments of action, making this technique particularly prevalent during the opening and closing phases. Because it is fleeting, punctuation does not seem forced or obtrusive. In its first and final phases, the design favors a hit-and-run approach to color scoring.

Punctual color emphasizes both minute actions and large-scale developments. At one end of the spectrum, the red lining in Robin's cape provides a flourish that climaxes his speech at Gallows Oak, when he swings his arm upward and exclaims: "And swear to fight to the death against our oppressors!" The grand gesture exposes the cape's scarlet lining, delivering a burst of complementary color (Figure 6.5). The same technique is expanded to punctuate King Richard's unveiling before Robin and his men. Richard opens his black cloak to reveal his saturated Flame Scarlet uniform, emblazoned with bright yellow (Dandelion or Sunshine) lions (Figures 6.6 and 6.7). His soldiers, too, open their cloaks, revealing bright white costumes emblazoned with red crosses. According to Rudy Behlmer, this visual effect was important enough to merit a noted historical

6.5. Robin's gesture delivers a burst of complementary color.

6.6 and 6.7. King Richard and his men reveal themselves, injecting strong red into the frame.

inaccuracy. Knights of the Crusades wore the red crosses on their backs when returning to England, but in this scene they bear the marks upon their chests "in order to make the revealment of the king and his nobles more effective dramatically."[11] Costume, once again, is the pivotal tool for generating spectacle, and color takes the central role in briefly punctuating the action.

By varying the functions of color across the film, *Robin Hood*'s design can grant narrative roles to Technicolor while keeping to a broad and assertive palette. Localized color scoring follows the character's fortunes during the second phase, and punctuation comes forward in the others. Large-scale color motifs, however, suffer. For example, red and green would seem to be good candidates for an adversarial motif, perhaps underlining the battle of the royals against Robin and his men. Though several scenes build up a thematic pattern of color, the design's commitment to variety blunts these associations. Robin's band consistently offers accents of blue, red, and yellow, and Sir Guy's foot soldiers wear the same brown and green colors common to Robin's men. Various knights, as well as Sir Guy himself, wear green at several points in the film.[12] Whereas the conservative use of red and orange allowed those colors to form precise patterns in *Lonesome Pine* and *A Star Is Born, Robin Hood*'s liberal palette diminishes the power of individual colors, discouraging finely tuned chromatic motifs.

Because of its cluttered palette, *Robin Hood,* when it reaches after thematically significant color, does so in an unusually bold and literal manner. The film's popularity (it is one of a handful of early Technicolor films with which most viewers are familiar) and the blatancy of its attempts at color motifs have skewed our historical understanding of Technicolor aesthetics. For instance, Richard Neupert, in his generally excellent discussion of Technicolor style, uses *Robin Hood* as an example of what he considers the rather clumsy way that narrative and color align in the classical era.[13] The view is exemplary of a general critical attitude toward "glorious" Technicolor. Against the background of our study, we might see *Robin Hood*'s thematic use of color as anomalous rather than typical, and appreciate how the shifting of functions enables a nimble narrativization of color.

The film's nearly symbolic use of color is most clearly illustrated by several peculiarly emphatic instances of red, and they merit analysis because they can help us counteract some common assumptions. At the conclusion of the second scene, Prince John offers Sir Guy a toast to affirm their designs upon the throne. As he sets down the decanter, Prince John knocks over his goblet of red wine. The camera follows the characters' surprised glances, tilting down to discover a puddle of deep, almost black, red wine on a stone gray floor. Neupert has analyzed this sequence as part of a motif that, for him, makes red "a major signifier of John's bloody treachery."[14] The spilled wine is "hardly a subtle foreshadowing of John's bloody reign," though it also helps characterize the would-be ruler as a "clumsy oaf who lacks the grace and finesse of a true leader like King Richard."[15]

For Neupert and others, this is typical of how Technicolor sought to narrativize color. Natalie Kalmus's discussion of red as symbolic of danger and blood in "Color Consciousness" supports this view.[16] From this perspective, the red motif "underlines and motivates the ensuing violence" when red accents occur in the tax-collection montage. The "newly butchered sides of beef" at the butcher's and the "roaring fireplace" in the blacksmith's forge might seem like clumsy "red for danger" signs.[17] I have already discussed the tax-collection sequence in connection with the contraction and expansion of the film's palette. The two brief scenes are dominated by muted colors and subdued variation (including red accents), setting up the far more vigorous explosion of red and green when Robin and Will Scarlett, the saviors, come thundering in on horseback. In fact, the vignettes represent a brief respite from the stronger contrasts in surrounding scenes. This is not to argue that the dashes of red, identified by Neupert, might not serve to develop the motif, but this function is not particularly pronounced. When function favors punctuation over motif, any rather subtle emphasis on red gets lost in the varied palette.

The pooled wine is clearly a symbol for the blood that Prince John's reign will spill, but such symbolism was not a common technique for binding color to narrative. This use of color is actually far less ambiguous than the motivic patterns set up by the restrained films. It recalls the literalness of *Becky Sharp* and *La Cucaracha*. *Robin Hood*'s shooting script indicates that, as originally planned, the connection between blood and wine would have been even more heavy handed, but also transitional. The shot of dripping wine was to be followed by this scene, eliminated from the final production:

> Dissolve To:
> WATERING TROUGH TRUCK SHOT
> We discover CLOSE-UP of rough flagstones and a fallen sword with blood dripping slowly down on them. TRUCK BACK to reveal a Saxon farmer lying half across a rough wood or stone watering trough with an arrow in his back, while in background four or five Norman horsemen are swiftly rounding up about twelve fine horses, bringing some out of the small barn, and herding them away.[18]

The color-symbol of the wine was originally linked directly to blood, and this was conceived as part of a transition to a series of vignettes illustrating Prince John's oppression. Like most obtrusive uses of color, this unusual symbolism was to be consigned to a transitional montage sequence. Indeed, because the color of the wine on the stone gray background is not particularly vivid (it is nearly black), the power of the motif rests on a sort of literary association of spilled wine with blood rather than on the visual charge of color.

Two subsequent scenes tap into the association of red with the spread of terror, and to stand out amid the busy color design, they are made extraordinarily vivid. They both occur in another montage, which links a series of atrocities perpetrated by Prince John's government. In one vignette, a knight who had ordered a Saxon hanged is struck in the chest

6.8 and 6.9. A bloodred sky and fuchsia wine create deliberate color motifs in the montage sequence.

by an arrow shot from off frame. The scene is drenched in red-orange light, motivated by an off-screen sunset; the legs of an unfortunate Saxon dangle in silhouette from the top of the frame (Figure 6.8). The shooting script describes these figures as forming "a grim, black silhouette against the blood-red sky."[19] The extreme use of colored light, mixed with near silhouette, anticipates the burning-of-Atlanta sequence in *Gone with the Wind*. It is certainly the most expressive use of colored light in the film. The bloodred backdrop and key light are, like the spilled wine, given a strong thematic charge. Color has been added to the conventional use of low-key lighting for representing a sinister act, creating a striking, painterly effect.

The next vignette takes place at the Saracen's Head tavern, where soldiers terrorize the owner and threaten his daughter. In a fairly low-key shot, two soldiers split open a cask, letting flow a torrent of bright, saturated Fuchsia Pink wine. The color of the wine, already quite artificial, is spotlighted, making it a major highlight in the composition. With the tavern keeper chained to the wall directly beyond the cask, the wine stands metonymically for his blood (Figure 6.9). The burst of red vividly punctuates the violent action, once again recalling the wine spilled when Prince John first hatched his plan.[20]

Compared to the bulk of Technicolor design in the 1930s, this chromatic motif is uncommonly deliberate and explicit. Neupert is correct to identify this use of red as an attempt to narrativize color, but we should also note the extreme stylization that marks these instances as a departure from Technicolor's typical methods. As noted earlier, the film's common technique for drawing attention to spectacular color involves revealing an array of colorful costumes and set pieces, most of which tend to be strongly motivated by the setting or event. By contrast, these examples depend on the bold expression of a single dominating hue. Red has been forced into the situation, making it unavoidably significant. These cases stand out from the rest of the film, indeed from the greater part of Technicolor production after 1935, because of the degree of color foregrounding and the method of showcasing a solitary hue. Red stands for Prince John's reign of terror, and this function is bought at the cost of very obtrusive manipulation. It is a technique that was largely abandoned after the demonstration films, and it returns only in the most outrageously stylized films of the 1940s, such as *Duel in the Sun* (1946).

Just as importantly, this particular motif is developed within a montage, not woven into the fabric of a fully developed dramatic scene. The sequence condenses Prince John's despotic rule into a swift succession of emblematic moments. In all, there are three vignettes, each ending with the interruption of a Norman evil by a well-timed arrow. The particulars of each scene are less important than the general impression of royal wrongdoings being righted by Robin Hood. Like the studio-makeover sequence in *A Star Is Born,* this montage offers the film's most pronounced manipulations of color. In reaching after the sort of literalness that characterized the demonstration mode, *Robin Hood* consigns it to montage, a context that helps it better integrate with classical style.

The boldness of these instances can blind the historian to the finesse of Technicolor aesthetics as they developed in the 1930s. More often, color supports narrative not through the development of full-blown color-symbols, but by being generally keyed to mood and by punctuating accents. This is the dominant method even in *Robin Hood,* especially during the second phase. When the austere image of Robin chained in Nottingham's dungeon gives way to Marian's apartment, the gentle reintroduction of color accents helps signal the transition to a more romantic tone; color parallels changes in lighting, setting, and the orchestral score. Color, though central to *Robin Hood*'s appeal, tends to be redundant when considered with other cues—integrated rather than clumsily laid on top. Indeed, this is a major distinction between an assertive film like *Robin Hood* and one from the demonstration mode; both feature broad palettes, but in assertive design, expressive choices do not so incessantly prioritize color. Varying the functions of color across the film allows *Robin Hood* to be spectacular and subtle by turns and to yoke a bold palette to basic storytelling tasks without appearing awkwardly overt.

Unweaving the Tapestry: A Close Analysis of the Banquet at Nottingham

This book has been largely concerned with illustrating the strategies for using color and the functions assigned to color in the classical feature. The analyses have included scenes and sequences that illustrate important trends in color design, but have not looked at the moment-by-moment texture of an extended design. *Robin Hood* offers an exceptional opportunity to unweave Technicolor's formal tapestry. In bringing our color vocabulary and our understanding of design options to bear on a single sequence, we can come to terms with how color works in the cinema to guide attention and cue our responses at every moment. Only close descriptive analysis can capture the complexity and richness of *Robin Hood*'s design and ground our observations. Few scenes present a more rewarding challenge to analysis than the Nottingham banquet, the film's first and most sumptuous display of color. In it, we can grasp how color works at a fine-grained level and how *Robin Hood* innovates both by elaborating opportunities for foregrounding and by bringing tactics for regulating color to a complex and assertive palette.

The scene begins with a display of regal pageantry as Prince John, Lady Marian, Sir Guy, the High Sheriff of Nottingham (Melville Cooper), the Bishop of the Black Canons (Montagu Love), and various Norman knights share the feast. Once it gets underway, the sequence swiftly plants information and sets the narrative ball rolling, moving fluidly from exposition to spectacular action. Prince John announces his villainous coup with a simple declaration: "I've kicked Longchamps out! From now on I am regent of England." Moments later, Robin storms into the hall, lays a deer carcass at John's table, and announces, "From this night on I use every means in my power to fight you." Prince John attacks, Robin escapes, and, amid a hail of arrows, Maid Marian flashes a concerned glance. The scene's challenge is to provide a color design that supports the spectacular pageantry and heroics while also guiding attention through some rather dense exposition.

In another scene transition exploited for color effect, the Nottingham banquet opens with two elaborate establishing shots. Together, they illustrate *Robin Hood*'s broadening of Technicolor's palette. Blue, red, green, and yellow mix and mingle in a vivid demonstration of color. Yet these colors are also carefully managed, helping ease the shift from the flamboyant opening into the scene's dialogue portion. As in most of the film, color is carried primarily by costume, and this allows it to be manipu-

6.10. The banquet hall in Nottingham Castle.

lated through staging and mobile framing. The director can fluidly shift emphasis by moving actors, thus helping integrate color with other elements of style. In concert with camera movement, sound, and character action, color leads the eye.

The first shot pans left across the hall from a high angle, presenting a master view of the set. Two long banquet tables run lengthwise down the center of the gray stone hall, Prince John's table sitting perpendicular to them at the far left. Color structures the shot. The take begins and ends on color accents, and the movement of color motivates the pan. The scene opens on a torch burning with a bright orange flame high above a large fireplace at the far right of the hall. This brilliant embellishment is quickly eliminated from the frame as the camera follows a line of waiters clad in flat Slate gray-blue and deep raspberry (Lipstick Red) uniforms, entering midground right. The waiters provide the key point of color, and their trajectory motivates the pan, guiding attention through the set until the second torch, fastened high on the wall in the left foreground, delivers a momentary flash of orange. The brief take ends just as the royal table comes into view, efficiently conveying the banquet's opulence and laying out the basic geography of the room (Figure 6.10). It also displays several of the key props for foregrounding color that the shooting script specifies, including the torches and "colorful banners . . . in brilliant hues."[21]

Not to let an opportunity for showcasing slip by, the first take is followed by a second, more detailed—but functionally redundant—establishing shot. This take covers the same ground as the first, but it is a masterpiece of color choreography, deftly guiding the viewer through details and toward the site of narrative interest. The framing returns to the first torch, this time somewhat closer to the flame, revealing a deep red and white flag just beyond (Figure 6.11). Instead of panning, the camera cranes downward and tracks left, exchanging and revealing new color accents. Immediately, the torch's orange flare is displaced by the roasting fire (directly below), and then another line of waiters, bearing trays of meat, enters from the right. Their movement again motivates the camera's. The waiters bring attention to the midground with a primary triad: Chinese Red shirts and grayish Stratosphere blue vests adorned with bright Dandelion yellow trim along the sleeves and tails. The viewer who grasped the grand sweep of the banquet in the first shot is invited to return to the start and revel in Technicolor detail, this time with just a bit more brilliance.

The track successively introduces and passes over distinct sources of color. While our attention is locked on the procession of waiters, the camera reveals yellow-hooded falcons on a perch, one of them with a bright emerald plume (Figure 6.12). The momentary burst of green moves off right, and the falconer's Sky Blue hat enters from the bottom. The color parade then modulates, adjusting our attention from the foreground to the midground and then to the background. Several waiters in a foreground medium shot pass out of the frame, and the midground is given over to a group of musicians in muted but rich costumes of brown, Lin-

6.11, 6.12, 6.13, and 6.14. The second establishing shot successively modulates color: from the torch to the falcons, and from musicians to men-at-arms.

coln green, and various tints of Cranberry (Figure 6.13). Swiftly, blue is reintroduced as the camera passes behind three men-at-arms in Azure Blue tights and brown jerkins (Figure 6.14). The palette contracts somewhat, offering a few well-defined variations.

Even in this very brief passage, color is thoroughly enmeshed with other elements of style. The waiters' costumes direct attention to their procession, which, in turn, motivates the camera movement. Similarly, the appearance of the musicians provides a shift in color while also helping tie the orchestral accompaniment to the diegesis. The score softens and modulates into strings and flutes that roughly correspond to the instruments on screen. The musicians' more sedate costumes initiate the transfer of color emphasis from the fore- to the mid- and background, aiding the transition into the main action of the scene. In like manner, by offering an on-screen justification for the music track, they tie it to the action at hand. Both sound and color begin to channel attention more directly to story events.

The exiting of the last waiter coincides with the onset of dialogue; an off-screen knight offers a toast to Prince John. As the music softens and the action begins, color contrast briefly recedes. But this simplifying of the foreground sets up a more varied palette at the rear of the dining hall, where the feast is in full swing. Knights and ladies seated at a dining table and facing away from the camera supply a particularly complex collection of accents. The scheme, which alternates cool and warm hues, is coordinated with a row of flags that emerges over Prince John's table in the far background. The palette's variety and order is remarkable. Seated from right to left are a knight in a Leaf Green cape, a lady in a burgundy dress and soft Pearlblush pink cowl, a knight in a burgundy cape, a lady in a Porcelain Blue gown with a soft pink cowl and a Leaf Green belt and hat, a Knight in a brown cape with a Lagoon green lining, a lady with a Golden Cream cowl, and so on. Contrast among the costumes is regulated by rather uniform shading: reds and yellows are toned down into gold and burgundy, and the brighter greens are quickly eliminated by the track. Thus, as the shot nears its destination, the array of color becomes more intricate, but also more carefully modulated. Color more pointedly flags narratively important portions of the set. Chromatic interest shifts first to the midground, where the knight proclaims his allegiance, then a more saturated spot of color marks out the far background, and the diners turn toward Prince John (Color Figure 21).

Prince John's table forms the apex of the set. As the track slows and the camera pans left, the prince's table, with its white cloth and deep red embroidery, offers the final stop in this tour of color. Centered on the wall behind it hangs a Cadmium Yellow gold curtain which coordinates with the lady's Golden Cream veil in the midground. If this fails to catch the viewer's eye, then the revelation of Sir Guy's bright Flame Scarlet and gold costume does the trick. As the knights rise and turn toward John (blocked from view at the rear), a glimpse of Sir Guy, well beyond the plane of focus, impels attention toward the background. The shot ends when a single waiter crosses in from the right foreground and the camera tilts downward to discover a hound tearing into a pile of bones, a none-too-subtle commentary on Prince John's voraciousness.

The opening of the Nottingham banquet does more than just extend chromatic display through a simple iteration of establishing shots. True, hue is deployed with greater variety, intensity, and richness than in previous major-studio three-color features. But color has also become more integrated with other stylistic registers, and it augments dialogue, music, and staging to engage us in the scene. *Becky Sharp* also draws on bold and varied costumes, but the demonstration mode never managed to so thoroughly blend color design with the system of style. The functions that color serves here are not radically new, but the design more fluidly incorporates these functions into the unfolding scene.

One familiar with the restrained mode would expect color to recede from emphasis as the scene continues. This is not the case. Rather than eliminate bright and saturated accents during dinner conversation, the cinematography and staging continue to manage a palette of contrasting hues. Wardrobe accounts for the majority of assertive colors. Sir Guy's costume is perhaps the most intense. His Flame Scarlet shirt is accented by metallic gold embroidery and trim, Sky Blue sleeves and collar, and deep red stones set in gold metal clasps. The outfit repeats the basic primary triad of the waiters' costumes, but with greater richness and saturation, especially in red hues that positively glow on the nitrate print. Each central character's costume offers an equally striking accent. Prince John's white satin shirt is studded with gold beads and blue stones and topped with a Bachelor Button blue hood. Marian's dress is a pattern of aqua and rust red on a black field. A black cape affixed by silver clasps with deep emerald green stones drapes her shoulders. The costume is finished with a Rich Gold cowl and crown. Her outfit coordinates with other costumes and props by gathering together hues representative of the entire palette and adding green to the gold, blue, and red triad (Color Figures 22 and 23).

So bold an array of color challenges the low-contrast harmonies that Kalmus favored. Instead of squelching contrast, the design achieves coordination by repeating hues across costumes. As usual, the female lead's ensemble is the linchpin. The blue lining inside Marian's cape coordinates with Prince John's blue hood, her gold cowl echoes the wall covering behind her, and her red and gold accents harmonize with Sir Guy's. When Robin enters, her emerald jewels, and the green component of the aqua pattern on her dress, provide the closest harmonies with the hero's Lincoln green attire. The coordination highlight's Olivia de Havilland's star presence, forecasts Marian's role as Robin's love interest, and follows Technicolor convention of organizing the mise-en-scène around a woman.

But beyond repetition, the design's color balance signals a new way of thinking about harmony in Technicolor. In concentrating heavily on gold, red, and blue, the mise-en-scène roughly adheres to the basic primary triad. As noted in the introduction, this triad secures harmony in the sense that, if combined, the hues would form a neutral gray. When properly distributed, yellow, red, and blue results in what Johannes Itten would call "harmonic equilibrium."[22] This kind of harmony, however, is different from that most often discussed by designers like Betancourt, Holden, or even Kalmus. They hoped to more simply mute differences of hue by insisting on analogous or split-complementary relationships. The high contrast of the primary triad resembles the juxtaposition of complementaries, but is somewhat less intense because it is dispersed among three hues. *Robin Hood* veers well away from Betancourt's "present trend toward taste" while still delivering a scheme defensibly harmonious. Equilibrium is displacing similarity.

Admittedly, describing the palette as a "triad" is reductive, since it implies the use of three well-defined hues. In fact, there is a good deal of variation within the individual hue families. Yellow modulates from Sir Guy's high-value, saturated gold trim to the brownish gold (Cadmium Yellow) wall covering. Blue shifts in tint between Sir Guy's Sky Blue collar and Prince John's Bachelor Button hood, and Marian's blue accents are mixed with green. Other colors are blended as well. The Bishop of the Black Canons, seated several places to Marian's right, is clad in his purple robe (between Royal Blue and Dahlia Purple), which blends red with blue.

Characterizing the scheme as a triad might also miss the small green details, which include lettuce on the bishop's plate, a knight's Leaf Green robe just visible beyond the bishop, or a small spray of grape leaves that Prince John fidgets with as he talks to Marian. Yet green, like purple, is clearly a minor note in a palette heavily dominated by red, blue, and yellow. The design achieves the impression of complexity by repeating and varying three central hues, avoiding flat-out complementaries and simple blocks of bold color while still delivering some fairly pronounced contrasts. Costumes deliver the "striking but consistently blended" color promised by the Warner Bros. advertisement.

When the central action kicks off, well-managed colors guide attention and support the drama. The principal characters seated at the head table are, from left to right, the High Sheriff of Nottingham, Sir Guy, Prince John, Marian, and the bishop. They constitute the center of interest, but saturated hues and color contrasts crop up all around them. At each end of the table, knights in Flame Scarlet provide strong visual magnets, as does a scarlet-caped knight immediately beyond the bishop. Most often, the framing is such that these figures are only briefly glimpsed in long shots; the medium shots and medium close-ups that carry most of the conversation eliminate potential distractions. Acceptable as embellishments at the start of the scene, these color magnets recede as serious dialogue gets underway. Tabletop items are similarly manipulated to suit the scene's development. At the start, Prince John's table is cluttered with bowls and platters of red gelatin and meat dressed with apples. Later, when a knight at another table addresses Prince John, the red accents have been removed. Now dominated by brownish gold serving pieces, the table has been neutralized as a source of color. In a manner reminiscent of the restrained mode, the reflective surfaces of these cups and pitchers introduce rather unobtrusive texture into the frame, a play of varied brightness, or dazzle, rather than hue.

When background accents do pop up, they often serve the scene. For example at the right end of the table the bishop, in blue-purple, is positioned just in front of a scarlet-clad knight. The effect is practical: it helps mark the bishop as an important character before he speaks. In a medium shot of Prince John and Marian, the contrast drives attention to the rear of the frame, cueing us to notice that the bishop is listening (Color Figure 22). Just before he interjects, two shots frame Sir Guy in the foreground with Marian and the bishop at rear. In the second of these shots, Marian has leaned slightly back, revealing the bishop more fully as he responds to her questions about Robin Hood: "Aye, an impudent reckless rogue." Color flags his position, preparing the way for the next cut, which brings the bishop into a medium shot as he continues. The visual magnet, encouraged by a wide, dynamic palette, has been harmonized with staging and performance and given a conventional function. *Robin Hood* features a broader and bolder palette than that found in most previous three-color design, but color is still attentively regulated from shot to shot.

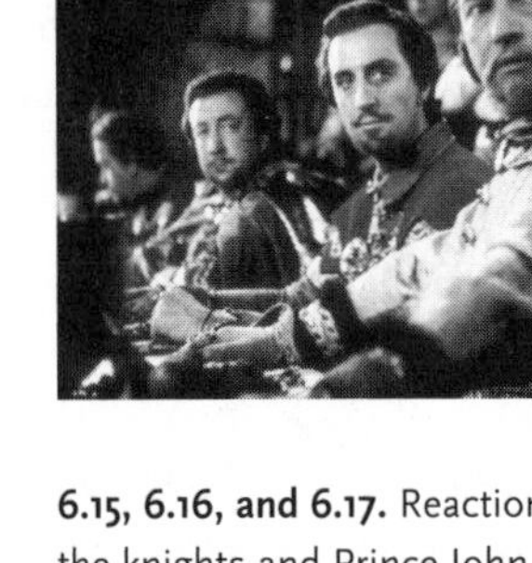

6.15, 6.16, and 6.17. Reaction shots from the knights and Prince John deliver jolts of color, set against Robin's more restrained frame.

Robin's arrival triggers the scene's first turning point, and the broad palette rushes forward to punctuate it. As the doors swing open, Robin fends off two men-at-arms and confidently strides into the hall, a deer across his shoulders. Two brief reaction shots blast bright color across the frame. In the first, a shot down one of the guest tables, a woman in a Dahlia Purple gown and another in a Candy Pink cowl contrast with the Sky Blue cape of the knight just beyond. In the foreground, a knight in a scarlet cape rears up and draws his sword, a punctual flash of red (Figure 6.15). The second reaction shot frames Prince John in the foreground and Sir Guy beyond him. The key colors here, Prince John's Bachelor Button blue hood and Sir Guy's Flame Scarlet shirt, repeat the accents of the previous setup (Figure 6.16). Just as Prince John turns, the scene returns to Robin, in long shot. These quick reactions deliver two jolts of blue and red, interrupting the more restrained brown and green compositions of Robin's progress (Figure 6.17).

The visual contrast helps emphasize the opposition between Robin and his foes, an opposition made more evident in the next cut. Robin is halted by a group of men-at-arms, who block him with silver battle spears. The crisscross of glinting silver is at the center of a nearly achromatic scheme dominated by gray and brown, with Robin's Lincoln green just peaking through. A cut back to Sir Guy and Prince John cracks the palette back open, reintroducing blue, red, and yellow. Robin's defense of the common people clashes with Prince John's exercise of elite power, and color underscores it. In a sense, the color design is opportunistic. This kind of contrast cannot be built into a meaningful pattern across such an assertive film, but at the local level, when practical, color can bolster a theme. One advantage of *Robin Hood*'s production design is that it can so easily justify splashes of high-value saturated color for punctual effects. The challenge, of course, comes in managing and controlling that palette.

In tune with the scene's development, color swells around grand actions and then retreats during tense confrontations. When Robin boldly approaches the head table, accompanied by Korngold's rousing theme, another tracking shot sweeps past color highlights. When the carcass is dropped in front of the prince, it lands next to a bowl of red gelatin; we find that color magnets have resurfaced on the table. Once the dialogue gets underway, this detail is again dispatched.

Color accents are controlled, but never absent, and *Robin Hood* innovates new schemes for ornamentation even amidst taut exposition. By including accents at the margins, and fields of color in close-ups, the scene keeps color an active and visible participant. As the confrontation between Robin and Prince John heats up, camera angles begin to consistently introduce conspicuous sources of color into the foreground. Generally, these details, quite low in value, do not become troublesome. For example, a rather low-angle shot of Sir Guy and Prince John, as he whispers to a guard, brings a large platter of grapes and apples into the lower foreground. Whether a matter of lighting or paint, the apples are quite deep red, not as bright as some of the red accents that adorned the table at the scene's start.

This technique becomes more noticeable, though, in a medium framing of Robin, seated at a table across from Prince John, that brings an apple into the extreme right corner. The accent, clearly complementary to Robin's Lincoln green outfit, is purely decorative, dressing out the composition as the hero begins his most important speech (Figure 6.18).[23] The pattern is magnified when a view of Robin, with his red apple at lower right, is directly followed by a view of Prince John's table, also with a red accent in the lower right. The tactic amounts to cutting around the fruit bowls to make decorative color prominent.

Significantly, in each shot the accent remains near the edge of the frame, usually toward the foreground, and well away from the character's face. In their endeavor to sustain color across the sequence, the designers decided that small touches of contrasting color, kept near the frame's

6.18. The apples are decorative accents placed at the margin of the frame.

perimeter, were acceptable. Reserved for the margins, these accents never intrude into the central area of interest, and they could be readily justified as part of the banquet setting. Both conditions help naturalize the device, guarding against the perception that color has been forced into the shot. That said, this kind of consistent ornamentation bespeaks a more flexible approach to color. The old rules for subordination are being bent, perhaps broken.

Decorative color also makes inroads into the background of important medium shots and close-ups. Technicolor design conventionally sought out harmonizing backgrounds for close-ups, especially of female stars. *Robin Hood* invigorates the technique with a more assertive palette and directed background lighting. For example, the medium shots of Prince John isolate him against the Cadmium Yellow curtain draped behind his chair. Contrast between this deep brown-orange gold and his Bachelor Button blue hood flirts with the complementarity of blue and orange. These colors intensify each other, an effect amplified by lighting that targets Prince John's hair and shoulders as well as the curtain. The bold but simple use of contrast lends a graphic punch to the closer takes of Prince John, and this helps him stand out from other characters.[24]

The same technique glamorizes Marian's close-ups, which use an extra to inject background color. An oddly cheeky squire clad in violet (between Royal Blue and Dahlia Purple) stands just beyond Marian's chair, creating an uncharacteristic background highlight in some longer shots of the group. Assertive design threatens to disperse attention. But the detail pays off later during Marian's close-up reaction shots to Robin. A patch of the purple appears in the rear left while soft facial lighting causes her gold cowl and crown to shimmer. In place of edge light, the illuminated purple velvet lends depth behind her shoulder (Color Figure 23). Moreover, this background accent bridges the aqua and rust red details on Marian's dress. Color harmony helps stylize the love interest's first close-ups. The color effect recurs when Robin fights his way out of the castle. Marian's squire exits, and the bishop rises to comfort her, his blue-purple robe providing the background for her close-up. Curtiz and his team routinely embellish Marian's close-ups with color, seizing on options opened up by a complex palette. Purple, it seems, struck an ideal harmony with de Havilland's features, and it returns in later scenes as part of her royal wardrobe.

The banquet sequence climaxes with Robin's spectacular escape from Prince John, giving us the chance to examine how Technicolor serves action. In the midst of a fight, *Robin Hood*'s vigorous color choreography joins a new emphasis on editing as a means of wielding contrast. The escape sequence mobilizes color to emphasize discrete actions, to unify short series of events, and to guide attention toward key areas of the frame during the swirl of movement. As the cutting becomes more rapid, color arrangements shift quickly, and costumes, so carefully arrayed in the opening shots, form swift contrasts and accents. The sequence divides roughly into three stages, each featuring several stunts. First, as Robin dodges the guard's surprise attack and scuffles with several knights, color alternates between high and low contrast. Sir Guy then attacks, setting off the scene's most intense concentration of hue. Finally, Robin flees the hall and covers his retreat with a shower of arrows, accompanied by punctual color accents. The palette pulses during the action, creating rhythm, intensifying the appearance of frenzied activity, and emphasizing stunts.

The first several shots exploit color to make images quickly legible and to help set a rhythm for the action. Robin's chair is struck with a spear, and in a long shot he rocks backward so that he can lift the chair as a shield. The shot is dominated by grays and browns; movement and focus draw attention to Robin's action. This relatively low-contrast image is juxtaposed with the assertive hues carried in a medium long shot of Prince John's table. The gold curtain is particularly prominent as Sir Guy rises and flings a candelabrum in Robin's direction. The intense red, blue, and gold provide a distinct beat of color before focus returns to Robin's composition. Color also guides attention by generating accents around each major character. Lady Marian, for instance, is the only central character whose costume is somewhat subdued, but she receives emphasis thanks to her purple-clad squire. Color guides viewers to the most important actions and reactions.

The next two stunts continue the rhythm of color bursts and recessions. As Robin repels the candelabrum with his chair and spins to face an off-screen attacker, the palette returns to brown and gray dominants, using Robin's Lincoln green as the major accent. Colors remain within these limits as a knight in a gray cape and a brown and tan jerkin rushes the camera, and Robin heaves a chair to strike him down. Aside from a few blue capes that pass quickly in the foreground, the unit of action is rendered with a fairly unified, workmanlike palette. High contrast returns for the next stunt, a skirmish between Robin and two knights in red and blue capes. Color energizes the fight as the capes flash. Red, blue, and green notes help unify the action as a distinct phase of the fight. Meanwhile, in Marian's last reaction shot, the bishop's purple robe helps her compete visually with the tumult's strong color.

The filmmakers begin to lay color on with a thicker brush as the action intensifies in the third stage. Once Robin has dispatched the knights, Sir Guy enters the fray in a flash of red, yellow, and blue. The next shot finds Robin upending several chromatically undistinguished men-at-arms (in brown and gray) and spinning around just in time to block Sir Guy's charge. The rhythm of color bursts accelerates. Sir Guy's colors prompt attention away from the men-at-arms as soon as he enters. With other portions of the frame dominated by gray and brown, color quickly accumulates around Robin and Sir Guy. Two knights in red capes join the clash from the rear while a third, in a green cape, cuts across the foreground. Then knights in blue, green, and blue-gray capes rush from the foreground, piling on top of Robin and creating a wash of cool hues. The capes overwhelm the frame and present color as a near abstraction. A perceptual jolt, like a sting on the music track, lays stress on the moment.

Robin sneaks out of the huddle unnoticed, and color contrast again dips momentarily as he brushes aside a single guard in a light blue cape. This sets up another explosion of color with a cut back to the huddle of knights. The medium shot is inundated with blue and gray tones as knights begin to back away from the center (Figure 6.19). They clear an opening to reveal Sir Guy, his red and gold breaking through the field of blue (Figure 6.20). Enraged, he glowers in Robin's direction. Color once more punctuates the series of actions, pulsing in a quickening rhythm. Sir Guy's spectacular red and yellow emergence from within a field of blue climaxes the succession of events.

The final stage of Robin's escape simplifies the dominant palette and employs very brief bursts of color to underscore discrete actions. Shots of Robin climbing up to a balcony and firing arrows into the crowd below are given over to the set's brown and gray tones. Extreme long shots of the hall reduce the individual costume colors to a muted array. But when, in long shot, one of Robin's arrows topples a soldier, a rush of extras in red

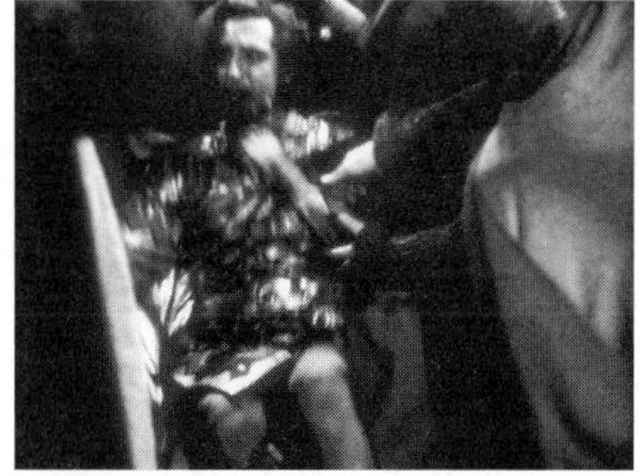

6.19 and 6.20. Sir Guy, in red, breaks through a huddle of blue capes, providing a brief climax within the fight.

robes and capes bring a dash of color to the foreground. Another arrow cuts down a guard, and as he falls, knights in purple and blue capes streak by. The tactic is repeated when soldiers and knights stream toward the hall's great door after Robin slips from the room. Into a low-angle shot of the door sweeps a crowd of knights in blue and red capes. Color flares just before a cut returns to Robin, framed against the gray stone walls of the castle. The dashes of color highlight quick actions, many of which are undercranked (sped up during filming). In this final stage, shots have been trimmed so that flashes of color stress the cuts.

Robin's daring escape from the banquet at Nottingham is somewhat reminiscent of the Duchess of Richmond's ball in *Becky Sharp.* In both cases, color is arrayed for a spectacular opening, modulated to provide visual interest during the scene's development, and then marshaled into a series of swift contrasts and vivid displays at the climax. But a key difference between the scenes is informative. *Becky Sharp* overtly arranges color as guests flee the ball, alternating reds and blues and building to a chromatic climax in which the redcoats, under red light, sweep past the camera. *Robin Hood* likewise uses color to embellish the sequence's climactic action, but it does not attempt obvious or rigid color scoring. Rather than impose a pattern of color upon the action, Robin's escape draws fluidly on the palette for a series of independent effects. Color is at once less obtrusively patterned and more freely manipulated. As in the film as a whole, color has found a place *among* the elements of style that energize the action instead of clumsily subordinating them to achieve a single chromatic effect. Close analysis lets us appreciate an orchestration of color that, during viewing, rushes by. The system works, and we sense a complete and ordered pattern of color that does not try to commandeer our attention.

Conclusion

When Warner Bros.' producers opted to employ three-color on their top-budgeted film of the season, the studio helped move Technicolor into a new phase. *Robin Hood* was the most ambitious Technicolor production to date, and it was designed to foreground color as a production asset. In this, the film broke with the restrained mode. *Robin Hood* works to renew spectators' awareness of color, drawing attention to it as an active element of film style. By contracting and expanding the palette from scene to scene, extending sequences of establishing shots that dwell on and reveal sources of color, and selectively introducing and removing hues within scenes, the film consistently nudges color forward.

But beyond these specific techniques, *Robin Hood* offers a fundamentally more diverse palette than those found in earlier films. With its emphasis on red, blue, yellow, and green, the film unavoidably deals in more complex harmonies and contrasts. Whereas the restrained mode favored differences in value and saturation, *Robin Hood* generates texture by varying hues themselves. The design methodically arrays contrasting colors as though to keep Technicolor's range ceaselessly on display. One reviewer seized on this color design as the film's primary attraction:

> It is only the brilliant, amazingly versatile use of color that puts suspense and excitement into *Robin Hood.* One is led from scene to scene wondering what new splash of tint and texture will be revealed, instead of wondering whether Robin will be captured. Not since *Becky Sharp,* has Technicolor been used to such effect. And this has twenty memorable color compositions for every one in *Becky Sharp.*[25]

Again, *Becky Sharp* is a good benchmark. In its verve for arraying and revealing color, *Robin Hood* resembles a demonstration film. Yet, perhaps because it is so easily motivated by the fanciful diegesis, color never appears quite so forced or consciously patterned as in *Becky Sharp.* Lavish though it is, the film is marked by a concerted effort to manage color so that it guides attention and enhances action. Color is also more thoroughly integrated into the system of style. Though color is prominent, the filmmakers do not as consistently grant it priority when developing effects. The restrained mode developed methods for unobtrusively manipulating color, and *Robin Hood* successfully brings them to an extravagant palette.

Robin Hood's color design also suggests a broadening of Technicolor's accepted definition of color harmony. As noted earlier, restrained films tended to rely on closely related hues or on different colors shaded and tinted into uniformity. Such decisions followed from Natalie Kalmus's rather general pronouncements that harmonious composition features the "judicious use of neutrals" and avoids a "super-abundance of color."[26] But *Robin Hood* presents another option. Assertive colors play off one another to create balanced but varied compositions. This practice points toward a more comprehensive definition of color harmony as the balance of contrasting hues. It seems likely that the general concept of defining harmony as an equilibrium of hues, an idea that dates back at least to Chevreul, held some sway with *Robin Hood*'s color designers. If so, this might have provided a rationale for packing the image with color accents: a red detail could balance a patch of green, and so forth.

Perhaps *Robin Hood*'s most prominent innovation is the marriage of Technicolor to the historical adventure genre. Clearly, the production's storybook gamut owes much to its generic identity. The *Hollywood Reporter* commended the accord between genre and color design:

> No more fitting subject for color than this period adventure tale has heretofore been found. The kaleidoscopic mixtures of strong tints are many and varied and they are used in striking harmony with the nature of the tale to make a brilliant and beautiful blending of action and visual opulence.[27]

Within a historical adventure, color foregrounding ceased to be a critical liability. Even the *New York Times* applauded the "tale of action" for its "eye-pleasing Technicolor."[28] Warner Bros. had hit upon a basic formula for exploiting the three-color process. Part of the film's longevity, including its popularity on early color television, may finally rest with its facility for showcasing color. *Robin Hood* forged a more flexible, dynamic, and compelling color style, an assertive mode of design that Technicolor would continue to develop throughout the 1940s in films such as *Blood and Sand* (1941), *The Black Swan* (1942), and *Meet Me in St. Louis* (1945), to name a few.

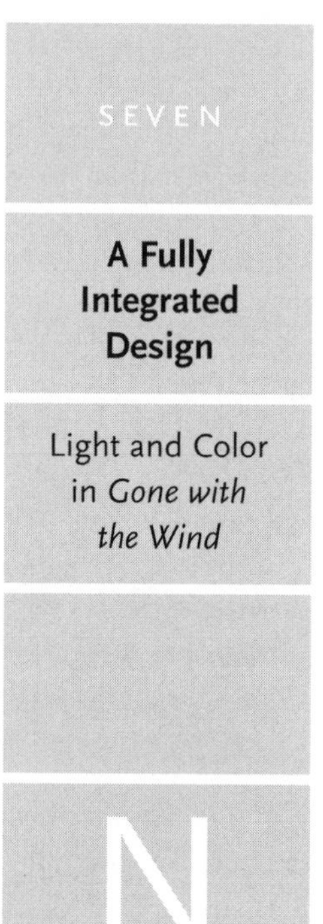

SEVEN

A Fully Integrated Design

Light and Color in *Gone with the Wind*

Nineteen thirty-nine was a breakthrough year for the Technicolor Corporation. Confidence in the three-color process was such that Technicolor embarked on a $1,000,000 expansion program that included the opening of a new laboratory and office building, nearly doubling the plant's capacity.[1] And in an even more meaningful development, the company's profits finally overtook its losses.[2] The acceptance of three-color was confirmed when the *Hollywood Reporter*'s annual exhibitor poll named three Technicolor features (*Jesse James, The Wizard of Oz,* and *Dodge City*) as the most lucrative releases in 1939.[3] But the year's crowning achievement came in December with the premiere of classical Hollywood's most expensive and popular production, *Gone with the Wind.*

According to Technicolor's executives, *GWTW* proved beyond question that color was essential to drama and spectacle. Corporate publicity declared that after seeing the film, audiences would become "conscious of the lack of color in the black-and-white pictures they subsequently view."[4] Although the *New York Times* critic maintained, "Color is hard on the eyes for so long a picture," the Hollywood establishment greeted *GWTW* as evidence that color had found its place.[5] At their annual ceremony, the Academy of Motion Picture Arts and Sciences presented two special awards: one to William Cameron Menzies for "outstanding achievement in the use of color for the enhancement of dramatic mood in the production of *Gone with the Wind,*" and another to Herbert Kalmus for "contributions in successfully bringing three-color feature production to the screen."[6] It had taken nearly a decade to put Technicolor on a firm commercial footing, but *GWTW* emerged at the end of the 1930s as an emblem of three-color's success.

With a budget of over four million dollars, Selznick International's production was by far Hollywood's most expensive feature to date.[7] *GWTW* was so big, and so long, that Selznick and Whitney counted it as the final two pictures in their Pioneer-Technicolor contract.[8] Selznick's staff estimated that color had added nearly $550,000 to the final budget, and the investment added a mark of distinction that helped justify a high admission price and a road-show strategy.[9] By the end of May 1940, the film had grossed an unprecedented twenty million dollars, which translated into a profit of eight million to be split between MGM and Selznick International.[10]

Selznick was well aware that *GWTW* could help bolster the Technicolor name, and he used his leverage to fight for autonomy from the Technicolor advisors, for more freedom to design the film as he and his crew saw fit. In his excellent book-length study of the film's production, David Alan Vertrees argues that Selznick created the position of "production designer" for William Cameron Menzies in order to exert greater control over the film and generate options that he could use in negotiating with other artistic personnel. According to Vertrees, "The role of production designer was invented by Selznick to supplant the parts played by the cinematographer and art director in the planning scheme . . . with a single technical authority whose opinions the producer could set against those of the director."[11] Selznick also used Menzies to thwart the meddling of the Technicolor staff. In January 1939, the producer wrote:

> something must be done immediately to correct the situation of the conflicting opinions about color among members of the art departments, officials of the Technicolor company, etc. . . . I should like to reiterate that Mr. Menzies is the final word on these matters and should be the arbiter on any differences of opinion. . . . It is up to Mr. Menzies to decide whether a pattern or color is going to be too obtrusive or is dangerous from any standpoint.[12]

Through Menzies, Selznick hoped to consolidate power over the film's visual design.

In railing against Technicolor's interference, Selznick articulated his ideas about color design. He sought color that would modulate with Scarlett's (Vivien Leigh's) changes in fortune. Beyond this, he envisioned a more dynamic design than he thought the Technicolor staff would allow. His ideas, laid out in a memo in March 1939, are worth quoting at length:

> I cannot conceive how we could have been talked into throwing away opportunities for magnificent color values in the face of our own rather full experience in Technicolor . . . despite the squawks and prophecies of doom from the Technicolor experts. . . . the proper telling of our story involves a dramatic and changing use of color as the period and the fortunes of the people change.
>
> Examine the history of color pictures: the one thing that is still talked about in Becky Sharp is the red capes of the soldiers as they went off to Waterloo. What made La Cucaracha a success, and did so much for the Technicolor Company, were the colors as used by Jones for his costumes. The redeeming feature of Vogues of 1938 was the marvelous use of color in the women's styles. The best thing about the Follies was the beautiful way in which colors of sets and costumes were blended, as in the ballet. . . .
>
> I am the last one that wants in any scene a glaring and unattractive riot of color—and I think I was the first to insist upon neutralizing of various color elements . . . so that the Technicolor process would not obtrude on dramatic scenes, but I certainly never thought that this would reach the point where a sharp use of color for dramatic purposes would be completely eliminated; nor did I ever feel that we were going to throw away the opportunity to get true beauty in a combination of sets and costumes.
>
> Presumably Bill Menzies is sufficient of an artist to so blend the colors that the scenes won't look like Italian weddings and so that where we use striking color, it will be used as effectively as Dietrich's costumes against the drab sand [in *The Garden of Allah*], or as the Zorina ballet. If we are not going to go in for lovely combinations of sets and costumes and really take advantage of the full variety of colors available to us, we might just as well have made the picture in black and white. It would be a sad thing indeed if a great artist had all violent colors taken off his palette for fear that he would use them so clashingly as to make beautiful painting impossible.
>
> Neutral colors certainly have their value, and pastel colors when used properly make for lovely scenes, but this does not mean that an entire

> picture—the longest picture on record—has to deal one hundred percent in neutral colors or pastel shades. This picture in particular gives us the opportunity occasionally—as in our opening scenes and as in Scarlett's costumes—to throw a violent dab of color at the audience to sharply make a dramatic point.[13]

Selznick reacted passionately against the restrained mode of design, but his final film tended to follow current trends and stands as a culmination of the 1930s Technicolor look. The examples he cited from *Becky Sharp* and *La Cucaracha* were exactly the sort of design from which Technicolor had departed so fundamentally in *The Trail of the Lonesome Pine* and thereafter. For *GWTW,* Selznick envisioned a style that would experiment with bold color, but would do so tastefully. Analysis of the film shows that it does, at points, move well beyond restraint in making color graphically active, but these innovations are firmly rooted within established principles of binding color to story. Moreover, the designs of *The Adventures of Robin Hood* and *The Wizard of Oz* show that Technicolor could be more flexible than the producer acknowledged. Even when *GWTW*'s color most fiercely bucked the trend of restraint, it was not so far from recent developments, and it still validated Technicolor's use in serious, prestigious melodrama.

As is well documented, *GWTW*'s crew underwent important changes during production.[14] Though the fire footage for the burning-of-Atlanta sequence was shot in December 1938, principal photography with major cast members did not begin until late January 1939. Production commenced with George Cukor as director and Lee Garmes as cinematographer. Ray Rennahan was the Technicolor cinematographer on the film, though Winton Hoch has been credited with overseeing "double screen" effects.[15] In mid-February, Selznick fired Cukor and replaced him with Victor Fleming, and he replaced Garmes with Ernest Haller a short while later. At the end of April, Fleming, suffering from exhaustion, left the production for two weeks, and Sam Wood took over principal direction until mid-May. After Fleming's return, he and Wood worked simultaneously. A generally accepted estimate is that Cukor directed 5 percent of the finished film; Fleming around 45 percent; Wood, 15 percent; William Cameron Menzies, who directed a second unit, around 15 percent; and the remaining 20 percent of the film split among various second units and specialists.[16] Jack Cosgrove and Clarence Slifer were responsible for most of the mattes and effects cinematography. Principal photography was completed in late June, and final retakes were finished in October 1939.

The sheer scale of *GWTW* presents a challenge to analysis. Thomas Schatz has aptly characterized the production as the film scholar's "proverbial 800-pound gorilla—an oversized nuisance that simply won't go away."[17] Though much ink has been spilled over *GWTW,* scholars, Vertrees aside, have tended to avoid serious analysis of the film. Perhaps this is because the mountain of popular literature can give the impression that more than enough attention has been lavished upon *GWTW.* In any case, the film's daunting length and the amount of data popularly available about it make it an unwieldy and cumbersome object of study.

This chapter focuses rather narrowly on *GWTW*'s innovations with respect to color cinematography and technology. Many of the film's tactics for handling color, such as the alternation of assertive and restrained color designs, the selective revelation of hue, the extension of establishing shots, and the manipulation of color to guide attention and punctuate action, have been discussed already, especially with regard to *Robin Hood.* The emphasis here is on how *GWTW* made use of improved film stock and other technological developments to extend the range of cinematographic devices available to Technicolor. Through the development of colored illumination, low-key lighting, and complex facial modeling, *GWTW* integrated striking color effects into the classical style and brought respected black-and-white techniques more fully within Technicolor's reach. As we will see, the film's true contribution to the Technicolor look was in the way it bound color to light.

Technological Developments and Selznick's Experimental Spirit

The film's gains in color cinematography were made possible by technological developments that came to fruition at the end of the decade. In early 1939, Technicolor introduced an improved negative stock. It was first employed, rather inauspiciously, on the promotional trailer for Twentieth Century–Fox's *Little Princess,* but Selznick's film brought the system to feature production in a far grander way.[18] Indeed, Selznick pushed Herbert Kalmus to deliver the new stock early, arguing, "On what better picture than *Gone with the Wind* would they want to demonstrate an improvement in quality. On what better picture than *Gone with the Wind* would they want to demonstrate saving in production cost?"[19] The new negative offered substantial gains in speed and, in turn, was touted as a major victory in the battle to bring flexibility to color lighting. Engineers at Technicolor and Eastman Kodak had managed to reduce the amount of light lost due to inefficient filters. Changes in filters alone allowed the Technicolor system to gain up to two f-stops that had previously been lost within the camera.[20] Additional responsiveness was probably achieved through techniques for sensitizing the negative.[21]

Ray Rennahan explained simply that the stock was "three times as fast as the old film under artificial light, and four times as fast to daylight."[22] According to Technicolor's head cameraman, this brought the average required illumination levels down to between 200 and 300 foot-candles, a marked reduction from the 500–600 foot-candles required since 1937.[23] Rennahan professed that the new stock brought Technicolor light requirements into the standard range of monochrome shooting before the introduction of Plus X in 1938. According to Fred Basten, the new stock helped reduce production costs, bringing *GWTW*'s lighting budget nearly $100,000 below that for *The Wizard of Oz*.[24] At last, it seemed, Technicolor could boast near parity with the black-and-white practice of only a few years earlier.

Evidence suggests, though, that Rennahan exaggerated. Articles from several years later paint a dimmer picture of three-color's responsiveness. For example, a report on tests of a new set of Technicolor stocks in 1950 claimed flatly that Technicolor required around 400–500 foot-candles of illumination, a far cry from Rennahan's 200–300.[25] Though a significant improvement for Technicolor, the process still lagged far behind monochrome, which, because of the revolution in high-speed panchromatic stock, had reduced light levels to around 75–100 foot-candles by 1940.[26] Joe Valentine, writing in 1948 about his cinematography for *St. Joan*, highlighted the difference between color and monochrome: "The highest key I ever used in black-and-white photography turned out to be the lowest key of lighting in the history of Technicolor. . . . ten lighting units must be used in color for two in black and white."[27]

Put in terms of film sensitivity, or ASA, the situation was no better. Adrian Cornwell-Clyne, the British historian of color film, put the speed of the Technicolor system in the 1940s at Weston 3 (approximately 8 ASA), and other experts agree that the speed was probably around 12 ASA.[28] This was still slower than the speed of ordinary 1920s negative stock, which lingered at around 20 ASA, and it was significantly less sensitive than Kodak's Super X stock, introduced in 1935, which offered a speed of 40 ASA.[29] Though the improved negative must have made color shooting more flexible, it appears that many of the process's early limitations would haunt Technicolor sets throughout the 1940s.

The new stock may not have been as revolutionary as Technicolor's representatives advertised, but it did have important implications for film style. The increase in speed meant that cinematographers could make greater use of smaller, more manageable lighting units. Incandescent lamps could be pressed into service to a limited degree. Rennahan pointed out that the stock allowed him to use inkie (incandescent) spotlights "for precise lighting of faces in close-ups."[30] Ernest Haller added that the use of smaller units and greater diffusion enabled him to "glamorize" close-ups. His assertion, quoted earlier, that Technicolor would be "more flattering than ever to women," pointed toward the aesthetic value accorded to incandescents. A study of studio lighting in 1942, presented to the Society of Motion Picture Engineers, explained that for close-ups on black-and-white sets, "the incandescent is usually indicated for soft, feminine effects, whereas the arc is often used for masculine characterization and to produce extreme gradations of illumination."[31] The new ability to use inkies and greater diffusion on modeling lights allowed Technicolor cinematographers to embrace these codes more readily.

GWTW probably offered the most thoroughgoing incorporation of incandescents into three-color production to date. Still, filtered incandescents were considered basically inefficient. In 1950, Arthur Arling noted, "When we filter incandescent lamps for regular Technicolor . . . we lose sixty percent of the light."[32] Not surprisingly, arc lights would remain the primary means of illumination until the early 1950s, when the Technicolor system was once again revised.

The new stock also opened up opportunities for effect lighting. As we will see, *GWTW*'s production crew exploited the increased speed for chiaroscuro and shadow effects. Rennahan admitted that *GWTW* involved so much "dramatic effect lighting" that it was "hardly fair to consider that our lighting averages would apply equally to more routine pictures where higher keyed, less dramatic lightings might be required."[33] Actually, Technicolor rarely received negatives exposed to their standards from Selznick International. Art director Lyle Wheeler remembered that "every reel in a Selznick film took Technicolor twice as long to process" because Selznick forced "them to change the density of the emulsion as they went along." Wheeler recalled Selznick exclaiming: "I don't want all the lights, I want natural lighting."[34] Selznick complained that Technicolor's "ideas of photography and what they consider ideal for their purposes are the exact opposite of what I like and what I think *Gone with the Wind* requires."[35]

GWTW's cinematographers often played at the extreme end of the stock's latitude. Haller was particularly impressed that the "shadow speed" of the stock had been increased, allowing him to decrease fill light without fearing that shadows would "vanish into inky blackness."[36] The new stock allowed for a more intricate use of shadow while maintaining detail, something that had eluded William H. Greene's chiaroscuro work in *A Star Is Born*. *GWTW* represented a culmination of 1930s efforts to achieve monochrome's expressive techniques in Technicolor. In challenging the Technicolor lab's exposure requirements, Selznick International's films became stylistic exemplars for the industry, the gold standard for effects lighting in color.

Rennahan also suggested that the new stock enabled the greater use of colored lighting. Improvements in color rendition, according to Rennahan, allowed for more extensive lamp, fire, and moonlight effects.[37] In fact, this sort of effect lighting had been employed frequently in earlier productions, most strikingly by Greene and Sol Polito in *The Private Lives of Elizabeth and Essex*, released in October 1939. Again, the producers of *GWTW* capitalized on the technology to extend earlier experiments. The flight-from-Atlanta sequence, for example, was particularly innovative for combining orange firelight effects with cold, bluish edge and modeling light, bringing together techniques that had been exploited independently in earlier films.

The scope of *GWTW* made it a proving ground for all types of effects work. Selznick International's visual-effects department, under the guidance of Jack Cosgrove, had been developing techniques for use with Technicolor for several years. According to photographic-effects specialist Clarence Slifer, who moved to Selznick International from Technicolor while assisting Cosgrove on *The Garden of Allah*, the department actually began planning for *GWTW* around the summer of 1936.[38] Each of Selznick International's Technicolor productions presented photographic problems and engendered solutions that were eventually used on *GWTW*. *The Garden of Allah* led to the development of matte painting techniques; *A Star Is Born* involved rear projection; *Tom Sawyer* and *Nothing Sacred* featured miniature projection and optical printing.[39] In retrospect, Slifer viewed the department's work as progressing toward the realization of *GWTW*: "Slowly we were getting the necessary tools to do the effects for *GWTW*. We were proving that these effects could be made so that the production could be designed to utilize them."[40]

A similar point can be made for Selznick International in general. For a studio with relatively limited resources, Selznick International had extensive experience with Technicolor. The organization benefited from a tightly focused creative staff well versed in the idiosyncrasies of Technicolor. This made Selznick International the ideal place to experiment with the new stock. *GWTW*'s terrifically high profile guaranteed that the studio would be setting standards for prestige productions and that its innovations in color and lighting would become benchmarks for the industry. Selznick's small company, with its reputation for experiment, was thus in position to produce an exemplar. The technical and aesthetic problems solved on *GWTW* represented gains for Technicolor production as a whole.

The Color Score

Whereas *Robin Hood* emphasized variety of hue at the cost of finely tuned color motifs and careful arrangements of highlight and shadow, *Gone with the Wind* fully explores the potentials for integrating vigorous color *and* emulating monochrome effects. A general overview of the film's color score helps us understand *GWTW*'s specific cinematographic innovations. Color design underscores broad plot articulations in the by-now-familiar manner. Most notably, the film moves between active and restrained palettes as Scarlett's fortunes change. In one of his famous memos, Selznick described his fundamental vision of color design to production manager Ray Klune and director Victor Fleming. The producer complained that the Twelve Oaks barbecue sequences had been "so neutralized that there will be no dramatic point made by the drabness of the costumes through the whole second half of the picture." Selznick planned to foreground hue at both at Twelve Oaks and the Atlanta Armory bazaar so that "the audience would have gasped at their beauty and would have felt a really tragic loss when it saw the same people in the made-over and tacky clothes of the war period." For the postwar period, Selznick suggested, "the picture should, by its colors alone, dramatize the difference between Scarlett and the rest of the people—Scarlett extravagantly and colorfully costumed against the drabness of the other principals and of the extras."[41] Like a typical Technicolor score, color would chart the changing circumstances of the characters.

In the finished film, color travels a path roughly similar to the one mapped out by Selznick's memo. In the first half, the barbecue and the bazaar represent high points for color variety; each sequence arrays and balances color highlights generally as *Robin Hood* did. The palette contracts as the tide of war turns against the South. Important scenes are keyed to subdued colors, but some accents, particularly red and blue, crop up as ironic reminders of the change that has come over the South. This general contraction sets up the eruption of red light that accompanies Scarlett and Rhett's (Clark Gable's) fiery escape from Atlanta. In turn, color accents drop out almost entirely once Scarlett returns to Tara and finds it stripped of its ornaments. A final shift in color temperature closes the first half as Scarlett faces the sunrise. In a shot apparently modeled on the final composition of *Snow White* (1937), her silhouette appears against the peach-tinted sky. The composition echoes the sunrise-sunset motif initiated when she and her father stood before Tara at the film's opening, and it underscores Scarlett's fresh hope in the midst of despair.[42]

After the intermission, the film reverts to a relatively restrained design that accentuates the somberness of Scarlett's struggle to keep Tara. Brighter accents generally signal a contrast to the O'Haras' meager lifestyle. Then, as Scarlett rises in business, her costumes and environment become more colorful, culminating with the richly appointed mansion that she and Rhett build in Atlanta. When Scarlett's closest friend, Melanie Wilkes (Olivia de Havilland), dies, the palette contracts one last time. The frame becomes nearly achromatic as Scarlett wanders through the fog back to her mansion. Their marriage finally disintegrates, and her and Rhett's last conversation before a foggy window holds color variation to an absolute minimum. This reduction suits the tragic turn and sets up one final flourish. The film's concluding moments reintroduce red notes, first by way of the mansion staircase and then in the deep pink-orange light of the sunrise that frames Scarlett's silhouette in the ultimate pullback. As at the end of the first half, the strong contraction of the palette grants extra force to the return of the sunrise motif.

Beyond this general correlation of color to the narrative arc, the film's design is noteworthy for its willingness to engage in nearly symbolic uses of color. For example, when two Atlanta matrons gossip about Scarlett's dealings with Yankees after the war, they are framed behind a large green teapot and cup, and the back wall of their parlor is bathed in vivid green light. The bizarre emphasis on green, admittedly buried within an elliptical montage, characterizes Atlanta's circle of society women as rife with jealous gossip. Similarly, Scarlett's costumes are prone to carry thematic charge. The pure white "prayer dress" she wears in the opening scenes helps establish Scarlett's youth and innocence, traits bitterly challenged by the trials of war and reconstruction (Figure 7.1). Red, then, is associated with passion and sexuality, especially in Belle Watling's (Ona Munson's) costumes and in the mise-en-scène of her brothel. After the war, Scarlett attempts to return to the colors of her prayer dress when she appears in white underclothes, a red bow in her hair. Rhett, though, angered by rumors of her liaison with Melanie's husband, Ashley Wilkes (Leslie Howard), commands Scarlett to wear a burgundy velvet dress to Ashley's

7.1. Scarlett's white prayer dress helps establish her youth and innocence.

7.2. She is forced to wear a red dress after her liaison with Ashley.

birthday party. Rhett angrily explains: "Nothing modest or matronly will do. Put on plenty of rouge. I want you to look your part tonight." (Figure 7.2) Such literal color meaning isn't a consistent feature of the film's design. Rather it opportunistically seizes on symbolic color when it can easily be accommodated by costume or by conventions for stylization.

Shaping Color with Light: Formal Innovation in *GWTW*

This general description gives a broad sense of how color fluctuates with the plot, but the film's great innovations involve the art of lighting. Color is a more flexible element of style in *GWTW* than in any other film of the 1930s. As in other features, color underscores narrative, punctuates actions and turning points, builds motifs, and foregrounds spectacular graphic qualities. But here, highlight and shadow (elements of tone) are as important as color in fulfilling these functions, and lighting effects commingle with color, forging a new cooperation between stylistic resources.

Color design is built around new opportunities opened up by technology. *GWTW* experiments with emphatically stylized lighting effects; it is a testing ground for style, evoking something of the exploratory character of *La Cucaracha* or *Becky Sharp.* Light molds the film's palette, and highlighting, shadow, and color temperature shape our perception of action and performance. By turns, *GWTW* both emulates the flexibility and precision of monochrome cinematography and reaches a new synthesis of color and light. In the remainder of our analysis, we will focus on the production's cinematographic innovations: colored lighting, low-key illumination, and complex facial modeling. In each case, *GWTW* expands the ambit of Technicolor's expressive devices and challenges us to grasp the complexity of color's interaction with light in the cinema.

It is hard to overstate the importance of colored lighting to *GWTW*'s color design. Well over half the examples that William Cameron Menzies cites in his handwritten notes on expressive color in *GWTW* involve the color temperature of light.[43] The film's use of colored light is even more significant if one recalls how use of the technique was generally discouraged after the experiments of *La Cucaracha* and *Becky Sharp.* Twenty-one of the film's seventy segments incorporate some degree of colored illumination or the play of color temperature. As we noted with regard to mid-1930s technology, the decision not to exploit the potentials of projected color was linked to Technicolor's bid for stylistic parity with black-and-white. Cinematographers like William H. Greene sought to prove that using color would not mean diverging from the respected techniques for controlling light and shadow. Rather than replace the delicate play of highlight and shadow with an all-out use of colored lighting, Technicolor cinematographers and designers most often opted to emulate monochrome effects.

Of course, the ban on colored light was never total. By the late thirties, the problem of colored illumination was one of motivation. Attempts to force projected color into a scene for emotional underscoring, as in *La Cucaracha,* had been largely rejected, but discrete effects seemed permissible if properly motivated. *Robin Hood* made fleeting use of red light for sunset and fire effects; *Elizabeth and Essex* extended the play of color temperature to the lighting of figures; and *The Wizard of Oz* found an excuse for multicolored light in the wizard's chambers. Discussions in the technical press regularly acknowledged the use of uncorrected high-intensity arcs and incandescents to simulate moonlight and lamplight. *GWTW* relied on accepted diegetic motivations for colored light—mainly lamplight, candlelight, moonlight, and firelight—and innovated by extending the manipulation of color temperature further than any previous production.

Early on, Selznick expressed concern about achieving the effect of warm candlelight in *GWTW.* In October 1938, Selznick wrote his general manager and production manager:

> I should like that whichever cameraman is finally decided upon to make some tests at an early date to see if we cannot do better at accomplishing a lighting effect of candlelight and other methods of illumination during the period of Gone With The Wind. All the period pictures that have been done in Technicolor to date look as though the scenes were lighted by electric light, and a good deal of mood is lost in consequence.[44]

Indeed, the contrast between cool and warm illumination is so well integrated into the film's visual style that it forms a basic option for graphic embellishment. The 1954 Technicolor print that I viewed, the only reissue that received Selznick's stamp of approval, is processed to emphasize the warm golden tones of candlelight. In most cases, the lighting effects are clearly motivated and redundant with other stylistic cues. To a certain extent, *GWTW* helps domesticate colored lighting for serious, dramatic production.

As Selznick noted, this type of lighting could convey a general mood, and in most instances the colored illumination is tied to the simulation of lamp-, candle-, or firelight. Many of these effects are simple and relatively unpronounced. For example, a burning fireplace motivates a soft glow of warm light in Rhett's room as he awaits Bonnie's birth. Amber lamplight adds warm accents to Scarlett's medium close-up in the scene immediately following her attack in the shantytown. This is, in turn, contrasted with the cold blue-white highlights on Frank's (her second husband's) face as he prepares to join the other vigilantes. The subtle play of color temperature helps accentuate the general atmosphere in much the way small variations in lighting key would function in black-and-white. More pronounced effects mark time or location. Cold blue moonlight sets the scene for Scarlett's nightmare in New Orleans and Bonnie's in London. These techniques became increasingly common after *GWTW,* and they had been well exercised in earlier efforts, especially *Jesse James,* released in January 1939.

More remarkably, the play of color temperature also serves specific expressive or dramatic functions. For instance, consider the introduction of the villain Jonas Wilkerson (Victor Jory) as Scarlett's mother, Ellen (Barbara O'Neil), returns home during the film's opening act. Wilkerson halts Ellen in her doorway, and color temperature creates a strong contrast. He receives very dim bluish highlights, and much of his figure is left in darkness; she, apparently lit by an oil lamp, is bathed in a warm amber key light. Ellen chides Wilkerson, telling him that Emmy Slattery (Isabel Jewell) gave birth to his child and that the child "has mercifully died." With that, she exits, and the camera dollies toward Wilkerson. A portentously deep chord sounds in the orchestral score and the light dims, leaving Wilkerson in cold white highlights, a pronounced eye light emerging near each pupil. Color temperature conveys Wilkerson's intrusion into the peaceful candlelit warmth of Tara's home life (Color Figure 24). Low-key modeling and beady eye lights lend the shot a sinister quality. Of course, the shift in color is redundant given the performances

7.3. A blue spotlight on Ellen's face contrasts with the warm candlelit background.

(Ellen's curt remarks and Wilkerson's expression), camera movements (the dolly-in signals that this character will have some significance), and music. Wilkerson is a threat, and style highlights his presence, paving the way for his attempt to usurp Tara. A very definite manipulation of colored light helps amplify that impression.

GWTW employs more ornate mixtures of color temperature for striking, punctual effects. The two standout examples each heighten scenes of mourning. Scarlett's first sight of her mother's bier after returning to Tara depends on the contrast of warm and cool light for its impact. In a frame dominated by cold highlights and deep shadows, Mammy (Hattie McDaniel) directs Scarlett's glance to a partially opened door through which peach-amber light can be glimpsed. The low-key setting accentuates the light, driving our attention toward the room. When Scarlett finally opens the door, an over-the-shoulder shot reveals the parlor suffused by the peach-amber light. Ellen's body, laid out on a table in the center of the room, forms a black silhouette against the warmly lit rear wall. Two candles, one at either end of the table, motivate the color. Ellen's face, though, is illuminated by a cold blue spotlight directed from overhead (Figure 7.3). A near-complementary contrast makes the spot of blue especially prominent against the amber background. In his notes, Menzies singled the scene out as an example of how "the arrangement of light and color values helped give a strong angular and moving composition."[45] The juxtaposition of color temperatures stylizes the composition, an effect heightened by restraint in surrounding shots. For the cinematographers and designers of *GWTW*, color temperature could be as central in shaping the image as highlight and shadow in black-and-white.

This blending of temperatures reaches its height toward the film's end in a scene that recalls Ellen's bier. In the sequence, Melanie comforts Rhett, who has locked himself in Bonnie's room to keep vigil over his dead daughter. A bravura balance of cool and warm light sources sculpts the performances and molds the architecture of the shot. After entering the room, Melanie emerges, only to collapse in Mammy's arms. Again, the bier is only glimpsed from the doorway, first as Melanie enters to talk Rhett into allowing a funeral, and again when she emerges. The lighting scheme is ornate, varying across four planes from the doorway into the depth of the shot: a dim foreground with amber highlights, an area of shadow and white highlights, a midground with warm and even amber light, and a background in cool blue. As characters move, the color contrasts lead the eye into Bonnie's room while the camera keeps us at the threshold.

The area immediately outside Bonnie's door is very low-key, a candelabrum set off to the right motivating some minimal warm highlights. When Melanie approaches the door, she moves from a warm foreground through darkness and finally into silhouette. The arrangement lets us keep track of Melanie and Rhett at the door as color contrast drives our interest farther back into the frame. Beyond an area of darkness, in the midground, Bonnie's bed is bathed in the warm peach-amber radiance of candlelight. The white bedspread, Bonnie's face and hands, and the red accent of her riding hat and gloves glow beneath the warm light. A chromatic gulf between the doorway and bed underlines the severity of Rhett's isolation. Farther back, a wall in the background is washed with cold blue light so that a fairy-tale mural barely shows through. As in the scene with Ellen's bier, the near-complementary play of cool and warm light anchors our vision to the center of the room. The arrangement of color elegantly separates planes and directs attention (Color Figure 25).[46]

The composition is an excellent example of how *GWTW* integrates color effects with virtuoso lighting, forging a link between two elements that were so often treated as opposed. Yet the pictorial effect is brief and punctual. The stylized design provides a quick visual payoff as Mammy leads Melanie to the room and gives a long description of Rhett's behavior since Bonnie's fall. The tactic is elliptical—typical for the second half of the film—and the glimpse of Bonnie's room offers a short, visually rich climax that helps balance the otherwise cursory treatment of events.

The same lighting situation supports Olivia de Havilland's performance when her character collapses after exiting the room, illustrating how the play of color temperature could be integrated with an actor's movement and expression. When she reappears at the doorway, the amber light outside the room has substantially increased. The shot begins with a medium framing, and as she opens the door, the amber light sweeps across Melanie's figure, catching her face and shawl. The wash of blue on the back wall in conjunction with the slight white edging on her shoulders and hair help intensify the color of the candlelight through contrast. As she moves left and closes the door behind her, the camera reframes, eliminating the white highlights. Melanie is lit entirely by frontal amber light that makes her flesh tones and shawl appear luminous while the detail in her deep blue dress is lost against the nearly pitch-black background (Color Figure 26).

The composition settles on a medium two-shot: Mammy on the left, Melanie on the right, and the candelabrum between them at the rear. Melanie explains that she has convinced Rhett to hold Bonnie's funeral, and Mammy replies: "I suspect the angels fights on your side, Miss Mellie. Hallelujah." As she begins to fail, Melanie turns toward the camera, moving away from the amber light and into hard white illumination projected from off-frame right. Her movement casts strong shadows across the left side of her face while the right takes on bright highlights. The cold new light source flattens her skin tones to pallid gray (Color Figure 27). She collapses. This change in color temperature is set off by an otherwise static lighting scheme. Mammy remains in a low-key setting with fairly minimal highlights, a choice that helps put more graphic weight on Melanie's side of the frame. The final shot of the sequence brings Melanie and Mammy into a medium close-up that continues the basic lighting scheme.

Colored illumination has been woven into the scene's dramatic fabric. Melanie's staging activates the cool light source at the moment she begins to faint. The shift in color that accompanies her turn away from the candelabrum is essential to her performance. De Havilland's face moves very subtly from a half smile to a drawn and exhausted expression as her character begins to fade. The lighting effect signals the sudden turn in health. Even the orchestral score lags behind the color effect, turning to a new theme only with the medium close-up that closes the scene. Staging, of course, is the strongest marker of this event, but the modulation of color temperature plays a particularly significant role. The color quality of the light clearly has been figured into the scene's staging. Within the acceptable diegetic parameters, colored lighting proved flexible enough to play a basic role in highlighting action and shaping the image.

If, on one front, *GWTW* pushes color effects forward, on another it conspicuously mimics distinguished black-and-white cinematography. In emulating monochrome effects, *GWTW* presents a culmination of experiments in low-key carried forward in *A Star Is Born.* With the faster stock and more flexible lighting units, the production incorporates stronger modeling and more complex shadow areas than any Technicolor film of the 1930s. As Selznick's memo suggested, low-key effects connoted "artistry" as opposed to simple "clarity"; they helped forge a prestigious Technicolor design. *GWTW*'s look would be equally measured against color and recent black-and-white prestige pictures. Selznick specifically advised his designers and cinematographers to view *Young Mr. Lincoln* (1939, shot by Bert Glennon) and *The Great Waltz* (1938, shot by Joseph Ruttenberg) as black-and-white models for what he hoped to achieve.[47]

A good number of *GWTW*'s shadow effects are fairly conventional for Technicolor and build on techniques developed in films like *Robin Hood, Elizabeth and Essex,* and even *Becky Sharp.* This is certainly true of the silhouette shots that stylize an image by emptying it of varied color and rendering a sharp contrast of light and shadow. During the Twelve Oaks barbecue, the reduction to silhouette suppresses and renews color. In an effect described by Menzies in his notes, Ashley and Melanie are briefly framed before a set of garden doors, and the backlight through the doors leaves them in silhouette. Then, as the couple steps out on a verandah overlooking the gardens, the frame is flooded with the bright green of the lawn and the pastel accents of costumed extras. For Menzies, this was a method of "overdoing" the brilliance of the barbecue "to contrast with the later drabness illustrating the disintegration of the south."[48] In technique and function, though, this effect reprises the silhouette-drawing scene in *Becky Sharp,* though more fluidly. Menzies embellishes the tactic during the scene of Melanie's labor by throwing black silhouettes against warm yellow-orange light coming through louvered blinds in her bedroom. The production designer rightly commented that the effect "intensified the feeling of a hot late afternoon," but the hard separation of light and shadow was hardly innovative.[49] The true breakthroughs in *GWTW*'s lighting design involve more intricate and complex shadows that carefully modulate detail.

At several points the cinematographers reduce light to extraordinarily low levels, but they achieve many of the most interesting shadow effects in moderate illumination. They overlay networks of highlights and transparent shadows onto mid-key scenes, and an often-restricted palette lends the shadows greater emphasis. These carefully graded lighting schemes support the dramatic rhythm as actors move in and out of highlights, and the light key gently shifts to underscore developments. The expressive possibilities of this kind of cinematography are best illustrated by Scarlett's parallel love scenes with Ashley in the first and second halves of the film. In the first, Scarlett gives Ashley a sash during his Christmas furlough, and in the second she visits him in the paddock and asks for help

7.4. A love scene ornamented by monochrome lighting techniques.

7.5. Highlights from Scarlett's tears echo the background raindrops.

paying the taxes on Tara. Though shot by different directors and cinematographers, these sequences both suppress color in favor of pronounced figure modeling. The intricate play of light and shade enlivens these quiet, dialogue-heavy love scenes.

In the scene directed by Cukor and shot by Garmes, Scarlett bids farewell to Ashley before a gray rain-streaked window in Aunt Pittypat's (Laura Hope Crews's) parlor.[50] The sequence adapts the restrained mode to more intricate modeling. Lighting contrast on the figures is accentuated by staging them before the window, which provides a backlight just below the level of Scarlett's key. This contrast exaggerates the impression of the dark foreground. In addition, the arrangement of the mise-en-scène creates a dark border that frames the couple in a vignette. Off-white curtain sheers catch light from beyond the window, but they are surrounded by heavy brown draperies that provide rich areas of darkness at the top of the frame. A small amount of fill picks out some of the folds in the drapes, but the overall effect is to form a dark border that graphically continues the silhouettes of two chairs in the lower foreground. Cukor and Garmes ornament the composition much the way they might have in black-and-white (Figure 7.4).

In close-ups, Garmes exploits the rain to create soft, shimmering highlights in the background, underscoring the bittersweet romantic tone. Scarlett's two final close-ups make the most of this. In the first, immediately after Ashley's kiss, the tears on Scarlett's face form highlights that are echoed by the raindrops in the background (Figure 7.5). The final shot dollies in on Scarlett's profile as she stands beside the window, watching Ashley depart, and the shadows of rain droplets streaking down the window are projected onto her face. These rain effects stylize the sequence by privileging the achromatic over hue. Despite all of *GWTW*'s bravura color effects, one of its most important cinematographic achievements lies in bringing to Technicolor this new level of control over highlight and shadow.

Fleming and Haller handle the paddock scene with a similar emphasis on lighting contrast. The greater part of the scene is staged within a small shed that opens up onto the warm red fields of Tara. Costume colors are overtaken by shadow while the high-key background delivers a wash of reddish brown in low saturation. With highlight and shade granted stylistic prominence, shifts in lighting support the dramatic trajectory. For example, once Ashley and Scarlett have settled into a medium long shot inside the shed, he recalls the war. With the mention of battle, the orchestral score shifts to a deep, ominous theme, and the image cuts to a medium close-up that deepens shadows and brightens the highlights on Ashley's face. A key light throws strong highlights onto the left half his face, and the right side is heavily modeled with a particularly strong shadow around his nose. The folds of his shirt, the edge of his shoulder, and the top of his hair all receive contrasting highlights. Each eye reflects two well-defined eye lights. Haller exploits high-contrast modeling to create an appropriately dramatic look for Ashley's description of combat: "I saw my boyhood friends blown to bits. I saw men crumple up in agony when I shot them" (Figure 7.6). As in Cukor and Garmes's earlier work, the scene integrates exacting control of highlight and shadow to underscore the action and mood.

Minute changes in light and color temperature support the scene's rhythm. Ashley's intense medium close-up is juxtaposed with a much softer treatment of Scarlett. Her reaction shot is much more finely graded, the highlights softened into shadow along her cheek (Figure 7.7). Whereas Ashley's composition featured a distinctly cool gray cast (carried by his clothing and the stone columns in the background), Scarlett's has a warm, almost rose, tint. Her background is taken up by the ground outside, which nearly matches the soft reddish tint of her calico dress. Softer treatment of the female lead follows general convention, but the lighting also helps underscore the scene's move away from Ashley's war remembrance and into a new phase in which he tries to comfort Scarlett. The change in color temperature amounts to trading one set of neutrals for another, but the effect is to further soften the image, making Ashley's medium close-up appear more severe by comparison. Color gently embellishes the lighting, accentuating the change of contrast.

The precise placement of highlights also means that as characters move, modeling supports their expressions. When Scarlett exclaims that

7.6. High-contrast modeling and steely colors suit Ashley's intense remembrance.

7.7. Soft highlights and warmer colors for Scarlett help move the scene in a new direction.

7.8 and 7.9. Scarlett dips into darkness and then snaps into light, punctuating her words to Ashley.

she would willingly abandon her father and sisters, she turns toward the camera and lowers her head, moving out of the range of her key light and into shadow (Figure 7.8). Then, as Ashley attempts to comfort her, and she demands that he run away with her, Scarlett quickly snaps her head upward, returning the highlights and punctuating the moment (Figure 7.9). More generally, the lighting key picks up as the would-be lovers move to the end of the shed, where they embrace and kiss. Here, fill light is more even and pronounced, setting off the kiss from the rest of the scene and allowing for a clearer view of facial detail.

The love scenes between Scarlett and Ashley are good examples of how *GWTW* developed the range of Technicolor lighting. In each case, the play of color is subordinated to lighting contrast. Though this had become a hallmark of the restrained mode, *GWTW*'s lighting schemes are more complex, and the staging within them is more fluid, than earlier efforts.

The effects that I have described may not seem particularly innovative in the context of monochrome cinematography, but for Technicolor they represent striking gains in the flexibility, precision, and intricacy of lighting style.

Convention may have guided both Cukor and Haller, and Fleming and Garmes, to make similar choices in staging and lighting.[51] Both the organization of highlight and shadow and the movement between soft and hard modeling are efficient ways to add variety and to underscore visually the character interactions in emotionally charged scenes. These techniques recur when Scarlett bars Rhett from her bedroom, when Rhett forces himself upon her, and, later, when she desperately tries to save their marriage as he packs his things. Melanie's attempt to comfort Rhett after Scarlett's fall down the mansion stairs follows the same protocol, including another rain-streaked window to provide backlight. This mode of lighting enlivens stormy romantic encounters and emphasizes brooding or sentimental dialogue sequences. And this style was adaptable. Since it does not reduce illumination enough to obscure details, the balance of shadow in mid-key sequences offered a practical option for more modest productions, films without *GWTW*'s stake in mannered, or pretentious, low-key effects.

GWTW also carries forward the strong experimental bent of Selznick International, and the filmmakers engage in far more adventurous lighting schemes, reducing illumination well below the stock's apparent threshold for rendering detail. At its extreme, the effect shrouds the image in darkness and obliterates color. The most fully developed sequence of deep chiaroscuro occurs at the end of the film's first half. As noted earlier, Scarlett's homecoming and her discovery of her mother's bier feature definite low-key that helps flatten out color. Things get even darker when Scarlett confronts her father in his office, and then, at the close of part one, wanders out to the garden, where she makes her oath to "never go hungry again". These scenes illustrate Selznick International's proclivity for pushing the boundaries of Technicolor lighting, and they help us pinpoint the gains achievable with the new stock and new lighting technology.

Cinematography during the office scene most thoroughly emulates black-and-white by nearly completely eliminating color from the frame. The first shot places emphasis entirely on highlights within a darkened frame. Gerald (Thomas Mitchell) is framed in medium long shot, seated before a large window, and after a gentle dolly forward, Scarlett enters and takes a drink of whisky from a decanter on her father's desk. The frame is lit entirely from behind the window by a cold white source that

7.10. Scarlett's meeting with her father thoroughly emulates black-and-white cinematography.

throws strong highlights on the left edge of Gerald's face, catching his silver hair (Figure 7.10). Once Scarlett enters, she picks up just enough highlights to distinguish her from the background and to catch some details of her dress and face. The familiar backlighting technique has been made more conspicuous by eliminating the frontal fill. Except for Ellen's jewelry box, which, glimpsed low in the frame on Gerald's desk, reflects just enough backlight to reveal its red color, all hue is reduced to a range of black and gray. The composition is more than a brief establishing shot; it runs a fairly lengthy forty-two seconds before the cut to medium close-up introduces more even illumination.

The clearest precedent for this Technicolor chiaroscuro is William H. Greene's work on *A Star Is Born,* and a comparison helps us appreciate the benefits of the new film stock. In the earlier film, the low-key effects could not offer substantial shadow detail or midtone. Though Greene aimed at complex effects, most often the results juxtaposed hard inky shadows with flat bright highlights. In the office scene, the highlights tend to be more minimal, and the shadows offer a greater range of detail before falling off into complete darkness. For example, in the shot described above, the edge light on Gerald generates a bright highlight along the edge of his face, and then softens into a dim shadow area within which his eye, nose, and cheek are distinguishable before they drop into blackness. Similarly, the shadows that cover Scarlett's face still allow a very minute highlight to distinguish a lock of hair on her cheek. When Scarlett walks toward the background and takes a seat next to her father at the end of the shot, she never once moves entirely out of highlight. The fine-grained differences between low-key in *A Star Is Born* and in *GWTW* specify what Haller meant by the increased "shadow speed" of the new stock. Gains in film sensitivity opened up new possibilities for staging in low light.

With this suppler control over tonal variation, directing viewers' attention becomes a matter of arranging highlights. When Scarlett learns that her father has saved only Confederate bonds, she lowers her head and turns back toward the window. This softens the light on her face; in the foreground, Gerald glances toward the left, picking up sharp, strong eye lights. The actors' movements briefly drive the highest point of contrast forward to Gerald (Figure 7.11). He scolds Scarlett for her comment about the worthless bonds, glances down, and then looks back into the eye lights when he suggests, "We must ask your mother." Scarlett, upon recognizing her father's dementia, raises her head toward the camera and into fuller facial light. As she glances forward, she catches her own eye lights at just the moment Gerald looks down (Figure 7.12). For an instant, the point of high contrast shifts back to Scarlett as she reacts. Gerald then glances up again, moving back into his highlights. The lighting scheme has pinpoint precision: the eye lights conduct us through the dark frame and buttress the scene's dramatic rhythm. Technicolor had never more closely approached the exactness of black-and-white cinematography.

The severe chiaroscuro of Tara's interior accentuates the burst of colored lighting as Scarlett steps out onto the porch and into a fairly strong red-orange key light. The spectacular return of color functions symbolically. It cuts through the murky gray and black low-key, signaling the onset of sunrise and recalling the motif set up at the start of the film. Conventional associations of dawn with renewed hope are layered with the graphic power of colored light. Music, too, stresses the moment, returning to *GWTW*'s main theme just as Scarlett comes into the light. All these stylistic registers coalesce to launch the climax of the film's first half. Low-key cinematography, however, remains unabated. Scarlett's oath before the rising sun is remarkably dark. As she rises up into a medium close-up, fill light provides barely enough illumination to reveal the contours of

7.11 and 7.12. Highlights shift from Gerald to Scarlett as she recognizes his dementia.

7.13. Remarkable low-key lighting for Scarlett's vow.

her cheeks and forehead. The shot juxtaposes strong shadows against the light, warm sky, but allows barely enough light to keep track of Scarlett's facial features (Figure 7.13).

The choice is exceptional for the final close-up before the intermission, much less for the composition that covers one of Scarlett's most important monologues. The shot sacrifices skin tone and facial detail in order to support the pictorial motif of a silhouette against the rising sun, a motif fully realized in the famous pullback that follows this close-up. The radical underexposure in this shot exemplifies *GWTW*'s testing of the new stock. The filmmakers seem to have overreached the system's sensitivity, producing a dim, murky image. But their willingness to shoot at the very margins of the system's latitude also marks a culmination of one trend in 1930s Technicolor design. The production is a testing ground for low-key, an experiment in trying out black-and-white techniques with the Technicolor camera, something from which most subsequent productions would retreat.

While many of *GWTW*'s lighting techniques emulate black-and-white effects, several sequences build a new kind of partnership between chiaroscuro and color. By spotlighting a piece of colorful mise-en-scène within an otherwise darkened frame, the filmmakers grant color a particularly powerful role. The technique may flag an important prop, as with the jewelry box on Gerald's desk during the office scene. The same device works expressively when Melanie visits Belle Watling, madam of the local brothel, in her carriage to thank her for harboring Ashley and Rhett after their raid on the shantytown. The carriage interior is black, as are the costumes, and this drives attention to Belle's Teaberry red lipstick and the shock of red hair that peaks from beneath her shawl. Highlighting makes these colors luminous in the darkness; their saturation is exaggerated by the low-key setting. The dialogue is an occasion for Belle to progressively reveal more and more color. As she discusses her child, she gradually parts her cape, revealing the bright Mandarin Red trim on her dress (Figure 7.14). Then, when she passionately denounces Scarlett as a "mighty cold woman," Belle removes her shawl, opens her cape, and begins powdering her chest. The action exposes her vivid Hyacinth Violet taffeta dress and red hair. Belle's half of the frame is deluged in saturated highlights as she bursts the confines of reserve and propriety. Color underlines character contrast, and the chiaroscuro lends it such exceptional intensity that it overwhelms the image.

This combination of low-key lighting and strong color culminates in the near abstraction of scenes staged on the Crimson red staircase of the Atlanta mansion. In low-key, the stairs offer regularly patterned alternations of deep, saturated Crimson and dark, impenetrable black. In reducing the palette to red and black, the staircase scenes capture the vigor of a high-contrast monochrome image, but with vivid color. This scheme first punctuates the shot of Rhett carrying Scarlett upstairs during his forceful seduction, but it recurs more powerfully when she collapses at the film's end. The camera dollies in from a long shot after she crumples on the stairs in her black dress, Rhett having finally left her. The stairs dominate the frame: their treads generate striking bands of color yet their risers are lost to shadow, creating a striped effect. Scarlett's dress forms an inky mass that interrupts the patterning of highlight and shadow (Color Figure 28). She buries her face on her arm, eliminating all flesh tones except for one hand that peeks out from her side.

The camera movement intensifies the monochrome color effect by filling the frame with Crimson and black as the voices of Rhett, Ashley, and Gerald (in an audio montage) beseech Scarlett to return to Tara. The reduction of color and light cooperate to make Scarlett's rise into close-up a brilliant revelation of light and texture. In lifting her head, she dramatically reintroduces flesh tone and engages sharp eye lights, punctuating her moment of decision (Figures 7.15 and 7.16). Color and low-key are equal partners. It seems fitting that a film so invested in expanding the ambit of Technicolor lighting should conclude with an exercise in combining color with shadow and shifting the key of illumination.

It is also appropriate that the *GWTW*'s penultimate shot showcases Scarlett's close-up, slowly revealing her face until her gaze locks on the brilliant eye lights. We have repeatedly observed the importance of appropriately lit facial details for reinforcing mood, performance, and character psychology. In the classical Hollywood style, there is nothing unusual about this emphasis on the close-up. For Technicolor, however, the pre-

7.14. Chiaroscuro intensifies the revelation of Belle Watling's red and violet dress.

7.15 and 7.16. The dramatic reintroduction of flesh tones punctuates Scarlett's decision to return to Tara.

cision and control of facial modeling here is just short of revolutionary. More than any color film of the 1930s, *GWTW* places graphic emphasis on the close-up and on the lighting of faces. We have already noted a good deal of detail about facial modeling, but a brief discussion of a few important techniques can help us understand *GWTW*'s innovations in this area.

It would be misleading to characterize facial modeling in earlier Technicolor films as entirely flat or featureless. Though high-key films like *The Goldwyn Follies* and *The Wizard of Oz* stayed with relatively flat and soft shading, other productions managed to obtain fairly intricate effects. Selznick International releases like *The Garden of Allah* and *A Star Is Born,* both shot by William H. Greene, exhibit a healthy share of dramatic facial lighting, and this is an important context for *GWTW.* For example, as discussed earlier, Esther and Norman's first kiss in *A Star Is Born* features a hard shadow that falls across half of her face, allowing an eye light to reflect through the darkness. The result is striking, though inflexible: the rest of Esther's face is lit without much contrast, and if she moved, she might be lost in an unforgiving shadow. Nonetheless, Greene's intent clearly is to stylize facial modeling to support the moment. When Esther drops into darkness during the kiss, the brief obliteration of facial detail punctuates the action. This is an unusual choice, but it demonstrates how a color cinematographer could save a place for tonal manipulation within Technicolor's restricted latitude.

Even within softer and higher-key settings, facial modeling could help serve performance with a degree of precision. Usually this was accomplished through eye lighting. When she contemplates abandoning her career to save Norman, Esther, framed in a medium shot with standard soft modeling, glances toward her Oscar and is moved toward tears. Her emotional shift is signaled, in part, when her glance meets up with two minute spots of light that reflect near her pupils. Similarly, in Esther's final close-up, the key light leaves half her face in even light while the right side is shaded around her cheek. Pronounced eye lights pick up her tears at the very end of the shot, after she introduces herself as "Mrs. Norman Maine." This technique is taken up much more boldly and consistently in *GWTW*, but it had been a tool of Technicolor lighting from quite early in three-color's history.

In 1939, Greene and Sol Polito achieved much more nuanced and intricate modeling effects in *The Private Lives of Elizabeth and Essex*. Evidence suggests that the Warner Bros. film, in production at the same time as *GWTW*, made use of the improved stock.[52] Greene and Polito's work anticipates many of *GWTW*'s techniques. They more readily mingle deep and soft shadow, and texture faces with an elaborate play of highlight and shading. To take one example, as Essex (Errol Flynn) sits next to his fireplace and discusses his love for the queen, an orange key light projects warm, even illumination onto the left of his face while his right cheek is strongly shaded. Highlights near the right of his nose and chin break through the shading. Moreover, the key light has a flicker effect to simulate fire, continually playing small halftone shadows across the highlights (Figure 7.17). This mixture of harder and softer shading, and the placement of highlights within shaded areas, typifies the complexity that Polito and Greene achieved in their modeling. Color cinematographers made immediate use of developments in lighting and stock to experiment with facial lighting.

Instead of viewing *GWTW* as breaking radically with standard practice, we should see it as refining and expanding this approach to facial modeling. Garmes, Haller, and Rennahan used the new stock to further extend the tonal range of their modeling and to integrate shifts in lighting more fully with performance and staging. Many of the specific techniques appeared in earlier films, and *GWTW* does rely on soft, simple, fairly pedes-

7.17. Complex modeling in *The Private Lives of Elizabeth and Essex.*

trian modeling for routine sequences. Yet the film also consistently brings forward more complicated designs, especially for Scarlett.

Virtuoso low-key effects are reserved for dramatic turns, but when the situation calls for glamorous effects, the new stock allows for exceptionally rich modeling. The formal elegance of Scarlett's close-up as she naps with the other belles at the Twelve Oaks barbecue signals a considerable advance in Technicolor lighting. Ernest Haller suggests an off-screen window blind by casting three diagonal shadows across Scarlett's face: one along her upper forehead, another from her right eye down across her nose, and a third along her chin. Alternating with these delicate shadows are soft highlights, an unprecedented use of diffused modeling lights in Technicolor (Color Figure 29). As Scarlett raises her eyes and glances left and right, she engages eye lights that create brilliant highlights near the center of the image. These lights help signal Scarlett's decision to sneak downstairs and corner Ashley. In its delicacy and exactitude, this lighting scheme far outstrips anything achieved in earlier three-color features. Of all of Scarlett's close-ups, this shot most clearly lends credence to Haller's claim, cited earlier, that the faster stock let the cinematographer use "little tricks of precision lighting he has used in monochrome to glamorize his stars."[53]

As in *A Star Is Born,* harder and more prominent modeling often surfaces for low-key dramatic sequences. Whereas Greene set single masses of undifferentiated shadow against equally flat areas of light, Haller, Garmes, and Rennahan layer brighter areas with cast shadows and break apart dark areas with highlights. Performances are transmitted through meticulous facial modeling, especially eye lighting. One of the basic schemes of facial modeling for color or black-and-white, and the one preferred for Scarlett, places the key light quite high and to the left, creating a bright triangular highlight directly below her right eye. This scheme

7.18. A fine network of shadows cast across Scarlett's face.

7.19 and 7.20. Scarlett moves into and out of light in rhythm with her performance.

forms a starting point from which expressive variations depart. When Scarlett discovers the burned-out remains of Twelve Oaks, for example, the triangular highlight is exaggerated by the elimination of fill along her right cheek. A fine network of cast shadows drift across her face as she glances around the great hall (Figure 7.18). Shading molds her face to suit the mood of the scene without straying too far from the standard beautifying lighting setup.

This scheme is repeated with greater precision when Scarlett steps forward to the ruins of the great staircase, her eyes filling with tears. The deep shadows of the banister posts pass over her face as she walks toward the stairs. Once in close-up, the right side of Scarlett's face is lost in darkness, aside from the highlight beneath her eye. Then, as she glances leftward, up the stairs, she turns more fully into the key light, moving out of shadow. The action also engages two pronounced eye lights in each eye, briefly illuminating her tears (Figure 7.19). Finally, she returns to the original position, darkening her face as she mutters, "The Yankees, the dirty Yankees" (Figure 7.20). As Vivien Leigh moves fluidly into and out of shadow, Ernest Haller orchestrates low-key facial light, varying the composition and shifting highlights in rhythm with her performance.

This brief discussion should give some idea of how facial illumination was developed in *GWTW.* In fact, the increased flexibility of lighting seems to have coincided with a special emphasis on facial detail. Sequences routinely culminate in close-ups of Scarlett, often with effects like those described above. Consider the persistence of this strategy in the first half of the film: Scarlett stares teary-eyed through a window at the end of the Twelve Oak's barbecue; her wedding concludes with a medium close-up of Scarlett crying; she watches Ashley return to battle after his furlough in medium close-up through a rain-streaked window; she curses her promise to care for Melanie in a close-up that accentuates the sweat and tears on her face, closing the sequence before the siege of Atlanta; she steps into an extreme close-up and into fairly intense eye lights as she climbs the stairs to Melanie's room to help her give birth; her discovery of the ruins of Twelve Oaks ends with the shot described above; her discovery of Ellen's body concludes with a heavily modeled medium close-up; and the penultimate shot before the intermission is the extremely dark close-up of Scarlett's oath in Tara's garden. Such emphasis on the star is common, but *GWTW* capitalizes on the classical convention with particular insistence. The film is a veritable workshop on the vicissitudes of the Technicolor close-up. Again, we can see *GWTW* as a culmination of the trend in 1930s Technicolor cinematography toward closing the gap between monochrome and color.

The Light at the Turn to Tara

In attending so closely to the cinematographic developments in *GWTW,* this analysis may seem to underplay the role of color. Certainly, an extended discussion of either the Twelve Oaks barbecue or the armory bazaar would reveal careful staging and the organization of a broad palette on par with the most skillful passages in *Robin Hood.* However, *GWTW*'s most formally adventurous sequences elaborate lighting innovations by emphasizing colored illumination. Hence, we should close this chapter with a short consideration of the flight from Atlanta, the visual apogee of the two-hundred-and-twenty-two-minute film. Specifically, Rhett and Scarlett's iconic kiss at the turn to Tara fully combines the tonal control that this analysis has focused on with unusually intense color.

The action is staged before a backdrop glowing with brilliant red-

7.21. Red light suffuses the establishing shot at the turn to Tara.

orange light, overturning the Technicolor convention for keeping backgrounds in unobtrusive cool colors. An establishing shot sets up the scene's basic palette. The extreme long shot frames Rhett and Scarlett's cart from a low angle as it works its way up a hill. Lining the roadway are several trees and a low fence, rendered in black silhouette against the red-orange sky. Billowing smoke, superimposed at the far left, serves as a marker of the characters' distance from Atlanta and a reminder of the diegetic motivation for the fiery sky. The sky itself modulates in value from a lighter tint near the ground to a deep, almost gray-black at the top of the frame. Though the frame is almost completely saturated in red with touches of black, Rhett's shirt and forehead catch white highlights. The color difference accents the main characters within this remarkably vivid setting (Figure 7.21). Subsequent compositions expand this palette only slightly by adding touches of cool blue modeling light.

The play of color temperature and shadow is fundamental to the closer shots of Rhett and Scarlett. Once Rhett steps off the cart and faces Scarlett, he is fully illuminated by a red-orange key light, and she receives minimal fill and some white highlighting along her face. Rhett's close-up uses a hard orange key light from off left so that the right side of his face is strongly shadowed. The top of his head and the backs of his shoulders are lit with contrasting cool, bluish white light. Scarlett's reverse shot, on the other hand, presents her shoulders and hair edged in red-orange, and her face is modeled by a steely white light from the right, leaving her left profile strongly shadowed. When the camera repositions behind Rhett, the juxtaposition of temperatures becomes more striking. Scarlett's coolly lit figure is sandwiched between vivid warm accents at fore and rear (Color Figure 30). The color temperatures reinforce each other. Contrast both makes the colored illumination pictorially forceful and visually translates character conflict.

Rhett and Scarlett's kiss forms the scene's climax, and the mixture of low-key lighting and projected color heightens the moment. The camera dollies forward to a medium-long shot of the couple, the fence railing a dark mass in the foreground. Rhett's facial modeling is provided by a red-orange source that highlights his forehead, the edge of his nose and mouth, and a patch under his eye, but leaves the rest of his profile in rugged shadow. As before, cool white light reflects along his back. Scarlett, facing right, is lit in red along her back and receives small highlights of white along her profile. It is true color chiaroscuro.

A cut in to a medium close-up places more weight on this facial modeling. When Scarlett resists Rhett's advances and turns away from him, she dodges out of her highlighting and is enveloped in shadow. Then, when Rhett declares his love, he grasps Scarlett's face, moving her so that the bright cool highlights return and she engages an eye light. The difference in color between the white highlights and the warm red-orange surroundings amplifies this play of facial modeling. Minute movements have consequences not only for tonal values but for hue as well. Shifting colors and highlights track the power struggle between the lovers.

After a third cut to a tight close-up, the hot points on Scarlett's face are softened to retain flesh tone, but they take on even greater graphic prominence. With nearly the entire frame in red and black, Scarlett's forehead and the edge of her nose, mouth, and chin receive the greatest contrast in the image. Indeed, they are the only sources of properly registered flesh tone (Color Figure 31). When Rhett kisses her, he blocks out these highlights and tilts Scarlett's head back so that she is suffused with the red-orange light. His movement forward into the key light creates a brief surge of red at the center of the frame. Each cut inward places successively greater stress on facial detail and the play of light. The strategy gives remarkable force to shifts in color, punctuating Rhett's kiss.

In stylizing this scene, *GWTW*'s production crew push color forward more forcefully than at any other point in the film. Ronald Haver reports that Fleming, Menzies, and art director Lyle Wheeler had to persuade Selznick not to reshoot the scene.[54] Selznick likely objected to color's obtrusiveness, its dominance over facial clarity. In a sense, this use of hue is a descendant of Robert Edmund Jones's early attempts to make colored light expressive. Red stands for passion in this scene in the same way that it connoted rage at the end of *La Cucaracha* or danger in the ball sequence in *Becky Sharp*. In those films, the technique of flooding the frame with red light is used only briefly, and uniformity of color creates a look that resembles a monochrome scene that has been tinted or toned. But in *GWTW* the color effect is integrated with more conventional expressive techniques of low-key modeling. By incorporating white and bluish highlights, and manipulating deep shadows, the cinematographers accommodate traditional methods of shaping the image within the red environment. The turn to Tara boldly brings together *GWTW*'s experiments in tonal control and colored illumination to showcase color as an expressive and pliant element of style. For once, one of Hollywood's best-remembered images seems worthy of its repute.

Conclusion

More than any other film, except perhaps *The Wizard of Oz, Gone with the Wind* is today remembered as a milestone in color feature production. This reputation was highlighted when New Line released a new dye-transfer version in 1998. Color was a key selling point for the release. Advertising proclaimed, absurdly, that the film would be presented "for the first time in its original Technicolor glory," and television spots dramatically wiped between the pale grainy images of an old duped print and the brighter, sharper picture of the reissue.

Criticism of the new print demonstrated popular conceptions about Technicolor and its importance to *GWTW.* One view presumed that the 1939 release had offered brilliant hues that did not survive into the latest incarnation. A critic for *Big Reel* complained, "It is a shock to see so many scenes with such muted colors, gone any resemblance of bright, rich, vivid tones."[55] Another view suggested that the film had pioneered a radical use of color to produce dramatic effects. *Variety*'s critic claimed:

> In its day, *GWTW* was darn-near avant-garde: a Technicolor film that used swatches of color to foreshadow tragedy, suggest moral failings (Scarlett the plantation coquette favors red hair ribbons), and just plain shock, as when a tracking boom shot at a railway depot follows Scarlett (in red) wading through a sea of tattered gray bodies.[56]

Of course, the dramatic organization of color was by no means new, and certainly not "avant-garde." As noted, the film departs from "bright, rich, vivid tones" for extended stretches of restraint. Still, each critic in his own way believes Technicolor to be central to the film's identity as a work of art. Over sixty years after its release, *GWTW* is popularly regarded as innovative in its use of color, though the exact nature of those innovations remains obscured by generalizations.

GWTW relies on techniques that we have already encountered. In a sense, it combines the restrained mode's power to develop chromatic motifs, exemplified by a film like *A Star Is Born,* with the emphasis on variety and ornamentation so vividly demonstrated by *Robin Hood.* More importantly, color design in *GWTW* was reconceived in relation to new cinematographic opportunities, and so it can best be understood in relation to lighting. The film's most vital innovations with regard to color lie in the way its cinematographers exploited technological gains to increase the precision and range of their lighting techniques.

The new film stock and new sets of filters helped extend Technicolor's latitude, making low-key lighting and precise modeling effects easier to achieve. The technology did not necessarily entail these achievements. In other cases, cinematographers used increases in film speed to save money, maintaining norms at lower light levels.[57] The norms of Technicolor lighting, however, were always subject to comparison with black-and-white, and during the 1930s, color cinematographers continually reached for parity with monochrome. In *GWTW,* Garmes, Haller, and Rennahan seemed intent on pushing the new film for all it was worth, experimenting with extreme low-key and creating elaborately lit close-ups. As the biggest prestige production of the decade, the film was particularly suited to such a mannered, carefully wrought approach to cinematography.

Lighting is also central to the problem of color design. Low-key illumination could effectively reduce the chromatic range, entailing restrained schemes that would single out important dashes of hue within a darkened frame. Near the start of principal photography, Selznick reminded Menzies of the important role that light could play with regard to mise-en-scène:

> As to the obtrusiveness of sets, it is my opinion, based upon very solid experience in Technicolor, that this is largely, if not entirely, a matter of the photography and lighting. Mr. Garmes is familiar with our desires in this respect, and is completely in accord with Mr. Cukor and myself on the obvious folly of the old-fashioned Technicolor photography that indulged in lighting every detail of a set with resultant and great distraction from the players.[58]

Selznick saw a more varied lighting as tightly linked with color design. Carefully directed pools of light could imitate candlelight and tone down or accentuate specific elements of the mise-en-scène. Certainly, the front hall of the Atlanta mansion, with its massive red-carpeted staircase, benefited from a lighting scheme that could modify its appearance. Gains in lighting facilitated greater control of set and costume color.

GWTW's most notable manipulations of color involve colored lighting. In simulating lamp-, fire-, and moonlight, the film makes color temperature a more pronounced element of style than earlier three-color features did. Colored lighting adds a new variable to highlight and shadow for shaping the image; it brings color firmly within the realm of the cinematographer's craft. In this area, *GWTW* follows the path opened by Robert Edmond Jones in *La Cucaracha*. But while Jones's designs forced color forward to serve broad expressive goals, *GWTW* usually tempers the device by providing a more plausible diegetic motivation and by reducing the range of hue to an opposition of cool and warm light. This is a familiar pattern of development for color style. Early experiments present a range of devices that are then reclaimed for feature production when they can be clearly motivated and made to work with established techniques. With the help of technological improvements, projected color is rendered more flexible; warm and cool components intermingle, often amplifying the kind of tonal contrast valued in monochrome. *GWTW* creates a new alliance between light and color at the level of cinematography.

In some cases, the film gives unusual precedence to projected color, though usually, as in the sunset and sunrise scenes, the effect is relatively brief and punctual. *GWTW* also experiments with its stylistic innovations by making them prominent for extended scenes. But color showcasing does not mean a loss of stylistic flexibility. The cinematographers effectively incorporate modeling effects that highlight performance and action. The tactic is indicative of *GWTW*'s experimentation with Technicolor style. At several points in the film, the filmmakers test limits to find the maximal level of stylization that can still accommodate standard functions of classical style. In Selznick's terms, the film indulges in "artistry" while striving to maintain "clarity."

To overemphasize *GWTW*'s most experimental or stylistically adventurous moments, however, would be misleading. At the time of its release, the film was praised not only for its spectacular effects, but also for controlling color and blending it with the narrative. *Time* proclaimed: "Technicolor (using a new process) has never been used with more effective restraint than in *GWTW*."[59] Similarly, Technicolor's promotional publication singled out the color design for inconspicuously supporting the story: "Perhaps the happiest conclusion of the color designing . . . is that although the picture runs almost four hours on screen it does not obtrude colorwise but remains beautiful and pleasing. The entire color key . . .

is extremely well used to convey mood, complement the characters and portray an era, without being blatant or claiming more than its rightful share of audience attention."[60]

The film's continued popularity as a Technicolor classic can obscure its place in the ongoing effort to secure a role for color during the 1930s and 1940s. Viewing *GWTW* as a milestone of color filmmaking does not acknowledge the way it builds on conventions and methods of earlier productions, nor does it help specify concrete areas of innovation. Like *Lonesome Pine* or *A Star Is Born, GWTW* helped demonstrate that color could serve drama and be integrated with respected formal techniques. From the perspective of this book, *GWTW* seems especially important for extending to Technicolor lighting a degree of flexibility that had previously been the province of black-and-white. If, as Technicolor declared, its process did not claim "more than its rightful share" of attention, this was, in part, because color could better cooperate with highlight and shadow.

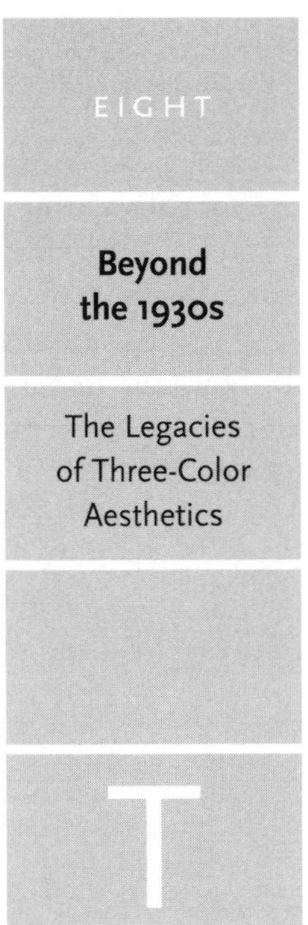

EIGHT

Beyond the 1930s

The Legacies of Three-Color Aesthetics

This book has argued that the 1930s were crucial in the development of color film aesthetics. Though fewer than forty live-action three-color features were produced during the decade, filmmakers and designers rapidly developed a series of formal solutions to the problem of color. Perhaps the most impressive aspect of their work has been its longevity. These methods for handling color formed a powerful baseline for subsequent Technicolor design. In our own time, at a much further historical remove, we can see that contemporary film artists seeking to integrate new digital techniques for manipulating color find themselves repeating strategies from the 1930s. In this closing chapter, I wish to revisit Technicolor aesthetics in order to suggest how they set the pattern for color design in the 1940s and to show their continued relevance to the most recent technological revolution in film color, digital intermediate.

The basic path of stylistic change during the 1930s was toward the integration of color, but also toward a greater flexibility and confidence in design. It is not surprising that conventions for handling color developed so swiftly. The stylistic norms of classical Hollywood cinema were firmly in place, and they set the horizon for color's use. More specifically, a set of conventions for proper and effective cinematography—developed for monochrome—bounded and influenced the ways that hue would be used in features. As we have seen, the Technicolor Corporation, by implementing a program of technological development and specifying aesthetic guidelines, actively sought to ensure that three-color could function within these frameworks. Cinematographers and designers engaged in a dialogue about how best to control color so that it would fulfill ideals of motivated spectacle, narrative centering, and unobtrusiveness. Once Technicolor was seen as an embellishment of existing practices rather than as a fundamentally different art, the development of color style could proceed fairly rapidly.

We have considered three modes of color design to be more or less distinct options. We should note, therefore, how much these modes overlap: each exhibits some tendencies of the others, and films could combine elements of each. The demonstration mode experimented with a range of techniques, many of which were reclaimed once they could be motivated and made to work with established aesthetic norms. After the demonstration films, the restrained mode largely closed down stylistic play and channeled color into less pronounced roles. That said, the restrained designs did not entirely turn away from color foregrounding. Rather, they tended to concentrate color display in transitions and in other scenes that seemed open to stylization. As three-color gained acceptance and as the body of conventions for harnessing it to the classical style developed, the palettes and the range of effects broadened once again, this time into the assertive mode, but built upon the lessons of restraint while doing so. Through all three modes, the most lasting uses of color followed the paths carved for other stylistic devices. These included the spectacular embellishment of transitions, the gentle directing of attention, the momentary highlighting of actions, the development of motifs, and the general correlation of color with the mood or tone of the drama.

In this sense, the course of color's adoption resembles the path followed by other formal innovations in Hollywood cinema. Specifically, color replays the dynamic that Lea Jacobs has uncovered with regard to effects lighting in features of the 1910s. Jacobs argues that striking lighting effects (Lasky lighting) in early Cecil B. DeMille films such as *The Cheat* (1915) and *The Heart of Nora Flynn* (1916) were carefully motivated and "made to dovetail with the culmination of the dramatic action." In describing what is distinctive about Lasky lighting, she contrasts it with the classical Hollywood cinema, in which "light works as a neutral element of the mise-en-scène," and in which the process of making it serve narrative "is much less obvious precisely because the mise-en-scène seems to exist apart from its signifying function." By developing narrative pretexts for the techniques, DeMille was "actually much more careful to motivate and integrate effects lighting than later classical filmmakers would be."[1] Without putting too fine a point on the comparison, we can draw a similar contrast between the deliberate designs of *Becky Sharp* and the less labored uses of color in *Robin Hood* or *Gone with the Wind.* Much of the energy expended in bringing color to the classical cinema was aimed at making color, like lighting, a neutral mise-en-scène element that could be flexibly manipulated and strategically brought forward. The rapid growth of stylistic precedents meant that later films could treat color with more fluidity. Perhaps, then, the movement from demonstration to acceptance and flexibility is a common trajectory for new visual technologies in Hollywood narrative cinema.

Refining the Design Modes: Options of the Early 1940s

This is not to suggest that Technicolor style had reached stasis by 1939. Like those of any other element of film style, the uses of color would continue to shift and develop. Rather, I would argue that the basic methods for handling color and assigning it functions—i.e., the terms under which filmmakers engaged with three-color—were set in place during the 1930s. The eclecticism of *GWTW*'s color design outlined the course that Technicolor would follow in the early 1940s. As live-action Technicolor found a comfortable niche in studio production, beginning with about fourteen features a year from 1940 through 1942 and increasing thereafter, there appeared a range of color design options, all operating within the general guidelines that we have charted.[2]

Immediately following the 1930s, filmmakers reworked and combined the restrained and assertive modes of design as well as their attendant strategies for color scoring and showcasing. A brief survey indicates some trends. Warner Bros.' military aviation film *Dive Bomber* (1941), for example, adheres very closely to the restrained mode nearly as strictly as *Lonesome Pine.* Restraint, in this case, has been generically moored to the masculine space of the military film. At the same time, MGM's melodrama biopic *Blossoms in the Dust* (1941) and the musical *Smilin' Through* (1941) are also both fairly restrained, but they take up different options within that mode. The former draws more heavily on the mode's color scoring and motif building potentials, while the latter uses color as a glamorous setting for Jeanette MacDonald, a look reminiscent of *Goldwyn Follies.* The successful series of Twentieth Century–Fox musicals starring Alice Faye, including *Down Argentine Way* (1940) and *That Night in Rio* (1941), also resemble *Goldwyn Follies* in drawing on tight harmonies to create a sense of high polish in exposition scenes. The big production numbers, however, showcase assertive and varied palettes. When not subjected to the demands of storytelling, color returns to the techniques of demonstration.

Assertive designs also remained vital. Adventures like Alexander Korda's production of *The Jungle Book* (1942) or Twentieth Century-Fox's more richly textured pirate film *The Black Swan* (1942) are reminiscent of *Robin Hood,* though not as insistent in their emphasis on variety. Rouben Mamoulian, committed as ever to exploring the possibilities of color scoring, directed Paramount's remake of *Blood and Sand* (1941). That film draws on an extraordinarily dynamic palette to forge dramatic effects in the vein of *GWTW.* Mamoulian shifts between moderate restrained and extremely assertive color to parallel the flow of action across the film, and cinematographers Ernest Palmer and Ray Rennahan provide low-key settings that mix shadow with strong chromatic accents.

American Cinematographer's "Photography of the Month" column, which ran from 1941 through 1943, extends and amplifies our sense of color style during the 1940s. With regard to Technicolor, the reviews confirm that the ideals and concerns of the 1930s remained important. For example, the critics clearly valued complex modeling and effects lighting in three-color. *The Jungle Book* was slighted for "a bit too much reliance on the traditionally flat Technicolor lighting," but of *Chad Hanna* (1942), Fox's Henry Fonda and Dorothy Lamour circus picture, the critic remarked: "The use of deep, full-bodied shadows as forceful elements of the composition was worth a million of the gutless semi-shadows with which color scenes are so often afflicted."[3] Similarly, color's potential to disperse attention remained a point of discussion. A close-up of Alice Faye in *That Night in Rio* was criticized for "the presence in the extreme background of an extra woman in a too strongly blue gown which, even though extremely out of focus, is still a sufficiently strong tonal intrusion to distract the eye from the star's face."[4] The musical *Louisiana Purchase* (1941) was similarly berated for settings that "like an irresistible magnet drew attention from the players to the background."[5] Despite the innovations in more intricate lighting and the success of more dynamic palettes during the late 1930s, concern with the dangers and limitations of three-color persisted in the 1940s.

In addition, the "Photography of the Month" columns pointed toward an awareness among *American Cinematographer*'s critics that films of the early 1940s employed a variety of distinct color styles. For example, in October 1941 the column noted:

> There are rapidly coming to be three clearly-marked schools of color-cinematography. One, exemplified by *Blood and Sand,* seeks to use color for strikingly dramatic effect; another, exemplified in *Blossoms in the Dust,* seeks to subdue color for realistic illusion; and the third, excellently exemplified by *Aloma of the South Seas,* seeks apparently to paint with a lavish brush for pictorial effect and dramatic illusion.[6]

These categories are inexact, overlapping distinctions of function, genre, and palette, but they capture the author's sense that several modes of Technicolor design coexisted. These "schools" were roughly aligned with genres. The modern drama *Blossoms in the Dust* was praised for "some of the most restrained use of color yet seen," whereas Paramount's exotic romance *Aloma of the South Seas* (1941) received commendation for "scene after scene" of "eye-arresting pictorial quality."[7] The categories resemble the restrained and assertive modes that I have identified for the 1930s, and the critic also tried to signal differences in the way color functioned: for realism, spectacle, or dramatic underscoring.

Though they admit a plurality of styles, the *American Cinematographer* critics expected that in all films the basic principles of harmony and unobtrusive coordination from the 1930s would serve the story. The color score of *Blood and Sand,* for instance, was heralded for making "color an integral part of the story and its telling" without "any obvious attempt at chromatic symbolism such as has in the past made other color films seem 'arty' and unreal."[8] The bold accentuation of drama with color, though it defined one style of design, could not become too conspicuous. *Billy the Kid* (1941), on the other hand, was criticized for "a feeling that the dominant chromatic value of a scene is jarringly out of key with its emotional content."[9] Similarly, *The Jungle Book* was praised for offering a "lavish" palette so "skillfully planned and photographed" that "it never becomes garish."[10] Even films oriented toward spectacle required tasteful balance. Otherwise, as in *Louisiana Purchase,* the design might be judged "a riot of color" that "forced itself into the foreground of the viewer's attention."[11]

The "Photography of the Month" reviews present a picture of diverse color styles coexisting within the borders of an overarching set of principles. In the years following *GWTW,* Technicolor features continued to draw on both the restrained mode and more assertive designs.[12] The conventions and strategies that developed during the 1930s seemed to be central to the kinds of effects and functions that the critics embraced. Three-color features of the 1930s laid a foundation of methods and techniques upon which filmmakers of the 1940s built.

Eclecticism and flexibility had always been built into Technicolor aesthetics. The general principles endorsed by the professional press and proffered by Natalie Kalmus never mandated a single, undifferentiated approach to color. This book has demonstrated the complexity and variety of 1930s Technicolor design. Though the restrained mode seems to have dominated production between *Becky Sharp* and *Robin Hood,* a broadening of options quickly followed it. In addition, the least flexible element of Kalmus's prescription in "Color Consciousness" was never consistently borne out in actual production. The color vocabulary, which Kalmus and others suggested would help design serve precise semantic functions, proved too literal from very early on. Color scoring was predominantly a matter of aligning noticeable contrasts and coordinations with particular events, an effect often integrated with music cues, lighting, or staging. It is this spirit of integration, of suppleness within limits, that explains the long life and influence of 1930s Technicolor style.

Renewing the Rainbow: The Birth of Digital Color

Recent history attests to the continued relevance of both Technicolor aesthetics and our methods for understanding them. Since the late 1990s, the rise of digital postproduction has engendered a renewed interest in color design, even if not a full return to the "color consciousness" of Natalie Kalmus's day. A film's palette and chromatic effects are increasingly determined after principal cinematography, in what has been called a "second stage of image creation."[13] The practice generally referred to as digital color grading involves scanning footage to create a digital intermediate that can be manipulated and then scanned back out onto film. The technique replaces the photochemical process of color timing with a more complex level of intervention. The earliest use of digital color techniques, in films like *Pleasantville* (1998) and *O Brother, Where Art Thou* (2000), replayed three-color's journey from brash demonstration to strict restraint.[14] Even more strikingly, when seeking to emulate Technicolor looks in his Howard Hughes biopic, *The Aviator* (2004), Martin Scorsese turned to cutting-edge digital techniques. *The Aviator* well illustrates how our new understanding of Technicolor design might illuminate contemporary practice as well as how a contemporary filmmaker can rework design modes to fulfill new functions.

The newfound flexibility of digital color raises an aesthetic question: what formal purposes should it serve? Cinematographer Dean Semler, discussing his experience with digital intermediate in the film *We Were Soldiers* (2002) notes, "The only problem with the process right now is getting lost in the number of choices you have."[15] Along with the breadth of options opened by digital grading comes the need to develop conventions and schemata for channeling the new technology. Stephen Burum (the cinematographer on *Mission: Impossible* [1996]) sums up the professional response articulated time and again in the pages of *American Cinematographer:* "The big question for the future is not whether film or digital technology will prevail, but rather how we can tell better stories with more interesting characters."[16] As in the 1930s, institutional rhetoric sets productive limits on the technology by invoking classical priorities of character and narrative. Faced with new devices for controlling color, filmmakers are again casting about for appropriate, respectable functions. One role of the early digitally graded films has been to set out concrete methods for yoking the technology to craft norms. Technicolor's precedent casts light on the current approaches to digital color.

Digital color grading enables filmmakers to isolate and manipulate areas of the frame, change the colors of particular objects, and dynamically adjust hue and saturation within a continuous shot. In most instances it has been a simple replacement for traditional photochemical color timing. For example, problems with lighting and weather on location were digitally corrected in sequences from action films like *Die Another Day* (2002) and *Gone in Sixty Seconds* (2000).[17] Early in the development of digital color grading, effects-heavy productions routinely incorporated digitally graded sequences into conventionally produced films. In a strategy reminiscent of interpolating three-color sequences into black-and-white films, the thriller *The Cell* (2000) featured fifty minutes of digitally graded footage to represent the hallucinations of a serial murderer.[18] Full-scale adoption of digital color depended, however, on establishing its value to a wide array of genres and production trends.

From a technological standpoint, the most important laboratory for digital technology has been Peter Jackson's *Lord of the Rings* (2001–2003) trilogy. As with *Gone with the Wind,* a superproduction provided a thoroughgoing test of the technology and encouraged experimentation. The economies of scale involved in producing three back-to-back features effectively turned the *Lord of the Rings* franchise into a research and development corporation. In a dynamic relationship reminiscent of that between Technicolor and Pioneer, Jackson and cinematographer Andrew Lesnie employed a prototype digital system manufactured by the UK-based 5D company. In turn, 5D, refined its Colossus system to meet the producer's needs, reasoning that this would make it more compatible with the norms of film production and more appealing to the industry.[19] Certainly these films are the most ambitious mixtures of film and digital technology, but a series of smaller, though high-profile, films in noneffects genres have played an equally important role as aesthetic prototypes.

The first American production to rely heavily on digital color grading was not an action film but Gary Ross's social satire *Pleasantville* (1998). This film revived the demonstration mode by making color manipulation part of its narrative premise: two 1990s teenagers bring color with them to the black-and-white world of a 1950s sitcom. The color manipulation was central to the film's market identity, as trailers stressed the mix of color and monochrome and posters featured the tagline "Nothing is as simple as black and white." Moreover, *Pleasantville* offered a far-reaching investigation into the problems of digital color for several firms in the postproduction industry. Cinesite Digital Imaging developed new software that allowed over 70 percent of the film to be scanned so that the producers could remove and then selectively reintroduce color.[20] Artists at an in-house postproduction service, Pleasantville Visual Effects, performed much of the color grading, but additional work was also parceled out to Cinesite Digital Studios, The Computer Film Company, and eFilm. Finally, Cinesite recorded the intermediary back to film, which was then processed by Deluxe Labs, where the prints were carefully monitored for color consistency. A prototype, *Pleasantville* catalyzed industry-wide research and development into digital color technology and techniques for handling the new medium.

Though *Pleasantville* strongly demonstrates digital color manipulation, few of its effects are well suited to conventional production. Digital color is harnessed to narrative, but obviously so. Color begins to emerge within the black-and-white universe when the teenagers introduce sexuality, passion, and free will into the sitcom's world of complacent sterility. The film's visual gimmick is founded on juxtaposing black-and-white and color elements within the same frame. Bold digital work (a True Red rose set against monochrome foliage or a high school girl's Candy Pink bubblegum in a black-and-white hallway) is justified by a rather narrow and specific high-concept premise. The film does little to suggest that digital color grading can cooperate rather than dominate a formal system, but as in *La Cucaracha* and *Becky Sharp,* this is not necessarily a failing. A demonstration film's aesthetic role is to draw industry attention to a new technology and suggest its spectacular and narrative potentials. Demonstration films leave to subsequent productions the job of integrating the device and developing paradigmatic conventions.

Pleasantville's demonstration was successful enough that, two years later, Kodak and Cinesite began offering their intermediate process to the open market, stressing its very broad applications. Speaking on behalf of Cinesite, cinematographer Allen Daviau proclaimed: "The growth of Digital Intermediate work is going to get the attention of everyone who shoots motion pictures . . . It's going to mean a lot more than a digital intermediary for effects work. It's going to work exactly as it does in lab procedures, except that now we're going to have a wonderful digital tool."[21] A number of celebrated noneffects films subsequently made extensive use of digital grading, including *Amelie* (2001) and *Frida* (2003). But *O Brother, Where Art Thou,* directed by Joel and Ethan Coen, was the film most recognized within the industry for its ambitious use of color grading.

The film's status as a prototype seems clear. *O Brother* was the first major Hollywood noneffects film to be scanned and manipulated in its entirety (the only prior film was *Star Wars: Episode I—The Phantom Menace* [1999], which used digital grading to integrate effects work). While promoting the film, cinematographer Roger Deakins became a virtual spokesman for Cinesite and the potentials of digital grading. Critical reaction to the film's look garnered him an Academy Award nomination for best cinematography, a nomination for outstanding achievement in cinematography from the ASC, and the award for best cinematography from the British Society of Cinematographers. The film played an important role in legitimizing digital color grading. It also helped Cinesite make the case that the process could be an extension of traditional cinematography, rather than a postproduction novelty. Work on the intermediate was organized as collaboration between Deakins and colorist Julius Friede; Deakins shot the film in a manner that would give him options in the postproduction phase.[22] *O Brother* was a pivotal film for validating digital grading and for providing a model for the integration of the process into Hollywood's prevailing creative hierarchy. Discourse in the critical and creative communities positioned the film as an exemplar of successful digital color design.

O Brother also returns to an aesthetic suited to exploiting and controlling the possibilities of digital color; its approach fits firmly within the restrained mode. In adopting this design mode for *O Brother,* the Coens and Deakins made a bid for the importance of color digital grading. On the one hand, desaturation has become a mark of virtuosity in color filmmaking since the 1960s (supported by lab techniques like bleach bypass, flashing, and silver retention—all of which were considered by the filmmakers before turning to Cinesite). The thinning of color is a contemporary sign of taste and differentiation, and the look was famously associated with the Depression-era settings in *Bonnie and Clyde* (1968). On the other hand, just as in the 1930s, restraint helps foreground departures from the palette, drawing attention to color as a compositional element and highlighting its dramatic functions. Digital color works as an extension of respected techniques when it is accented. Deakins confirms this understanding of the film's strategy: "The technology enabled us to create a look that supported the mood of the story. . . . I wish there was more discussion about how we can tell more compelling stories and less hype implying that different techniques and uses of technology will replace or diminish the cinematographer's role in telling stories."[23]

The film's color design highlights the new digital tools while assigning them well-established functions. Loosely modeled on the *Odyssey, O Brother* follows the journey of three escaped convicts in the American South during the 1930s. The film's look is partly motivated by its Dust Bowl–era setting. Deakins and Friede removed green from footage that was shot in Mississippi during its verdant summer months, desaturated the palette, and worked in a rather narrow range of warm browns and earth tones.[24] This stylized environment helped the filmmakers establish that digital tools could handle routine formal tasks without commanding undue attention. Digitally desaturated backgrounds give figures greater prominence, thus directing attention. Leaving particular colors untouched (like the color-magnet red cans of Ulysses's "Dapper Dan Pomade") helps graphically underline motifs. Elsewhere, Deakins and Friede vary the saturation and value of the ever-present brown and orange foliage to parallel and emphasize dramatic turning points. During the trio's somewhat mystical encounter with a baptism ritual, and their seduction by the sirens, the mise-en-scène color shifts in a manner akin to the way a change in lighting might accentuate a dramatic passage. The digital-grading suite, these sequences submit, can be a team player with other elements of style, suiting the mood of the story without unduly dominating the proceedings.

In moving from demonstration to restraint, *Pleasantville* and *O Brother* suggest that the introduction of digital grading followed the aesthetic tread of Technicolor, and they remind us of the interplay between film form and the promotion of technology. In Scorsese's *The Aviator,* however, the intersection between new technology and Technicolor style is bold and intentional. Scorsese is the most historically minded contemporary American filmmaker, and reaching back to Technicolor aesthetics served as both an authorial mark and an indicator of period in his biopic. Inspired in part by the Technicolor sequences in Howard Hughes's 1930 epic *Hell's Angels,* Scorsese rendered the first act of his film in a simulation of two-color and transitioned to a three-color look for the remainder. Though Technicolor had briefly revived dye-transfer printing in the late 1990s, the company again shut the production line down in 2002. Ironically, Scorsese, the traditionalist, worked digitally for the first time with the company's Technicolor Digital Intermediates (TDI) subsidiary to achieve his retro look. The result is a modified, contemporary revision of Technicolor design.

Creation of the digital Technicolor look involved collaboration between Scorsese, visual-effects supervisor Rob Legato, cinematographer Bob Richardson, Technicolor digital colorists Steve Arkle and Stephen Nakamura, and TDI vice president of research and development Josh Pines. Scorsese began by screening Technicolor films for his staff, including *The Toll of the Sea, The Black Pirate,* and *Follow Thru* (1930) in two color, and *La Cucaracha, Becky Sharp,* and *Robin Hood.*[25] Development of the virtual Technicolor style was then shared out among the staff, and it moved through several phases. Rob Legato arrived at versions of two- and three-color by manipulating photographs on his laptop using Photoshop, and then consulting with veteran Technicolor expert Dr. Richard Goldberg. Arkle used Legato's experiments to digitally treat the high-definition video dailies that Scorsese screened during production. The problem of creating these effects for the final film, however, fell to Pines, who developed digital filters (look-up tables, or LUTs) to emulate two- and three-color looks. The LUT is an algorithm that actively translates the original image into a new color space. When digitally grading the film, Richardson and Nakamura viewed the footage through Pines's LUTs, and then adjusted colors, shadows, and details from shot to shot. All of this information was "baked in" to a final negative from which prints were produced.[26]

The process represents an important technical advance in the practice of digital color grading. Pines's work, in particular, breaks new ground: filmmakers can apply an overall color look to a film by using LUTs rather than relying on intensive shot-by-shot intervention from the colorist.[27]

The LUT creates a baseline look, and colorists are free to manipulate scenes and sequences as needed within that color space. Ron Ames, Legato's partner on the project, explains: "We can now emulate a look created with film stock and processes that no longer exist using today's stock and digital technology."[28] If so, the new developments may have profound implications for film preservation and for the creation of "restoration" prints of Technicolor features.

In *The Aviator,* however, the Technicolor emulations aren't historically accurate reproductions so much as creative interpretations of the original looks. There was no direct path between the original Technicolor processes and the final effects in the film. Rather than duplicate the colors of a nitrate master, as a preservationist might, Scorsese's team drew on a range of films for inspiration and engaged in a sort of creative digital conversation with one another. Legato's Photoshop prototype became Pines's model for his LUTs. On the set, Scorsese consulted Arkle's high-definition dailies, which created a Technicolor look through entirely different means. Moreover, as this book demonstrates, the Technicolor look is a complex and multifaceted style that cannot really be reduced to the characteristics of the three-color camera or the dye-transfer process. Richardson's lighting doesn't strictly emulate styles of the 1930s and 1940s, and Dante Ferretti's set designs make reference to period aesthetics but conform to the demands of contemporary style, with its roving camera and overt compositions. Scorsese's initial impetus was to evoke viewing experiences in the 1940s and 1950s that he describes as "formative for me in a very primal way."[29] Rob Legato explains that his aim was to create something like the effect of using a Technicolor camera and film stock with contemporary lighting technology and contemporary camera mobility.[30] In the end *The Aviator*'s palette does not re-create a specific style, but pays tribute to the director's subjective memory of color film.

Different sequences in the film echo different moments in color's Hollywood history. *The Aviator*'s most overt and artificial color designs are not achieved digitally but through colored illumination. A red light in Hughes's (Leonardo DiCaprio's) screening room washes the screen in deep scarlet as he sinks into psychic torment. While *La Cucaracha* might be one source for this style, the effect is closer to the bold use of colored light to signal a character's distress, used memorably in 1950s melodramas like Nicholas Ray's *Bigger than Life* (1956), and Vincente Minnelli's *Some Came Running* (1958). Scenes with Ava Gardner (Kate Beckinsale) reference high-gloss 1940s productions like the Fox musicals or John Stahl's *Leave Her to Heaven* (1945), while early sequences in the Cocoanut Grove refer to two-color spectacles of the early 1930s, most notably *The King of Jazz* (1930). Elsewhere, Scorsese's color effects are strongly contemporary. At the start of his screening-room retreat, Hughes is alternately bathed in blue or placed before the projection booth so that flares of blue light outline his dimly illuminated figure. The forcefully stylized use of blue light, and intentional lens flares, has been a key element of 1990s Hollywood cinema.

Perhaps the most important effect of Scorsese's digital emulations is that they call attention to color's manipulation and, by extension, to the intentionality of the film's designs. The knowing artifice of digital color in *The Aviator* alerts the viewer that color is an active choice and not, as is the norm in contemporary cinema, a formal default. In this sense, the technique returns to color something of the novelty it enjoyed in the 1930s and 1940s; color ceases to be transparent. The film's major shift in digital color is motivated by chronology. The years 1927 through 1936 are rendered through Pines's two-color LUTs, and 1937 though 1947 utilize the three-color emulation. The point of transition takes place one-third of the way through the film, and it coincides with a narrative turning point, the introduction of Juan Trippe (Alec Baldwin) president of Pan Am, and Hughes's nemesis for the remainder of the film. The main effect of the two-color LUT is to eliminate pure greens and blues and translate them as various shades of turquoise and aquamarine. The major change after the transition, then, is the forceful addition of green to Scorsese's palette, abetted by the presence of strong and deep blues. Generally, the three-color LUT saturates the primaries, giving precedence to reds and greens, and heightens contrast between adjacent colors. Legato described the look as "a palette with a much reduced and compressed color fidelity"; a caption in *American Cinematographer* pointed out, more simply, "vivid, ultra-saturated colors of the three-strip look."[31] This is Technicolor as popularly remembered.

Each look departs enough from contemporary norms to become noticeable, but Scorsese modulates the obtrusiveness of his manipulation. Flesh tones, for instance, seem relatively immune to stylization. Nowhere does the film simulate the pale matte-finish skin tone proffered by Technicolor's two-color processes and on display in *The Toll of the Sea* and *The King of Jazz.* Seriously compromising the stars' images might have been considered too risky for such a high-profile production. Sky and foliage, on the other hand, prove particularly sensitive to treatment by the LUTs, and they are important signals to the viewer that color has been manipulated. In a scene inspired by the golfing musical *Follow Thru,*

Hughes courts Katharine Hepburn (Cate Blanchett) on a golf course featuring blue-green grass and an aqua blue sky. Errol Flynn (Jude Law) taunts Hughes by muddling the carefully arranged blue-green peas on his plate, and the aviator crashes an airplane in a blue-green beet field, only to rush home to a foyer filled with blue-green shrubs. In each case the transformation of normative color reminds the viewer of digital alteration, spurring our awareness of color in general. According to Legato, the two-color LUT could have been tweaked to lessen the alteration of greens, but Scorsese preferred the compromise.[32] The effect is similar to the brief expansions of the palette in the restrained mode, which keeps color from drifting entirely from our attention. Indeed, the effects of digital grading can easily go unnoticed by viewers, and each of our films offers a means for making the technology at least momentarily opaque.

The three-color portion of the film is markedly less artificial, but color nonetheless comes forward, in part through contrast with the earlier scenes. A cluster of scenes that foreground green and blue with red accents highlights the transition into three-color and demarcates a new phase of the story. Ferretti's design for Juan Trippe's office, the first interior set viewed in the three-color LUT, features strong deep Midnight blue walls painted with murals of maps featuring green accents. Already forceful, the design has special prominence because it offers the film's first strong blue and green contrast. Similarly, Hepburn's Pistachio green dress in the next sequence comes as a revelation, heightened by its play against her Cherry Red lipstick and auburn hair. Scorsese exploits his film's new colors for spectacular emphasis by featuring them on his major female characters. Moments later, Ava Gardner is introduced wearing an arresting black, blue, and red dress, and Hughes has an obsessive-compulsive episode in a gleaming green marble bathroom. The climax of this introduction to three-color comes as Hughes and Hepburn drive to her Connecticut estate (Color Figure 32). In a shot that Legato calls the film's strongest three-color Technicolor moment, grass and foliage are now powerfully saturated bright green; sky and ocean are pure blues.

The palette references the couple's two-color golf date, creating a nice symmetry between the beginning and the turning point of their relationship. At the same time, whereas the previous three-color revelations are powered by their contrast with the two-color emulations, the saturation in this sequence appears artificially heightened. The scene serves as notice that in moving to full color, Scorsese does not intend to underplay digital intervention. Compositions with saturated greens, blues, and reds continue to advertise themselves as "treated," marked as "Technicolor" rather than simply rendered in color. The gains for digital intermediate here are important. Setting the manipulations within a prestige picture, and offering the double motivation of auteurist flourish and period authenticity, *The Aviator* legitimizes the technology without letting it disappear.

For dramatic purposes, Scorsese also draws on the three-color LUTs tendency to exaggerate red-green contrast. In so doing, he offers an interesting revision of Technicolor color scoring. In Gardner's fierce argument with Hughes after she discovers that he has bugged her home, cutting to red accents on a green set punctuates her attack. Gardner wears a Lipstick Red blouse and a Deep Red velvet skirt for the occasion, a choice that echoes the Technicolor practice of keying designs around the lead woman's costume. The set's palette is dominated by greens and gold browns, creating an aggressive complementary contrast with Gardner. When the scene enters a shot-reverse-shot pattern it trades between Gardner's vibrant reds and Hughes, centered in a remarkably symmetrical set that features matched Emerald green furniture on either side of him, a green and beige patterned carpet, and a softer green rear wall. The back-and-forth between the characters reaches a fever pitch when Hughes proclaims that he cares for Ava and will remove all the bugs. Exasperated, she yells, "Bullshit" as the camera cuts back to a reestablishing shot from just behind her, bringing a brilliant bouquet of red roses into the center foreground. The reds of her costume align with the roses in a graphic spike that punctuates the argument's turning point, a moment emphasized by a brief pause in dialogue, as well as by the interruption of the shot-reverse-shot. The next shot returns to a frontal medium shot of Ava, as she redirects her line of questioning: "What do you mean ALL the bugs?"

The bouquet of roses, also glimpsed in the scene's opening tracking shot, is exactly the kind of chromatic echo Technicolor designers might plant for emphasis. The striking and sudden convergence of prop and costume gives the moment a direct, sensual intensity and lends it the air of a carefully determined design. The technique recalls the alignment of green accents during June's confrontation of Jack after her brother's death in *Lonesome Pine*. And the flourish of red, motivated within the set, to underline rage has been with us since Pancho flared his red serape to wrap Chatita during their dance-duel in *La Cucaracha*. Mamoulian replays the effect when he gives Carmen (Linda Darnell) a red scarf to brandish in anger during *Blood and Sand*, and Alice Faye was similarly equipped with a red handkerchief for her rebuff of Cesar Romero in *Week-End in Havana* (1941). We have seen similar punctual cutting in the Duchess of Richmond's ball and in *Robin Hood*. In this moment, Scorsese reawakens one of Technicolor design's richest techniques and foregrounds it using new technology. The effect takes on a special charge because the film's digital manipulation has granted color a kind of opacity. Because the three-color LUT compresses the range of hue and heightens color contrast, we are especially aware of the film as being designed; we sense an agency behind the image, though the logic of design is not always so overt. The technique is also transformed by the speed and punch of Thelma Schoonmaker's rapid editing. It is a true marriage of contemporary style and classical method.

In so explicitly playing with the new technology, Scorsese participates in what David Bordwell has termed the "intensified" style of contemporary Hollywood. While still embracing the goals of narrative-centered continuity, contemporary filmmakers indulge in a more overt and eclectic approach to form than their classical counterparts.[33] Like Scorsese's use of split-screen, Steadicam, and elaborate crane shots, his use of color draws from the modern American filmmaker's toolbox. As much as the film is a throwback to classical techniques, it is also another chapter in Scorsese's collaboration with Richardson, which yielded strikingly state-of-the-art looks in *Casino* (1995) and *Bringing Out the Dead* (1999). The development of digital grading represents less a return to Technicolor style than an example of how contemporary popular cinema can embrace a wide range of devices, not least those of the Technicolor era.

Nonetheless, *The Aviator* also shows the continued vitality of three-color aesthetics. On one hand, Scorsese successfully aligns a new color technology with dramatic goals by reaching back to Technicolor schemata. On the other, the creative dynamic that surrounds digital grading mirrors that of three-color; in both cases, filmmakers responded to new color technology by exploring formal options that would both integrate and showcase it. More generally, in making color the creative province of postproduction, digital grading has encouraged contemporary filmmakers to experiment with consistent "looks" or modes of design more intensively than in the recent past. Certainly, important film stylists (Scorsese among them) have kept color alive since the passing of Technicolor's empire in the 1950s. In our current historical circumstance, however, digital grading promises to replenish color's power in much the way Technicolor must have during the 1930s. If so, and films like *The Aviator* and *O Brother* suggest it, then the way of thinking about color analysis proposed by this book should become newly relevant.[34]

To paraphrase Victor Shklovsky's famous discussion of Tolstoy, digitally graded films promise to remove color from the automatism of conventional perception, to prick our color conscience.[35] In doing so, however, the digital films are not merely breaking new ground but returning to the fertile possibilities of the past. In the rush to describe how new technologies are changing film form, the case of color grading is a reminder that one way to understand the digital "revolution" is to view it against a historical background that emphasizes continuities and ancestry as well as innovation. Indeed, analytical methods shaped through contact with classical cinema may help us capture nature of contemporary film color.

If my approach to Technicolor films of the 1930s can help chart the directions of new technology, there is reason to hope that it might also aid a more precise understanding of color design in all eras. It seems clear, for example, that with the introduction of Eastmancolor in the 1950s and the subsequent extension of color to most feature productions in the 1960s, its status as a device shifted and developed.[36] Our knowledge of classical strategies can help us specify these changes with new diligence. Likewise, though particular auteurs have long been lionized as color stylists, we have suffered from a poverty of context. We might better understand the innovations of Douglas Sirk or Vincente Minnelli, for example, by considering their films in relation to the traditions of classical design, the norms and options that we have uncovered here.

I hope that this book has confirmed the value of close analysis for the study of color. Scholars working on Technicolor have often relied on Kalmus's "Color Consciousness" and the reiteration of its principles in the 1950s by the Society of Motion Picture Engineers to characterize classical color design. These principles are certainly important for understanding how filmmakers conceived of color, but close analysis reveals a much richer network of functions and strategies. The task of carrying out such analysis can be particularly demanding because color resists easy methods of coding or even notation. In undertaking this study, I intended to give a fuller account of the classical style and, in the process, to develop a worthwhile method for tracking color in film. We are now in a better position to explain that sense of plentitude and inevitability that graces Technicolor design. Ultimately, only by raising our own color consciousness, by renewing our awareness of cinematic color, can we hope to fully acknowledge and grasp it.

APPENDIX 1

Types of Prints Consulted and Variables in Color Reproduction

For this book I have consulted four types of prints: nitrate dye-transfer prints, dye-transfer prints on safety stock, photochemical reproductions of Technicolor films, and a print utilizing the new dye-transfer process. Each kind of print, and the method used for viewing it, has a particular status with regard to color reproduction, and so these variables warrant explanation.

Ideally, analysis would be based on well-preserved 35 mm nitrate dye-transfer prints. Even here, though, there is room for variation. Because Technicolor engineers continually sought to update and improve their processes, dye-transfer reissues may alter the color characteristics of the original release. Though little precise information is available, it is clear that throughout the 1930s and 1940s the Technicolor staff researched and implemented improvements in the mordants (chemicals that help dye bind to the release stock), the emulsion of the matrix stock, and the dyes themselves.[1] Similarly, during the 1930s and 1940s, to improve contrast and shadow definition on release prints, they were treated with a halftone black-and-white image before the dyes were transferred. This practice was phased out between the mid-1940s and early 1950s, and this may have lead to greater apparent color saturation in later prints.[2] Thus, one cannot assume that even a pristine nitrate dye-transfer print necessarily maintains the colors presented to the original spectators. Nitrate dye-transfer prints consulted for this project include *La Cucaracha* (1934), *The Trail of the Lonesome Pine* (1936), *The Goldwyn Follies* (1938), and *The Adventures of Robin Hood* (1938); all are held by the University of California–Los Angeles (UCLA) Film and Television Archive.

The production of nitrate film stock, a very flammable medium, was phased out in the early 1950s, and many surviving Technicolor films are available only on the "safety stock" that replaced nitrate. These prints may depart from the density and vibrancy of color on nitrate, though preservation experts admit that the difference is impossible to quantify.[3] The 1954 print of *GWTW* that I consulted was a 35 mm dye-transfer safety print. I have also made use of some 16 mm safety prints that Technicolor manufactured for nontheatrical markets. The reduction from 35 mm to 16 mm inevitably involves a loss of visual information, and in some cases, an apparent cropping of the image. According to Richard Haines, Technicolor's quality control for 16 mm was not as consistent as that for 35, resulting in color fringing and registration problems and color variation from reel to reel.[4] Yet because the dye-transfer colors are stable over time, and since Technicolor produced these prints, a well-made 16 mm print can provide valuable information and function as a useful point of reference. In the analyses that follow, I have made use of a privately owned 16 mm version of *La Cucaracha* and a print of *The Adventures of Robin Hood* held by the Wisconsin Center for Film and Theater Research.

At a third remove from the ideal print are reproductions of Technicolor films using photochemical processes like Eastmancolor. These versions present a distinct set of problems because the processes rely on different means for producing color. Where Technicolor's dye-transfer printing mechanically dyed the image on the release stock, processes like Eastmancolor depend on coupler development, that is, the formation of dye by the interaction of chemicals within various layers of the emulsion. These multilayer films are far more complex, both physically and chemically, than the materials used by Technicolor.[5] Since the great majority of color films available today are Eastmancolor versions, we must be aware of the differences between them and a Technicolor original.

Dr. Richard Goldberg, vice president of research and development for Technicolor during the 1950s, oversaw the reformulation of the dye-transfer process for use with Eastmancolor stock, and he has expert knowledge of the differences between the processes. Goldberg explained to me that one strength of dye-transfer was color separation, or the ability to precisely control individual color components. Release prints would be dyed three times with a different matrix, a sort of rubber stamp, carrying yellow, cyan, and magenta dye. Each matrix could be independently controlled to alter tone scale and color rendition, and the density of each dye could be modified to control color contrast. Further, the matrices used to produce prints were made from the original negative. The processing of Eastmancolor stocks, on the other hand, involves the creation of internegatives and interpositives, steps between the original negative and the final print, leading to interimage contamination, or "cross-talk," between the various layers of color. As an example, Goldberg noted that Eastmancolor printing has difficulty withholding cyan information from flesh tones, which should be very rich in magenta and yellow.[6] For similar reasons, yellows in Eastmancolor tend more toward orange than in Technicolor.[7] Most significantly, the complexity of the chemical reactions in Eastmancolor film is responsible for the well-known problem of color fading, in which the image loses its blue information and takes on a pinkish or salmon tint. Color in a Technicolor print has much greater stability, partly because Technicolor prints are comparatively simple.[8]

The point of this discussion is not to disparage Eastmancolor and other photochemical processes, but to point out some differences between them and Technicolor dye-transfer. Indeed, this is a very complex issue that would require a lengthy detour into chemistry and physics to address with any kind of rigor. For our purposes, we must note only that an Eastmancolor print of a Technicolor film inevitably departs from the color rendition of the original. Until recently, however, the only option for preservationists seeking to produce new prints of Technicolor films was to use this technology. The prints of *Becky Sharp* (1935) and *A Star Is Born* (1937) that I consulted were color-positive preservations created by the UCLA Film and Television Archive under the guidance of Robert Gitt and Richard

APPENDIX 2

Chronological Filmography: Three-Color Features of the 1930s

Variety Review Date	Title and Crew	Producer/Distributor
1934		
Feb. 20	*The Cat and the Fiddle* Sequence: Final Reel Camera: Harold Rosson Director: William K. Howard	Metro/MGM
- and -	*La Cucaracha* (short) Color: Robert Edmond Jones Camera: Ray Rennahan Director: Lloyd Corrigan	Pioneer Pictures/RKO
Mar. 20	*House of Rothschild* Sequence: Final Reel Camera: Peverell Marley Director: Alfred Werker	Twentieth Cent./UA
May 29	*Hollywood Party* Sequence: Disney's "Hot Chocolate Soldiers" Camera: James Wong Howe Director: Harry Rapf	Metro/MGM
Nov. 13	*Kid Millions* Sequence: Final Reel Camera: Ray Rennahan Color: Willy Pogany Director: Roy Del Ruth	Samuel Goldwyn/UA
1935		
Mar. 27	*The Little Colonel* Sequence: Final Reel Camera: Arthur Miller Tech. Camera: William Skall Director: David Butler	Fox/Fox
June 19	*Becky Sharp* Color: Robert Edmund Jones Camera: Ray Rennahan Director: Rouben Mamoulian	Pioneer Pictures/RKO

Variety Review Date	Title and Crew	Producer/Distributor
1936		
Feb. 26	*Trail of the Lonesome Pine* Color: Natalie Kalmus Tech. Camera: William H. Greene Camera: Robert C. Bruce Director: Henry Hathaway	W. Wanger/Paramount
June 24	*The Dancing Pirate* Color Designer: Robert Edmond Jones Color: Natalie Kalmus Camera: William Skall Director: Lloyd Corrigan	Pioneer Pictures/RKO
Oct. 14	*Ramona* Color: Natalie Kalmus Tech. Camera: William Skall Camera: Chester Lyons Director: Henry King	Sol Wurzel/Fox
Nov. 25	*The Garden of Allah* Color Designer: Lansing C. Holden Color: Natalie Kalmus Tech. Camera: William H. Greene Camera: Hal Rosson Director: Richard Boleslawski	Selznick Int'l./UA
1937		
Jan. 13	*God's Country and the Woman* Color: Natalie Kalmus Tech. Camera: William Skall Camera: Tony Gaudio Director: William Keighley	First Natl./WB
Mar. 17	*Wings of the Morning* (UK) Color: Natalie Kalmus Tech. Camera: Ray Rennahan, Jack Cardiff Camera: Henry Imus Director: Ray Enright	New World/Fox
Mar. 24	*When's Your Birthday?* Animated Sequence Director: Harry Beaumont	RKO

Variety Review Date	Title and Crew	Producer/Distributor
Apr. 26	*A Star Is Born* Color Designer: Lansing C. Holden Color: Natalie Kalmus Camera: William H. Greene Director: William Wellman	Selznick Int'l./UA
July 21	*George VI Coronation* (UK)	Brit. Movietone/Fox
Aug. 4	*Vogues of 1938* Color: Natalie Kalmus Camera: Ray Rennahan, Winton Hoch Director: Irving Cummings	Walter Wanger/ UA
Aug. 25	*Victoria the Great* (UK) Sequence: Final Reel Tech. Camera: William Skall Camera: Freddie Young Director: Herbert Wilcox	Herbert Wilcox/RKO
Oct. 13	*Ebb Tide* Color: Natalie Kalmus Color Assoc.: Morgan Padelford Tech. Camera: Ray Rennahan Camera: Leo Trover Director: James Hugan	Lucien Hubbard/Par.
Dec. 1	*Nothing Sacred* Color: Natalie Kalmus Color Assoc.: Henri Jaffa Camera: William H. Greene Director: William Wellman	Selznick Int'l./UA
Dec. 29	*Snow White* Animated	Walt Disney/RKO
1938		
Jan. 19	*The Divorce of Lady X* (UK) Color: Natalie Kalmus Camera: Harry Stradling Director: Tim Whelan	London Films/UA
Feb. 2	*The Goldwyn Follies* Color: Natalie Kalmus Color Assoc.: Henri Jaffa Color Designer: Richard Day	Samuel Goldwyn/UA

Variety Review Date	Title and Crew	Producer/Distributor
	Tech. Camera: Ray Rennahan	
	Camera: Gregg Toland	
	Director: George Marshall	
Feb. 16	*The Adventures of Tom Sawyer*	Selznick Int'l./UA
	Color: Natalie Kalmus	
	Tech. Camera: Wilfred Cline	
	Camera: James Wong Howe	
	Director: Norman Taurog	
- and -	*Gold Is Where You Find It*	First Natl./WB
	Color: Natalie Kalmus	
	Tech. Camera: Allen M. Davey	
	Camera: Sol Polito	
	Director: Michael Curtiz	
Mar. 23	*Her Jungle Love*	G. Arthur/Paramount
	Color: Natalie Kalmus	
	Camera: Ray Rennahan	
	Director: George Archainbaud	
Apr. 20	*The Drum/Drums* (UK)	London Films/UA
	Color: Natalie Kalmus	
	Color Designer: Zoltan Korda	
	Tech. Camera: Aldo Ermini	
	Camera: George Perinal, Osmond Borradaile	
	Director: Zoltan Korda	
Apr. 27	*The Adventures of Robin Hood*	First Natl./WB
	Color: Natalie Kalmus	
	Color Assoc.: Morgan Padelford	
	Tech. Camera: Ray Rennahan	
	Camera: Tony Gaudio, Sol Polito	
	Director: Michael Curtiz, William Keighley	
Aug. 17	*Valley of the Giants*	Lou Edelman/WB
	Color: Natalie Kalmus	
	Color Assoc.: Morgan Padelford	
	Camera: Sol Polito	
	Director: William Keighley	
Oct. 26	*Men with Wings*	W. Wellman/Paramount
	Color: Natalie Kalmus	
	Color Assoc.: Henri Jaffa	
	Camera: William H. Greene	

Variety Review Date	Title and Crew	Producer/Distributor
	Director: William Wellman	
Oct. 26	*Sixty Glorious Years* (UK)	Herbert Wilcox/RKO
	Color: Natalie Kalmus	
	Camera: Freddie Young	
	Director: Herbert Wilcox	
Dec. 14	*Heart of the North*	Brian Foy/WB
	Color: Natalie Kalmus	
	Color Assoc.: Morgan Padelford	
	Tech. Camera: Wilfred Cline	
	Camera: L. William O'Connell	
	Director: Lewis Seiler	
Dec. 21	*Sweethearts*	Hunt Stromberg/MGM
	Color: Natalie Kalmus	
	Color Assoc.: Henri Jaffa	
	Tech. Camera: Allen Davey	
	Camera: Oliver T. Marsh	
	Director: W. S. Van Dyke II	
- and -	*Kentucky*	Gene Markey/Fox
	Color: Natalie Kalmus	
	Color Assoc.: Henri Jaffa	
	Tech. Camera: Ray Rennahan	
	Camera: Ernest Palmer	
	Director: David Butler	
1939		
Jan. 11	*Jesse James*	Nunnally Johnson/Fox
	Color: Natalie Kalmus	
	Color Assoc.: Henri Jaffa	
	Tech. Camera: William H. Greene	
	Camera: George Barnes	
	Director: Henry Johnson	
Jan. 25	*Mikado* (UK)	Gen. Film/Universal
	Color: Natalie Kalmus	
	Tech. Camera: William Skall	
	Camera: Bernard Knowles	
	Director: Victor Schertzinger	
Feb. 22	*The Little Princess*	Gene Markey/Fox
	Color: Natalie Kalmus	
	Color Assoc.: Morgan Padelford	
	Tech. Camera: William Skall	

Variety Review Date	Title and Crew	Producer/Distributor
	Camera: Arthur Miller Director: Walter Lang	
Mar. 8	*The Ice Follies of 1939* Sequences: Final Reel Tech. Camera: Oliver Marsh Camera: Joseph Ruttenberg Director: Reinhold Schünzel	Harry Rapf/MGM
Apr. 12	*Dodge City* Color: Natalie Kalmus Color Assoc.: Morgan Padelford Tech. Camera: Ray Rennahan Camera: Sol Polito Director: Michael Curtiz	Robert Lord/WB
Apr. 26	*The Four Feathers* (UK) Color: Natalie Kalmus Color Designer: Zoltan Korda Camera: Georges Perinel, Osmond Borradaile Director: Zoltan Korda	London Films/UA
Jun. 21	*Land of Liberty* (sequences)	MPPDA/MGM
Aug. 16	*The Wizard of Oz* Color: Natalie Kalmus Color Assoc.: Henri Jaffa Tech. Camera: Allen Davey Camera: Harold Rosson Director: Victor Fleming	Mervyn LeRoy/MGM
Sep. 6	*The Women* Sequence: Fashion Show Camera: Oliver Marsh, Joseph Ruttenberg Director: George Cukor	Hunt Stromberg/MGM
Oct. 4	*The Private Lives of Elizabeth and Essex* Color: Natalie Kalmus Color Assoc.: Morgan Padelford Tech. Camera: William H. Greene Camera: Sol Polito Director: Michael Curtiz	Robert Lord/WB
- and -	*Hollywood Cavalcade* Color: Natalie Kalmus	Darryl Zanuck/Fox

Variety Review Date	Title and Crew	Producer/Distributor
	Color Assoc.: Henri Jaffa Camera: Allen M. Davey Director: Irving Cummings	
Nov. 8	*Drums along the Mohawk* Color: Natalie Kalmus Color Assoc.: Henri Jaffa Tech. Camera: Ray Rennahan Camera: Bert Glennon Director: John Ford	Raymond Griffith/Fox
- and -	*Over the Moon* (UK) Color: Natalie Kalmus Camera: Harry Stradling Director: Thorton Freeland	London Films/UA
Dec. 20	*Gone with the Wind* Color: Natalie Kalmus Color Assoc.: Henri Jaffa Production Designer: William C. Menzies Tech. Camera: Ray Rennahan, Wilfred Cline Camera: Lee Garmes, Ernest Haller Director: George Cukor, Victor Fleming	Selznick Int'l./MGM
- and -	*Gulliver's Travels* Animated	Max Fleischer/Par.
Dec. 27	*Swanee River* Color: Natalie Kalmus Camera: Bert Glennon Director: Sidney Lanfield	Kenneth Macgowan/Fox

APPENDIX 3

Pantone Numbers for Color Names

Air Blue	15-4319
Algiers Blue	17-4728
Almond Cream	13-1017
Almond	16-1432
American Beauty	19-1759
Antique Bronze	17-1028
Apricot Wash	14-1230
Apricot	15-1153
Aqua Gray	15-5205
Arcadia	16-5533
Ash Rose	17-1514
Ash	16-3802
Atmosphere	16-1406
Azure Blue	17-4139
Bachelor Button	14-4522
Baltic	16-5123
Bark	16-1506
Barn Red	18-1531
Beechnut	14-0425
Beeswax	14-0941
Beige	14-1118
Bermuda	14-5416
Biscay Bay	18-4726
Bisque	13-1109
Bittersweet	17-1663
Blithe	17-4336
Blossom	14-1513
Blue Green	13-5412
Blue Grotto	15-4421
Blue Haze	15-4707
Blue Turquoise	15-5217
Bog	14-0418
Bonnie Blue	16-4134
Brick Red	19-1543
Bright Gold	16-0947
Bright Green	15-5534
Brilliant Blue	18-4247
Buff	13-1024
Burgundy	19-1617
Burnt Orange	16-1448
Burnt Sienna	17-1544
Cadet Gray	17-4111
Cadet	18-3712
Cadmium Yellow	15-1340
Camel	17-1224
Cameo Blue	16-4414
Cameo Brown	16-1516
Candy Pink	14-2307
Cantaloupe	15-1239
Capri Blue	17-4728
Capri	15-4722
Caramel	16-1439
Cardinal	18-1643
Cascade	14-5713
Celestial Blue	14-4210
Cement	14-0708
Cerulean	15-4020
Chalk Pink	13-1904
Champaign Beige	14-1012
Charcoal Gray	18-0601
Cherry	17-1563
Chili	18-1448
Chinese Red	18-1663
Cinnamon	19-1436
Citrus	14-0955
Classic Blue	19-4052
Clay	15-1231
Cloud Blue	14-4306
Cloud Pink	13-1406
Cobalt	16-4127
Copper	16-1325
Coral Blush	14-1909
Cranberry	17-1545
Cream Pearl	12-1006

Cream	12-0817
Crimson	19-1762
Crystal Blue	13-4411
Crystal Gray	13-3801
Curry	16-0982
Cyan Blue	16-4529
Cypress	18-0322
Daffodil	14-0850
Dahlia Purple	17-3834
Dandelion	13-0758
Dark Blue	19-4035
Dark Purple	19-2524
Dawn	12-0811
Dawn Pink	15-2205
Deep Blue	19-3847
Deep Lake	18-4834
Deep Purple	19-3323
Deep Red Brown	19-1321
Deep Sea	17-5513
Delphinium Blue	16-4519
Desert Dust	13-1018
Dewberry	18-3533
Directoire Blue	18-4244
Dove	15-0000
Dresden Blue	17-4433
Drizzle	16-4402
Dusk	17-3910
Dusty Pink	14-1316
Dusty Rose	17-1718
Ecru	11-0809
Eggplant	19-2311
Emberglow	17-1547
Emerald	17-5638
Ethereal Blue	15-4323
Feather Gray	15-1305
Fiery Red	18-1664
Flame Scarlet	18-1662
Foliage Green	18-6011
Forest Green	17-0230
Forget-Me-Not	15-4312
Fuchsia Pink	15-2718
Fuchsia Purple	18-2436
Garnet	19-1655
Georgia Peach	16-1641
Geranium Pink	15-1922
Geranium	17-1753
Golden Apricot	14-1401
Golden Cream	13-0939
Golden Fleece	12-0288
Golden Glow	15-1050
Golden Yellow	15-0953
Gray Mist	15-4706
Gray Sand	13-1010
Gull Gray	16-3803
Gunmetal	18-0306
Harvest Gold	16-0948
Hazel	17-1143
Honey Gold	15-1142
Horizon Blue	16-4427
Hyacinth Violet	18-3331
Hyacinth	17-3619
Ice Green	13-5414
Imperial Blue	19-4245
Inca Gold	17-1048
India Ink	19-4019
Indigo	19-3215
Ink Blue	19-4213
Iris	14-3805
Ivory Cream	13-1011
Ivory	11-0907
Jacaranda	17-3934
Jade Lime	14-0232
Juniper	18-6330
Lagoon	16-5418
Larkspur	17-4421
Lavender Mist	16-3307
Leaf Green	15-0332
Leather Brown	18-1142
Lemon Chrome	13-0859
Lemon Drop	12-0736
Lilac Gray	14-3904
Lilas	16-1708
Lime Green	14-0452
Lipstick Red	19-1764
Lyons Blue	19-4340
Madder Brown	19-1331

Magenta	17-2036	Periwinkle	16-4032
Mahogany	18-1425	Persimmon Orange	16-1356
Majolica Blue	19-4125	Persimmon	16-1544
Mandarin Red	17-1562	Pink Flambé	18-2133
Maple Sugar	15-1316	Pink Mist	13-2805
Marigold	14-1050	Pistachio Green	13-0221
Maroon	18-1619	Plume	13-4809
Mars Red	18-1655	Pompeian Red	18-1658
Mauvewood	17-1522	Poppy Red	17-1664
Meadow Green	16-0233	Porcelain Blue	14-4512
Medium Blue	18-4432	Porcelain Green	17-5421
Melissa Pink	14-2311	Powder Blue	14-4214
Midnight	19-4127	Prism Violet	19-3748
Mineral Red	17-1537	Purple Haze	18-3718
Mistletoe	16-0220	Purple Orchid	18-3027
Moonbeam	13-0000	Quarry	15-4305
Morning Glory	15-1920	Radiant Yellow	15-1058
Moroccan Blue	19-4241	Raspberry	18-1754
Mulberry	17-3014	Rattan	14-1031
Murmur	12-5203	Raw Umber	17-1422
Neutral Gray	17-4402	Red Earth	18-1444
Niagara Blue	17-4123	Rich Gold	16-0836
Nutmeg	18-1326	River Blue	15-4720
Ochre	14-1036	Rose Shadow	13-1906
Olympian Blue	19-4056	Rose Wine	17-1623
Orchid	15-3214	Rosewood	19-1532
Overcast	14-0105	Royal Blue	19-3955
Oxblood Red	19-1524	Saffron	14-1064
Pale Banana	12-0824	Sage	16-0421
Pale Gold	15-0927	Sand	15-1225
Paprika	17-1553	Scarlet	19-1760
Parrot Green	15-0341	Seafoam Green	12-0313
Pastel Lilac	14-3812	Shamrock	15-6432
Pastel Yellow	11-0616	Shell Pink	16-1632
Peach	14-1227	Silver Cloud	15-4502
Peacock Blue	16-4728	Silver Gray	14-0000
Peacock Green	16-5413	Silver Lining	14-4501
Pearl Blue	14-4206	Sky Blue	14-4318
Pearl	12-1304	Slate Gray	16-5804
Pearlblush	12-1207	Slate	16-4408
Pebble	14-1112	Smoke	14-4505
Pecan Brown	17-1430	Snapdragon	13-0840
Peridot	17-0336	Spectra Yellow	14-0957

Spray	13-6007	Tidal Foam	14-0210
Starlight Blue	12-4609	Tigerlily	17-1456
Steel Gray	18-4005	Tomato	18-1660
Stone Blue	16-4114	True Red	19-1664
Stone Green	17-0123	Turquoise	15-5519
Storm Blue	17-4716	Turtledove	12-5202
Storm Gray	15-4003	Ultramarine Green	18-5338
Stratosphere	14-4508	Ultramarine	17-4037
Strong Blue	18-4051	Vapor Blue	14-4203
Sunburst	13-1030	Vibrant Green	16-6339
Sunset Gold	13-0940	Vibrant Orange	16-1364
Sunshine	12-0727	Vivid Blue	17-4432
Tabasco	18-1536	Wedgwood	18-3935
Tarragon	15-0326	Wheat	13-1016
Teaberry	18-1756	Willow	16-0632
Teal	17-4919	Yellow Cream	12-0738
Terra Cotta	16-1526	Yolk Yellow	14-0846
Thistle	14-3907		

Notes

Chapter One

1. Barry Salt, *Film Style and Technology,* 2nd ed. (London: Starword, 1992), 78–79.

2. Gunning, "Colorful Metaphors: The Attraction of Color in Early Silent Cinema," *Fotogenia,* no. 1 (1994): 253.

3. Ibid., 250–251.

4. Roderick Ryan, *A History of Motion Picture Color Technology* (New York: Focal Press, 1977), 16–18.

5. Salt, *Film Style and Technology,* 78, 124, 150–151.

6. Ryan, *Motion Picture Color Technology,* 16–17, 19.

7. Salt, *Film Style and Technology,* 79–80; Ryan, *Motion Picture Color Technology,* 26–30.

8. Herbert Kalmus, *Mr. Technicolor* (Absecon, N.J.: MagicImage Filmbooks, 1993), 25.

9. Thompson, *Breaking the Glass Armor* (Princeton, N.J.: Princeton Univ. Press, 1988), 7–11.

10. Bordwell, "Story, Causality, and Motivation" in *The Classical Hollywood Cinema,* ed. David Bordwell, Janet Staiger, and Kristin Thompson, 19–23 (New York: Columbia Univ. Press, 1985). This overview of motivation draws on Bordwell's discussion of how the concept might be applied to classical Hollywood cinema. As he explains, genre is the most common type of transtextual motivation for this mode of cinema, and artistic motivation most often is limited to momentary displays of artfulness. For a discussion of motivation with regard to a broader range of film modes, see Thompson, *Glass Armor,* 15–21.

11. For an ideological criticism of color, see Edward Buscombe, "Sound and Color" in *Movies and Methods,* ed. Bill Nichols, 2:83–92 (Berkeley and Los Angeles: Univ. of California Press, 1985); Steven Neale, *Cinema and Technology* (Bloomington: Indiana Univ. Press, 1985); and Mary Beth Haralovich, "All that Heaven Allows: Color, Narrative, Space, and Melodrama," in *Close Readings,* ed. Peter Lehman (Tallahassee: Florida State Univ. Press, 1990).

12. For a definition of classical style, I draw on the influential volume by Bordwell, Staiger, and Thompson, *The Classical Hollywood Cinema: Film Style and Mode of Production to 1960.* During the studio era, the classical Hollywood style set the guidelines for the adoption and employment of color. This cinema tended to sustain a set of narratively oriented functions for film style, as well as a historically

bounded set of norms, but favored different devices, color among them, at different times.

13. Joseph Albers, *Interaction of Color,* rev. ed. (New Haven, Conn.: Yale Univ. Press, 1975), 1.

14. Rudolf Arnheim, foreword to Augusto Garau, *Color Harmonies,* trans. Nicola Bruno (Chicago: Univ. of Chicago Press, 1993), vii.

15. Charles A. Riley II, *Color Codes* (Hanover, N.H.: Univ. Press of New England, 1995), 1.

16. Albers, *Interaction of Color,* 1.

17. Rudolf Arnheim, *Art and Visual Perception* (Berkeley and Los Angeles: Univ. of California Press, 1974), 344.

18. John Gage, *Colour and Culture* (London: Thames and Hudson, 1993), 8.

19. Ibid., 27, 58. Gage explains that this set of assumptions about color persisted for early medieval spectators who identified as purple not a specific hue but "a thick quality of probably silk cloth, which might be of almost any colour, including white and green" (27).

20. For a detailed criticism of various attempts to restore *GWTW,* see Craig S. Cummings, "Tampering with Tara: The Desecration of *Gone with the Wind,*" *Big Reel* (January 1999): 122.

21. Richard May, interview with the author, Los Angeles, Calif., July 18, 1996; also quoted in Bill Desowitz, "*GWTW:* Is Brighter Better?" *Los Angeles Times,* June 7, 1998.

22. Robert A. Harris, interview with the author, Bedford Hills, N.Y., March 24, 2004.

23. Desowitz, "Frankly, My Dear, You're a Bit Blurry," *Los Angeles Times,* July 7, 1998.

24. Ibid.

25. Ibid.

26. Desowitz, "Is Brighter Better?"; Cummings, "Tampering with Tara," 122; Glenn Lovell, "Frankly, My Dear, This Is No Improvement," *Variety,* June 22–28, 1998, 51.

27. In ascertaining a general sense of Technicolor design, I have been aided by reference to the Tom Tarr collection of original 35 mm Technicolor frames held by the Margaret Herrick Library at the Academy of Motion Picture Arts and Sciences (Los Angeles). This extensive collection consists of slide-mounted frames that Technicolor maintained for reference purposes. The frames were especially useful in providing background information about films that have not survived.

28. David Bordwell and Kristin Thompson, *Film Art,* 5th ed. (New York: McGraw-Hill, 1997), 30–31. Other estimates suggest the difference is even greater. Mathias and Patterson propose that color negative film (as opposed to the positive print referred to by Bordwell and Thompson) would have the equivalent of 3,048 scan lines (Harry Mathias and Richard Patterson, *Electronic Cinematography* [Belmont, Calif.: Wadsworth, 1985], 57).

29. Paul Zelanski and Mary Pat Fisher, *Color,* 2nd ed. (Englewood Cliffs, N.J.: Prentice Hall, 1994), 79–80; Mathias and Patterson, *Electronic Cinematography,* 112–134.

30. This description assumes that red, blue, and green function as primaries in the video system. As we will see, these are not the same as the "painter's" or pigment primaries used in basic color theory.

31. Zelanski and Fisher offer a CIE (Commission Internationale d'Éclairage, or International Commission on Illumination) chromaticity diagram that compares the chromatic ranges of film and video. Whereas video can actually achieve more saturated blue than film, and near identical saturation in red, green falls far short. The greatest divergence between the two appears in the ranges of cyan, yellow, and magenta (*Color,* 80–81).

32. Leatrice Eiseman and Lawrence Herbert, *The Pantone Book of Color* (New York: Abrams, 1990).

33. This description is based on Warner Bros.' 1998 dye-transfer reissue.

34. This description refers to the MGM home entertainment DVD released in 1998.

35. C. L. Hardin, *Color for Philosophers* (Indianapolis: Hackett, 1988), 88; Zelanski and Fisher, *Color,* 86.

36. Hardin, *Color for Philosophers,* 89, 182–183.

37. Jules Davidoff, *Cognition through Color* (Cambridge, Mass.: MIT Press, 1991), 109.

38. Ibid., 126.

39. Ibid., 129.

40. Davidoff notes that, in the human visual system, categorizing bounded surfaces (shapes) takes precedence over categorizing surface color, and that shapes are more rapidly read than colors (*Cognition through Color,* 173).

41. Albert Munsell, *A Color Notation,* 6th ed. (Baltimore: Hoffman Brothers, 1926), 11.

42. Eiseman and Herbert, *Pantone Book of Color,* 7.

43. Publications include *The Pantone Professional Color System Selector* and *The Pantone Textile Color Selector.*

44. Zelanski and Fisher, *Color,* 80.

45. The value of this approach has been demonstrated by Edward Branigan in his analysis of Jean-Luc Godard's *Deux ou trois choses que je sais d'elle* (1966–1967). In "The Articulation of Color in a Filmic System" (*Wide Angle* 1, no. 3 [1976]: 20–31), one of the few thoroughgoing analyses of color in a single film, Branigan uses the language of color theory to explain the nature of Godard's choices.

46. Munsell, *Color Notation,* 18–31; Zelanski and Fisher, *Color,* 15–17. I will use the more common term "saturation" to describe the purity of a color.

47. Zelanski and Fisher offer a clear explanation of this phenomenon (*Color,* 16–17).

48. Johannes Itten, *The Art of Color* (New York: Van Nostrand Reinhold, 1973), 17.

49. Faber Birren presents a brief but complete discussion of color circles and their development in *Principles of Color* (Atglen, Pa.: Schiffer, 1969, 1987), 9–26. For a more detailed historical account, see Gage, *Colour and Culture,* especially 153–176.

50. For examples of filmmakers' reliance on the standard color wheel, see Natalie Kalmus, "Color Consciousness," *Journal of the Society of Motion Picture Engineers,* August 1935, 142–143, 147; Gilbert Betancourt, "Present Color Trend Is toward Subdued Hues," *American Cinematographer,* August 1937, 317.

51. In painting, this is not actually the case. Zelanski and Fisher point out that while photographic processes rely on yellow, cyan, magenta, black, and white to approximate most visible colors, in paint it is impossible to generate such a range from any three primaries (*Color,* 15).

52. As with the designation of primaries, the traditional color circle's distribution of complementaries does not strictly accord with the actual mixtures. In practice, blue and yellow, not blue and orange, yield a monochromatic gray. Gage notes that although observations from the eighteenth century onward suggested red and blue-green, or blue and yellow, as complementaries, the "by now canonical circular arrangement and the doctrine of secondary mixtures made green the almost universally accepted 'complementary' of red" (*Colour and Culture,* 172). The theory most often taken up by artists and color primers, thus, does not square with physical research.

53. Any number of authors can be consulted for a fuller account of these terms and concepts. Worthwhile discussions are found in Zelanski and Fisher, *Color,* 11–15; Birren, *Principles of Color,* 11–26, Itten, *Art of Color,* 34–37; and Arnheim, foreword to Garau, *Color Harmonies,* x–xii. There are a slew of explanations for the perception of a cool-warm or advancing-receding opposition between red-orange and blue-green. In addressing the issue, C. L. Hardin notes the following possibilities: red and yellow are associated with fire, whereas blue and green are associated with water; shortwave light (blue and green) focuses on the retina like light from a more distant object, but long waves (red and yellow) focus like light from a closer object; and the human eye is less sensitive to the reflective energy of blue than of yellow. Further, he notes that subjects viewing warm hues, after adapting to gray surrounds, show elevated vital signs. Subjects exposed to cool hues show lowered vital signs (*Color for Philosophers,* 131–133).

54. Birren, *Principles of Color,* 26–35. See also Gage, *Colour and Culture,* 172–174.

55. M.-E. Chevreul, *The Principles of Harmony and Contrast of Colours,* trans. Charles Martel, 2nd ed. (London: Longman, Brown, Green, and Longmans, 1855; New York: Garland, 1980), 11–18. See also explanations in Birren, *Principles of Color,* 26–35, and Zelanski and Fisher, *Color,* 51–52.

56. Chevreul, *Harmony and Contrast,* 62.

57. Zelanski and Fisher, *Color,* 92–103. I draw on Zelanski and Fisher because

they offer particularly clear and direct descriptions. However, nearly any basic color primer is bound to rehearse these concepts. For discussions that are more historically proximate to Technicolor production, see Walter Sargent, *The Enjoyment and Use of Color* (New York: Charles Scribner's Sons, 1923; New York: Dover, 1964), 191–193; Sterling McDonald, *Color Harmony* (Chicago: Wilcox and Follet, 1949), 46–59. McDonald's book is particularly interesting because he draws on these conventions of harmony to deal, almost exclusively, with problems of interior decoration.

58. Zelanski and Fisher, *Color,* 94.

59. Ibid.

60. Ibid., 103.

61. N. Kalmus, "Color Consciousness," 142.

62. Chevreul, *Harmony and Contrast,* 78.

63. Zelanski and Fisher, *Color,* 97.

64. Itten, *Art of Color,* 119.

65. Ibid., 22–23, 118–119.

66. Arnheim, *Art and Perception,* 359.

67. Ibid., 361. It should be noted that Arnheim sees this property of complementaries as a potential problem for composition. A complementary or triad scheme tends to be "so self-contained and self-sufficient" that it "subordinates only with difficulty into a larger color scheme" (361).

68. N. Kalmus, "Color Consciousness," 147.

69. For cogent criticisms of theories of harmony, see Albers, *Interaction of Color,* and Arnheim, *Art and Perception,* especially 346–350.

70. These case studies are supported by extensive background viewing. Of the thirty-six live-action three-strip features released from 1935 through the end of 1939, I have been able to study all but seven. The films I have not viewed are: *The Dancing Pirate* (1936), *Her Jungle Love* (1938), *Sixty Glorious Years* (1938), *Heart of the North* (1938), *Hollywood Cavalcade* (1939), *Over the Moon* (1939), and *Swanee River* (1939). I have also consulted prints of thirteen features released between 1940 and the end of 1942, and video versions of seventeen others from these years.

Chapter Two

1. For accessible yet detailed discussions of the earlier two-color processes, see H. Kalmus, *Mr. Technicolor,* 21–90; Richard Haines, *Technicolor Movies: The History of Dye Transfer Printing* (Jefferson, N.C.: McFarland, 1993), 1–17; Fred Basten, *Glorious Technicolor: The Movie's Magic Rainbow* (Cranbury, N.J.: A. S. Barnes, 1980), 19–46; and Ryan, *Motion Picture Color Technology,* 77–82. In addition to these sources, I am drawing on Joe Schmit's unpublished "History of the Technicolor Imbibition Process for Color Motion Pictures" (1991).

2. Haines, *Technicolor Movies,* 4–7.

3. Schmit, "Imbibition Process," 2; Haines, *Technicolor Movies,* 8–13.

4. H. Kalmus, *Mr. Technicolor,* 82.

5. Joseph Arthur Ball, "The Technicolor Process of Three-Color Cinematography," *Journal of the Society of Motion Picture Engineers,* August 1935, 127. Ball presented this paper at a meeting of the Technicians Branch of the Academy of Motion Picture Arts and Sciences, May 21, 1935. It also appears in the Academy Technician's Branch *Technical Bulletin,* May 31, 1935, 1–10.

6. H. Kalmus, *Mr. Technicolor,* 91.

7. For explanation of the three-color Technicolor camera, see William Stull, "Explanation of the Trichrome Technicolor," *American Cinematographer,* January 1935, 8–9, 12, 14; Ball, "Three-Color Cinematography," 127–138; and Basten, *Glorious Technicolor,* 199–204.

8. Schmit, "Imbibition Process," 5. This description is based primarily on Schmit, though equivalent discussions can be found in Haines, Ball, and Basten.

9. Ball, "Three-Color Cinematography," 132.

10. Schmit, "Imbibition Process," 6–7.

11. John F. Kienninger, "Track Printing, Blank Processing, and Transfer," *Educational Program of Lectures Given to Release, Rush, and Answer Print Viewers by Technicolor Motion Picture Corporation: Lecture Three,* February 1956, 4; located in the Technicolor Collection, Margaret Herrick Library, Academy of Motion Picture Arts and Sciences, Los Angeles, Calif. See also Schmit, "Imbibition Process," 7.

12. Kienninger, "Track Printing," 6; Schmit, "Imbibition Process," 7–8; Dr. Richard Goldberg, interview with the author, July 19, 1996.

13. According to Schmit, this order was encouraged because magenta, "being the most important record for resolution, was transferred last to prevent its diffusing during subsequent transfers" ("Imbibition Process," 7).

14. Haines suggests that the bipack records were not as sharp as the green record because they received reflected light, hence the gray ghost, printed from the green record, could offset this softness (*Technicolor Movies,* 24).

15. H. Kalmus, *Mr. Technicolor,* 94.

16. Haines, *Technicolor Movies,* 18–19.

17. H. Kalmus, *Mr. Technicolor,* 95.

18. *Fortune,* "What? Color in the Movies Again?" October 1934, 162, 164.

19. Ibid.; H. Kalmus, *Mr. Technicolor,* 96.

20. H. Kalmus, *Mr. Technicolor,* 96.

21. Ibid., 97.

22. *Fortune,* "Color in the Movies?" 164; *Time,* "Whitney Colors," May 27, 1935, 28. *Fortune* put the average cost of a short subject at $15,000.

23. *Fortune,* "Color in the Movies?" 164.

24. Robert Edmond Jones, "The Crisis of Color," *New York Times,* May 19, 1935.

25. Norris Houghton, "The Designer Sets the Stage," *Theatre Arts Monthly* 20, no. 12 (December 1936): 968.

26. Jones, "Crisis of Color."

27. Ibid.

28. Ibid.

29. Ibid.

30. Ibid.

31. Andrew Boone, "Pictures in Full Color Open New Era in Movies," *Popular Science* 126, no. 5 (May 1935), 14.

32. Ibid.

33. Ibid., 15.

34. Henri Coulon, "Color Control for Color Film," *American Cinematographer*, May 1934, 11.

35. Ibid., 11, 19.

36. Ibid., 11.

37. L. O. Huggins, "The Language of Color," *American Cinematographer*, July 1934, 108.

38. Ibid., 117.

39. Ibid., 118.

40. *Fortune*, "Color in the Movies?" 95, 96.

41. H. Kalmus, *Mr. Technicolor*, 83.

42. John Belton, "Color and Realism," (paper presented at the Society for Cinema Studies Conference, University of Southern California, 1992), 4.

43. Ibid., 3, 4.

44. Ibid., 4, 5.

45. Ibid., 6.

46. Ibid., 6, 8.

47. *Technicolor News and Views*, "Color Director's Work Important," May 1939, 3. Herbert Kalmus's second wife disputed Natalie's history. She suggested that although Herbert encouraged her to attend an art program in Zurich, "she never did enroll in that school—or any other of which there is a record." Instead, Eleanore suggests, Natalie depended on "informal study, absorbing what Europe had to offer" (H. Kalmus, *Mr. Technicolor*, 193).

48. N. Kalmus, "Color Consciousness," 147.

49. *Technicolor News and Views*, "Importance of Color Control Service Growing," February 1941, 1.

50. *Technicolor News and Views*, "Color Director's Work," 3; and "Importance of Color Control," 3. In addition to Padelford and Jaffa, *Technicolor News and Views* lists Robert Brower, William Fritzsche, and Richard Mueller as staff members. In 1939, Monroe W. Burbank appears on the list, but he is left out of the 1941 discussion. Similarly, the 1941 article introduces Henry Staudigl as staff member. It seems likely that most of these consultants were assigned short subjects or assisted Kalmus, Jaffa, and Padelford during this period. William Fritzsche and Robert Brower would both handle feature films in the mid to late 1940s.

51. N. Kalmus, "Color Consciousness," 145.

52. Richard Neupert, "Technicolor and Hollywood: Exercising Restraint," *Post Script*, Fall 1990, 23.

53. I refer to the *Journal of the Society of Motion Picture Engineers* version of "Color Consciousness," since it is the most accessible.

54. N. Kalmus, "Color Consciousness," 141.

55. Ibid., 140.

56. Ibid., 141, 142.

57. Neupert, "Technicolor and Hollywood," 26.

58. Ibid.

59. N. Kalmus, "Color Consciousness," 139, 140.

60. Ibid., 142.

61. Ibid., 142,43.

62. Ibid., 146.

63. Ibid., 143.

64. Ibid., 142.

65. Ibid.

66. Ibid., 146.

67. Ibid.

68. Ibid.

69. Ibid., 147.

70. Ibid.

71. Society of Motion Picture and Television Engineers, *Elements of Color in Professional Motion Pictures* (Los Angeles: SMPTE, 1957), 44. See also Adrian Cornwell-Clyne, *Colour Cinematography,* 3rd ed. (London: Chapman & Hall, 1951), 653–656.

Chapter Three

1. H. Kalmus, *Mr. Technicolor,* 99.

2. Ibid.; Richard Jewell, "RKO Film Grosses, 1929–1951: The C. F. Tevlin Ledger," *Historical Journal of Film, Radio, and Television* 14, no. 2 (1994): microfiche supplement.

3. This production history is available in a number of sources. For a concise and detailed discussion, see Anthony Slide, "The Return of *Becky Sharp,*" *Films in Review* (March 1985): 148–153.

4. Robert Gitt and Richard Dayton, "Restoring *Becky Sharp,*" *American Cinematographer,* November 1984, 101.

5. *Time,* "Whitney Colors," 34.

6. William Stull, "Will Color Help or Hinder?" *American Cinematographer,* March 1935, 100.

7. Ibid., 107.

8. Rouben Mamoulian, "Some Problems in Directing Color Pictures," *Journal of the Society of Motion Picture Engineers,* August 1935, 150. Mamoulian's essay is also included in the *Technical Bulletin* of the Academy Technicians Branch, May 1935, 18–21; in *International Photographer,* July 1935, 20–21; and in Richard Koszarski, *The*

Hollywood Directors, 1914–1940 (Oxford: Oxford Univ. Press, 1976), 288–293. A condensed version appeared as "Colour and Emotion" in *Cinema Quarterly,* Summer 1935, 225–226.

9. See Jones, "Crisis of Color," and Frank Nugent, "One More Word on Color," *New York Times,* May 19, 1935.

10. Slide, "Return of Becky Sharp," 151.

11. Stull, "Help or Hinder?" 107.

12. Ibid., 106.

13. Mamoulian, "Directing Color Pictures," 151.

14. Ibid., 150.

15. The earlier adaptations, all entitled *Vanity Fair,* included a 1911 Vitagraph production, a 1915 feature distributed by the Kleine-Edison Feature Service, a 1922 British production produced by H. B. Parkinson, and another in 1923, distributed by Goldwyn. The most recent, released in 1932 and featuring Myrna Loy in the role of Becky, had been produced by M. H. Hoffman and distributed by Allied Pictures.

16. David Robinson, "Painting the Leaves Black," *Sight and Sound* 30, no. 3 (Summer 1961): 126.

17. Mamoulian, "Directing Color Pictures," 151.

18. Gitt and Dayton, "Restoring *Becky Sharp,*" 100. My discussion of the reconstruction draws heavily on this thorough and detailed article. For a brief discussion of the Italian material, see "Lookin' Sharp," *American Film,* July–August 1985, 9. According to Gitt, a complete subtitled print was uncovered at the Netherlands Filmmuseum, but only after completion of the film restoration (Gitt, interview with the author, 2005).

19. Gitt and Dayton, "Restoring *Becky Sharp,*" 104.

20. Ibid.

21. The color change in reel four also noticeably affects the Imperial Blue accents on George's collar, which can be seen clearly at the end of reel three, during the silhouette scene. When reel four commences, these blue accents have shifted to deep black.

22. Gitt interview.

23. Rouben Mamoulian, "Colour and Light in Films," *Film Culture* 21 (Summer 1960): 74.

24. After an insert shot of a curtain blowing over a candelabrum, Mamoulian repeats the lighting change over a reverse angle of the dance floor. This time the effect is even more pronounced, as women with saturated blue, green, and red gowns catch the spotlighting.

25. Neupert, "Technicolor and Hollywood," 27.

26. Mamoulian, "Directing Color Pictures," 151.

27. Vincente Minnelli makes an even more striking use of this kind of reversal during the "Trolley Song" number in *Meet Me in St. Louis* (1944). In that case, however, the palette is extraordinarily dense and varied, and it forms a much

more consistent contrast with Esther's (Judy Garland's) predominately black outfit. Minnelli freely exploits the greater latitude offered by the musical to stretch the rules of emphasis that Kalmus recommended and Mamoulian echoed in his writing.

28. It remains one of *Becky Sharp*'s great peculiarities that the chromatic centerpiece should come so early in the film, leaving little room for further development. Indeed, Mamoulian seemed to recognize this when he declared that the scene was the climax toward which he developed the palette, and then remained silent about any other portion of the film. In fact, this is indicative of the film's terrible unevenness. It still seems astonishing that the same production could boast such intense attention to detail in the ball scene yet also contain what Anthony Slide called "surely the worst error in continuity ever perpetrated in the history of the cinema" ("*Becky Sharp,*" in *Magill's Cinema Annual 1982*, ed. Frank Magill [Englewood Cliffs, N.J.: Salem, 1982], 406). In the final reel, Becky's second-story apartment prominently features people passing by her window.

29. *Hollywood Reporter,* review of *Becky Sharp,* June 14, 1935, 3.

30. *Variety Film Reviews,* review of *Becky Sharp,* June 19, 1935. Note: The *Variety* reviews I cite are those collected in *Variety Film Reviews,* volumes 2–5 (New York: Garland, 1983). The collected reviews are organized chronologically by their original date of publication. Hereafter, references to *Variety* reviews will note the source as *Variety Film Reviews* and give the original date of publication.

31. Ibid.

32. J.C.M. [John Chapin Mosher], The Current Cinema (review of *Becky Sharp*), *New Yorker,* June 22, 1935, 53.

33. Ibid.

34. Don Herold, review of *Becky Sharp, Life,* August 1935, 43, 45.

35. Andre Sennwald, review of *Becky Sharp, New York Times,* June 14, 1935.

36. Ibid.

37. *Variety,* "Color Has Producers on the Fence; Paint Brush Boys Future Big Shots?" June 19, 1935, 1, 67.

38. Karl Hale, "Learn About Shooting Color from *Becky Sharp,*" *American Cinematographer,* July 1935, 312.

39. Herold, review of *Becky Sharp,* 45.

40. J.C.M., review of *Becky Sharp,* 53.

41. Sennwald, review of *Becky Sharp.*

Chapter Four

1. Denis Morrison, "Color at the Crossroads," *Variety,* June 2, 1937, 5.

2. H. Kalmus, *Mr. Technicolor,* 105.

3. Ibid.

4. *Variety,* "Color's Future Depends on Costs," July 13, 1935, 5.

5. H. Kalmus, *Mr. Technicolor,* 110.

6. *Variety,* "Writers Turned Loose on *Goldwyn's Follies,*" June 2, 1937, 5. More recent scholarship suggests that Technicolor cost an average of around 30 percent more than black-and-white during the mid-1930s. See Gorham Kindem, "Hollywood's Conversion to Color," in *The American Movie Industry* (Carbondale: Southern Illinois Univ. Press, 1982), 153; Basten, *Glorious Technicolor,* 61.

7. *Hollywood Reporter,* "Exhibitor Poll Results, the 12 Best Money Pictures of 1937," December 31, 1937, 33; *Variety,* "U.S. Evaluations of Box Office Picture, 1937's Top Pix Grossers," January 5, 1938, 1.

8. Arthur Ungar, "Analysis of Top Films and Stars," *Variety,* January 4, 1939, 5.

9. *Hollywood Reporter,* "Box Office Winners for 1939," December 30, 1939, sec. 2, 10.

10. For a discussion of prestige pictures as a production trend in the 1930s, see Tino Balio, "Production Trends," in *Grand Design: Hollywood as a Modern Business Enterprise, 1930–1939,* ed. Tino Balio, 179–211 (New York: Scribner's, 1993; Berkeley and Los Angeles: Univ. of California Press, 1995).

11. Richard Neupert also refers to "color restraint" when discussing Technicolor style. However, his use of the term refers to a basic set of rules that broadly informed all Technicolor color design from the 1930s through the 1950s. In my argument, the restrained mode refers to a more specific style that coexisted with other methods for treating color. The restrained mode was dominant between 1936 and 1939, but thereafter existed as one style among several. See Neupert, "Technicolor and Hollywood," 21–29.

12. *American Cinematographer,* "Why All This Hubbub regarding Color," August 1936, 327.

13. Ibid.

14. *American Cinematographer,* "Just What Is So Mysterious about Color?" October 1936, 414.

15. "Hubbub regarding Color," 327.

16. "Mysterious Color?" 424.

17. Ibid., 425.

18. "Hubbub regarding Color," 327, 334, 335.

19. "Mysterious Color?" 426.

20. The nature of this conflict seems to replay the tension between studio personnel and sound engineers during the late 1920s and early 1930s. See James Lastra, "Standards and Practices: Aesthetic Norm and Technological Innovation in the American Cinema," in *The Studio System,* ed. Janet Staiger (New Brunswick, N.J.: Rutgers Univ. Press, 1995), 215, 219, 222.

21. Dr. Richard Goldberg, interview with the author, September 1996.

22. Cornwell-Clyne, *Colour Cinematography,* 132.

23. Goldberg interview, September 1996. See also Cornwell-Clyne, *Colour Cinematography,* 132, which suggests that Technicolor's effective speed before 1940 was Weston 3, approximately equivalent to 4 ASA.

24. Salt, *Film Style and Technology,* 195–196.

25. *Journal of the Society of Motion Picture Engineers,* "Report of the Studio Lighting Committee," January 1937, 39. See also Salt, *Film Style and Technology,* 196.

26. In the 1930s the industry considered a temperature of approximately 6,500° Kelvin (11,240° Fahrenheit) as standard for daylight. See *Journal of the Society of Motion Picture Engineers,* "Glossary of Color Photography," May 1935, 437. The actual color temperature of sunlight can vary somewhat. For example, Cornwell-Clyne indicates that a uniform overcast sky has a temperature of about 6,500–7,000°K (11,240–12,140°F), but late afternoon sun (around 4:30) dips to about 4,700°K, or 8,000°F (*Colour Cinematography,* 86). Contemporary color emulsions that are balanced for daylight usually respond to a temperature of 5,600°K (9,620°F). See Kris Malkiewicz, *Cinematography,* 2nd ed. (New York: Prentice Hall, 1989), 66.

27. Winton Hoch, "Cinematography in 1942," *Journal of the Society of Motion Picture Engineers,* October 1942, 99. Ernest Palmer notes simply that the use of interchangeable filter units or special film stocks balanced for interior and exterior use was "not considered practical with the three color system," leading to the reliance on arc lighting ("The Inkie's Place in Technicolor Lighting," *American Cinematographer,* July 1941, 323).

28. David Bordwell, "Technicolor," in *Classical Hollywood Cinema,* ed. Bordwell, Staiger, and Thompson, 354.

29. W. Howard Greene, "Low Key Lighting May Be as Easy in Color as It Is in Monochrome," *American Cinematographer,* April 1938, 146.

30. William Skall, "Artificial Sunlight Simplifies Technicolor Exteriors," *International Photographer,* October 1936, 14.

31. Ibid., 16; Peter Mole, "Arc Lights for Color," *International Photographer,* October 1935, 23.

32. C. W. Handley, "The Advanced Technic of Technicolor Lighting," *Journal of the Society of Motion Picture Engineers,* August 1937, 169.

33. These figures are based on a presumed 42 percent reduction. As noted earlier, monochrome sets averaged 250–400 foot-candles.

34. Handley, "Advanced Technic," 177.

35. Mole, "Lighting Equipment for Natural-Color Photography," *International Photographer,* June 1936, 16; William Skall "Simplifying Color Lighting," *International Photographer,* March 1936, 12; William H. Greene, "Creating Lighting Effects in Technicolor," *International Photographer,* January 1937, 11; James Wong Howe, "Reaction on Making His First Color Production," *American Cinematographer,* October 1937, 411.

36. Greene, "Creating Lighting Effects," 10, 11.

37. John Huntley, *British Technicolor* (London: Skelton-Robinson, 1948), 55. Also cited in Duncan Petrie, *The British Cinematographer* (London: British Film Institute, 1996), 43.

38. Ray Rennahan, quoted in *American Cinematographer,* "Faster Color Film," August 1939, 356.

39. Broadside refers to the side arcs, which provided general illumination, and in this case might also cover the overhead scoops.

40. *American Cinematographer,* "Faster Color Film," 356.

41. Salt, *Film Style and Technology,* 197. For a detailed discussion of the use of exposure readings in Technicolor cinematography, see Ralph A. Woolsey, "Lighting and Exposure Control in Color Cinematography," *Journal of the Society of Motion Picture Engineers,* June 1947, 548–553. Technicolor's light meters were calibrated in hundreds of foot-candles.

42. C. W. Handley, "History of Motion-Picture Studio Lighting," in *A Technological History of Motion Pictures,* ed. Raymond Fielding (Berkeley and Los Angeles: Univ. of California Press, 1967), 123.

43. William Stull, "Technicolor Bringing New Charm to Screen," *American Cinematographer,* June 1937, 236.

44. Greene, "Creating Lighting Effects," 11.

45. Howe, "His First Color Production," 411.

46. Mole, "Natural-Color Photography," 17.

47. Ibid.

48. Howe, "His First Color Production," 409.

49. Ray Rennahan, "Natural Color Cinematography Today," *American Cinematographer,* July 1935, 288.

50. Skall, "Simplifying Color Lighting," 20.

51. Stull, "Technicolor Bringing New Charm," 236.

52. Greene, "Creating Lighting Effects," 25.

53. Rennahan, quoted in Stull, "Technicolor Bringing New Charm," 236.

54. Russell Conant, "Basic Principles of Color Separation," *Educational Program of Lectures Given to Control Department Film Technicians by Technicolor Motion Picture Corporation: Lecture Five,* September 1955, 17, 18; Technicolor Collection, Herrick Library, Los Angeles.

55. Nancy Smith, "The New Max Factor Technicolor Make-Up" *International Photographer,* June 1936, 10.

56. *International Photographer,* "Color Make-Up: New Factor Development Solves Color Problem," June 1937, 27.

57. Max Factor, "Make-Up for the New Technicolor Process: An Interview with Max Factor," *American Cinematographer,* August 1936, 331. Not surprisingly, the terms "skin tone" and "flesh tone" referred to Caucasian coloration. Factor noted, "Special make-ups for racial groups are also being made," adding, "Make-ups have already been devised for South Sea Islanders, Eskimos, Negroes, Orientals, and other types" (334). In general, discussion of the quality of skin tone reproduced by the Technicolor process is limited to white performers.

58. Ibid., 334.

59. Ibid.

60. Ibid., 331.

61. Ibid., 331, 334.

62. Haines, *Technicolor Movies,* 35.

63. Stull, "Trichrome Technicolor," 9; Goldberg interview, September 1996.

64. Goldberg interview, July 1996; Schmit, "Imbibition Process," 5.

65. Goldberg interview, July 1996; Richard May, interview with the author, July 18, 1996.

66. Schmit, "Imbibition Process," 4; Cornwell-Clyne, *Colour Cinematography,* 465.

67. Goldberg interview, July 1996; Schmit, "Imbibition Process," 4.

68. *Variety Film Reviews,* review of *Ramona,* October 14, 1936.

69. Betancourt, "Present Color Trend," 317. More recent research suggests that this is a wholly inaccurate view of color history. In fact, early peoples had limited palettes based on earth tones. For a discussion, see Zelanski and Fisher, *Color,* 115–118.

70. Betancourt, "Present Color Trend," 352.

71. Ibid.

72. Howe, "His First Color Production," 409.

73. Ibid., 408.

74. Ibid.

75. Greene, "Creating Lighting Effects," 25.

76. Ibid.

77. Herbert Aller, "Color Marches On," *International Photographer,* May 1936, 17.

78. Fox's novel (1908) was adapted for the stage in 1912 by Eugene Walter. It was adapted for film by the Broadway Picture Producing Co. in 1914, in a production starring Dixie Compton; it was filmed again, in 1916, by the Jesse L. Lasky Feature Play Co., in a production directed by Cecil B. DeMille and starring Charlotte Walker; and it was also filmed in 1923, by Famous Players–Lasky, in a production directed by Charles Maigne and starring Mary Miles Minter (Patricia King Hanson, ed., *American Film Institute Catalog of Motion Pictures Produced in the United States,* volume F3, *Feature Films, 1931–1940,* 2251–2252 [Berkeley and Los Angeles: Univ. of California Press, 1993]).

79. *Variety,* "Picture Grosses," March 18, 1936, 6, 8, 9, 13.

80. *Variety,* "Wanger's First for UA All Set," July 15, 1936, 5.

81. Terry Ramsaye, ed. *International Motion Picture Almanac, 1937* (New York: Quigley, 1937), 942–943.

82. *Variety Film Reviews,* review of *The Trail of the Lonesome Pine,* February 26, 1936.

83. *American Cinematographer,* "Is All This Color Ballyhoo Justified?" August 1936, 373.

84. *Variety,* advertisement for *The Trail of the Lonesome Pine,* February 26, 1936, 14.

85. John Fox Jr., *The Trail of the Lonesome Pine* (New York: Charles Scribner's Sons, 1908), 7.

86. The hue of this costume shifts from scene to scene. In the second segment, an exterior scene, the dress appears to be flat black. However, in some interiors and close-ups, especially in segment twenty-four, set in Jack's Gap Town office, the outfit takes on a deep blue cast. I suspect that the dye in the costume (or costumes) was a composite black, which is rendered bluish under the slightly higher-temperature arc lights, but appears black in true sunlight. In either case, the dress remains an unobtrusive hue.

87. Raymond Palmer, "Technicolor on the Way to Its Greatest Triumph in *Trail of the Lonesome Pine*," *International Photographer*, January 1936, 20.

88. Because of the scarcity of prints, I have been unable to obtain frame enlargements for *Lonesome Pine*.

89. See, for example, my discussion of *GWTW* in Chapter 7.

90. *Variety*, "Picture Grosses," 8.

91. R. Palmer, "Greatest Triumph," 20.

Chapter Five

1. H. Kalmus, *Mr. Technicolor*, 122–123. Selznick International produced five features to honor the original Pioneer contract: *The Garden of Allah* (1936), *A Star Is Born* (1937), *Nothing Sacred* (1937), *The Adventures of Tom Sawyer* (1938), and *Gone with the Wind* (1939), which was counted as two features.

2. Ronald Haver, *David O. Selznick's Hollywood* (New York: Knopf, 1980), 206.

3. Tino Balio, "Production Trends" in *Grand Design*, ed. Balio, 207.

4. *Variety*, advertisement for *A Star Is Born*, May 12, 1937, 14.

5. Lansing C. Holden to David O. Selznick, "*A Star Is Born*—Color", November 2, 1936. Selznick Administrative: Production Files, 1936–1941, *A Star Is Born*—Color, 225.19. David O. Selznick Collection, Harry Ransom Humanities Research Center, University of Texas at Austin (this collection of documents is hereinafter referred to as Selznick Production Files, *A Star Is Born*).

6. David O. Selznick to Hal Kern, January 30, 1937; John Hay Whitney to David O. Selznick, January 28, 1937. Selznick Production Files, *A Star Is Born.*

7. Salt, *Film Style and Technology*, 199.

8. Haver suggests that Holden's position was created because Selznick International's heavy schedule of color production required "someone on the premises at all times to work out the kinks and rough spots in the color scripts and schemes" (*Selznick's Hollywood*, 196). If so, the position does not seem to have lasted, since Holden is not credited with color-design work on any other Selznick film.

9. Whitney to Selznick, January 28, 1937. Selznick Production Files, *A Star Is Born.*

10. Lansing C. Holden, "Designing for Color," in *We Make the Movies*, ed. Nancy Naumburg (New York: Norton, 1937), 239.

11. Ibid.

12. Ibid., 240–241.

13. Ibid., 243.

14. Haver, *Selznick's Hollywood,* 198.

15. Holden, "Designing for Color," 242, 243.

16. *Variety Film Reviews,* review of *A Star Is Born,* April 28, 1937.

17. Lansing C. Holden to David O. Selznick, November 2, 1936. Selznick Production Files, *A Star Is Born.*

18. Holden, "Designing for Color," 243.

19. Mattie delivers the line "House all covered up with movie magazines, and the other day I caught her talking to a horse with a Swedish accent" just after Esther reaches for the magazine and begins reading.

20. According to Haver, this effect is actually a glass painting by Jack Cosgrove.

21. The final sequence, in which Esther attends her latest premiere at Grauman's, affirming her commitment to Hollywood, features red-orange spotlights as well as the name "Vicki Lester" spelled out in yellow lights. Perhaps here the motif reaches closure, riding alongside the repetition of Grauman's, the site Esther first visited upon arriving in Hollywood.

22. The film garnered a total domestic gross of $1,355,713 (Series 6C: Played and Earned Figures, 1919–1950; United Artists Corporation Collection, Wisconsin Center for Film and Theater Research, State Historical Society, Madison). Despite the box-office success, the film cost $1,800,000 and lost $727,500, "the most Sam Goldwyn had ever lost on a single picture" (A. Scott Berg, *Goldwyn* [New York: Knopf, 1989], 305).

23. *Variety Film Reviews,* review of *Goldwyn Follies,* February 2, 1938.

24. Marion Squire, "The Girl's Eye View," *Variety,* February 23, 1938, 6.

25. Because of the scarcity of prints, I have been unable to obtain frame enlargements of *Goldwyn Follies.*

26. The opening number of *Louisiana Purchase* (1941) offers an example.

27. Robert Edmond Jones, "The Problem of Color," in *The Emergence of Film Art,* ed. Lewis Jacobs (New York: Hopkinson and Blake, 1969), 206.

28. Ibid., 209.

29. Richard Neupert also notes this example in his discussion of color's relationship to narrative in Technicolor ("Technicolor and Hollywood," 27).

Chapter Six

1. *Variety Film Reviews,* review of *God's Country and the Woman,* January 13, 1937.

2. *Variety Film Reviews,* review of *Gold Is Where You Find It,* February 16, 1938.

3. Rudy Behlmer, "From Legend to Film," introduction to *The Adventures of Robin Hood,* Wisconsin/Warner Bros. Screenplay Series (Madison: Univ. of Wisconsin Press, 1979), 33.

4. Ungar, "Top Films and Stars," 10.

5. Ibid., 10, 11.

6. Behlmer, "From Legend to Film," 20.

7. Lincoln green is not a Pantone color, but is the hue specified by the shooting script for the costumes of Robin and his men. The hue appears to fall somewhere between Pantone's Parrot Green and Peridot.

8. *Film Daily,* advertisement for *The Adventures of Robin Hood,* April 26, 1938, 5; ellipses in the original.

9. See, for instance, Garau, *Color Harmonies,* 2–5. Johannes Itten succinctly described the odd nature of complementaries: "They are opposite, they require each other. They incite each other to maximum vividness when adjacent; and they annihilate each other, to gray-black, when mixed—like fire and water" (*Art of Color,* 78).

10. A magnificent exercise in balancing complementaries is offered in segment twenty-three when King Richard, in disguise, meets the bishop. Complementary costumes of yellow and lavender assure that king and bishop are the most visually conspicuous characters, and it communicates the tension between them.

11. Behlmer, *Adventures of Robin Hood,* 214–215.

12. Jean-Loup Bourget suggests that a general distinction between the aristocrats and the common people is carried by the textures of the costumes they wear. He notes that the peasants wear matte colors, whereas the rich are adorned in brilliant silks and satins. This seems accurate to a degree; however, it is also clear that particular hues are not consistently associated with a single class of characters. See Bourget, "Esthétiques du Technicolor," in *La Couleur en Cinéma,* ed. Jacques Aumont (Paris: Cinématheque français, 1995), 113.

13. Neupert, "Technicolor and Hollywood," 25–26.

14. Ibid., 25.

15. Ibid.

16. Ibid.; N. Kalmus, "Color Consciousness," 143.

17. Neupert, "Technicolor and Hollywood," 26.

18. Behlmer, *Adventures of Robin Hood,* 60.

19. Ibid., 95.

20. Neupert also notes this as an example of the red motif.

21. Behlmer, *Adventures of Robin Hood,* 68.

22. Itten, *Art of Color,* 22.

23. A dolly in to medium close-up eliminates the detail when Robin begins to explain his plans ("I'll organize a revolt, exact a death for a death").

24. Interestingly, the effect is lessened after Robin's arrival; background illumination on the curtain is reduced, giving it a more ordinary brown look. The difference may well result from a simple lapse in continuity, but the change illustrates the importance of lighting to color balance and registration.

25. Meyer Levin, "The Candid Cameraman," review of *The Adventures of Robin Hood, Esquire,* August 1938, 82.

26. N. Kalmus, "Color Consciousness," 142.

27. *Hollywood Reporter,* "*Robin Hood* Boxoffice Natural," April 26, 1938, 43.

28. Frank Nugent, review of *The Adventures of Robin Hood, New York Times,* May 13, 1938.

Chapter Seven

1. *Technicolor News and Views,* "Technicolor Expansion Program in Operation," April 1939, 1, 3; Basten, *Glorious Technicolor,* 90.

2. H. Kalmus, *Mr. Technicolor,* 118.

3. *Technicolor News and Views,* "Three Technicolor Pictures Lead Exhibitor Poll," January 1940, 1.

4. *Technicolor News and Views,* "Audiences Becoming 'Black and White Conscious,'" January 1940, 1.

5. Frank Nugent, review of *Gone with the Wind, New York Times,* December 20, 1939.

6. *Technicolor News and Views,* "Special Award Bestowed for Color Process," March 1940, 1, 3.

7. Aljean Harmetz, *On the Road to Tara: The Making of "Gone with the Wind"* (New York: Abrams, 1996), 16; Haver, *Selznick's Hollywood,* 299. Harmetz reports the cost as a flat four million dollars; Haver offers the more specific figure of $4,085,790.

8. H. Kalmus, *Mr. Technicolor,* 122.

9. H. Ginsberg to David O. Selznick, June 26, 1939. Selznick Administrative: Production Files, 1936–1942, *Gone with the Wind*—Technicolor, 192.5. David O. Selznick Collection, Harry Ransom Humanities Research Center, University of Texas at Austin (hereinafter, Selznick Production Files, *GWTW*—Technicolor). Harmetz, *Road to Tara,* 101.

10. Haver, *Selznick's Hollywood,* 309.

11. Alan David Vertrees, *Selznick's Vision: "Gone with the Wind" and Hollywood Filmmaking* (Austin: Univ. of Texas Press, 1997), 182.

12. David O. Selznick to William Cameron Menzies, cc. Ginsberg, Cukor, Garmes, and Klune, January 28, 1939. Selznick Production Files, *GWTW*—Technicolor.

13. David O. Selznick to R. A. Klune, cc. Mr. Fleming, March 13, 1939. Selznick Production Files, *GWTW*—Technicolor.

14. For thorough discussions of the film's production, see Haver, *Selznick's Hollywood,* 236–311; Harmetz, *Road to Tara;* and Vertrees, *Selznick's Vision.*

15. W. G. C. Bosco, "Aces of the Camera: Winton Hoch, A.S.C.," *American Cinematographer,* January 1947, 13.

16. Vertrees, *Selznick's Vision,* 203. Here Vertrees relies on interviews that Ray Rennahan and Ray Klune gave to Gavin Lambert for his book *GWTW: The Making of "Gone with the Wind"* (Boston: Little, Brown, 1973). Vertrees's commitment to these figures gives them some additional authority, since he had recourse to an annotated shooting script that listed the director for each shot.

. For a discussion of color design in *Pleasantville* and *O Brother,* see Scott ns, "A New Color Consciousness: Color in the Digital Age," *Convergence* 9, (Winter 2003): 60–76.

David E. Williams, "Firepower in Post," *American Cinematographer* 83, no. 2 ary 2002): 50.

"The Future of Filmmaking: The Future as Seen by Cinematographers," *an Cinematographer* 81, no. 9 (September 2000): 82.

John Pavlus, "No Holds Barred," *American Cinematographer* 83, no. 11 (No- r 2002): 45; Christopher Probst, "New Products and Services: A Digital tion," *American Cinematographer* 81, no. 9 (September 2000): 151.

ean Oppenheimer, "Toying with Visuals in Post," *American Cinematogra-* no. 9 (September 2000): 56.

)ebra Kaufman and Ray Zone, "A Legacy of Invention: Cinematographers ng the Growing Possibilities of Postproduction Are Continuing a Time- d Tradition," *American Cinematographer* 83, no. 5 (May 2002): 73.

ob Fisher, "Black-and-White in Color: The Comedic Fantasy *Pleasantville* a Unique Opportunity for the Digital and Photochemical Production o Momentarily Merge," *American Cinematographer* 79, no. 11 (November)–62, 64–67.

ephanie Argy, "Cinematographer's Computer Age: Cinematographers al Effects Experts Assess the Impact of Digital Technology on the Creative *American Cinematographer* 80, no. 8 (August 1999): 76.

b Fisher, "Escaping from Chains," *American Cinematographer* 81, no. 10 2000): 36–40, 42, 44–49.

erican Cinematographer, "Future of Filmmaking," 79.

her, "Escaping from Chains."

n Pavlus, "High Life," *American Cinematographer* 86, no. 1 (January 48.

detailed discussions of the digital color processes used in *The Aviator,* l Goldman, "Scorsese's Color Homage," *Millimeter,* January 2005, 14–18, 26; and Pavlus, "High Life."

dman, "Color Homage," 22; Pavlus, "High Life," 50.

lman, "Color Homage," 26.

., 14.

Legato, interview with the author, February 15, 2006.

us, "High Life," 50.

o interview.

d Bordwell, "Intensified Continuity: Visual Style in Contemporary lm," *Film Quarterly* 55, no. 3 (2002): 16–28.

urse, unlike Technicolor, digital grading is not the product of a single and so no progression of color design can be neatly attributed to a omotional effort. Rather, it seems likely that the market pressures as-

17. Vertrees, *Selznick's Vision,* ix.

18. *Technicolor News and Views,* "New High Speed Film Is Now in Use," April 1939, 2. Though *GWTW* was reportedly the first film to go into production using the new stock, it was probably not the first to be released. Both *The Private Lives of Elizabeth and Essex* and *Drums along the Mohawk* were produced with the new stock in 1939, and they were released in October and November, respectively, of that year. In nearly all publicity and commentary, however, *GWTW* was touted as the first feature to use the newly improved system. See *Technicolor News and Views,* "New Negative Is Predicted" November 1939, 2.

19. David O. Selznick to Henry Ginsberg, November 7, 1938. Selznick Production Files, *GWTW*—Technicolor.

20. Cornwell-Clyne, *Colour Cinematography,* 133.

21. Goldberg interview, September 1996.

22. *American Cinematographer,* "Faster Film," 355.

23. Handley, "Advanced Technic," 177; *American Cinematographer,* "Faster Film," 355.

24. Basten, *Glorious Technicolor,* 98. The author estimates lighting costs for *Oz* to be $226,307 and notes that this was "nearly $100,000 more than for *GWTW.*" However, he provides no citation for this figure.

25. Leigh Allen, "New Technicolor System Tested by Directors of Photography," *American Cinematographer,* December 1950, 414.

26. Salt, *Film Style and Technology,* 196.

27. Joe Valentine, "Lighting for Technicolor as Compared with Black and White," *International Photographer,* January 1948, 7.

28. Cornwell-Clyne, *Colour Cinematography,* 132; Goldberg interview, September 1996. Conversions of the Weston scale to ASA are based on the conversion table in Arthur C. Miller and Walter Strenge, eds., *American Cinematographer Manual,* 3rd ed. (Hollywood: ASC Holding Corp., 1964), 244.

29. Salt, *Film Style and Technology,* 195.

30. *American Cinematographer,* "Faster Film," 356.

31. R. G. Linderman, C. W. Handley, and A. Rogers, "Illumination in Motion Picture Production," *Journal of the Society of Motion Picture Engineers,* June 1943, 336.

32. Allen, "New Technicolor System," 424.

33. *American Cinematographer,* "Faster Film," 355.

34. Mary Corliss and Carlos Clarens, "Designed for Film: The Hollywood Art Director," *Film Comment,* May–June 1978, 56.

35. David O. Selznick to Henry Ginsberg, February 28, 1938. Selznick Production Files, *GWTW*—Technicolor.

36. Corliss and Clarens, "Designed for Film," 356.

37. Ibid.

38. Clarence Slifer, "Creating Visual Effects for *G.W.T.W.,*" *American Cinematographer,* August 1982, 789, 835.

39. Ibid., 836.

40. Ibid.

41. Selznick to Klune, March 13, 1939. Selznick Production Files, *GWTW*—Technicolor.

42. In a memo to Menzies, Selznick urged his production designer to see *Snow White* particularly for "the last shot of Snow White and her prince riding off." In the film, they are silhouetted against a strong sunset. From David O. Selznick to W. C. Menzies, May 12, 1939. Selznick Administrative: Production Files, 1936–1942, *Gone with the Wind*—Art Department (Memos to William Cameron Menzies &# [*sic*]), 177.9. David O. Selznick Collection, Harry Ransom Humanities Research Center, University of Texas at Austin (hereinafter, Selznick Production Files, *GWTW*—Art).

43. William Cameron Menzies, "Notes on Color in *Gone with the Wind*." Selznick Administrative: Production Files, 1936–1942, *Gone with the Wind*—Menzies, William Cameron, BK359, 185.8. David O. Selznick Collection, Harry Ransom Humanities Research Center, University of Texas at Austin (hereinafter, Selznick Production Files, *GWTW*—Menzies).

44. David O. Selznick to Mr. Ginsberg and Mr. Butcher, cc. Mr. O'Shea, October 18, 1938. Selznick Administrative: Production Files, 1936–1942, *Gone with the Wind*—Cameramen, 177.15. David O. Selznick Collection, Harry Ransom Humanities Research Center, University of Texas at Austin (hereinafter, Selznick Production Files, *GWTW*—Cameramen).

45. Menzies, "Notes on Color." Selznick Production Files, *GWTW*—Menzies.

46. Ray Klune complained to Selznick that Fleming wasted an hour and a half rearranging the furniture in Bonnie's room for this shot after rethinking the setup he had approved the night before. Ray Klune to David O. Selznick, June 4, 1939. Selznick Production Files, *GWTW*—Art.

47. David O. Selznick to Ray Klune, June 7, 1939; David O. Selznick to Victor Fleming, March 20, 1939. Selznick Production Files, *GWTW*—Cameramen.

48. Menzies, "Notes on Color." Selznick Production Files, *GWTW*—Menzies.

49. Ibid.

50. Cynthia Molt, *"Gone with the Wind" on Film* (Jefferson, N.C.: McFarland, 1990), 275.

51. For a discussion of the film's stylistic consistency, see Vertrees, *Selznick's Vision*, 53–115. Vertrees convincingly argues that Menzies's designs were but one element that Selznick used to control and shape the film to his conception. Very few of Menzies's storyboards were adopted unaltered into the final production.

52. *Technicolor News and Views*, "New Negative," 2. The article quotes Herbert Kalmus's remarks to the Society of Motion Picture Engineers in October 1939. In describing the new Technicolor stock, Kalmus reported that, in addition to *GWTW*, *The Private Lives of Elizabeth and Essex*, *Drums along the Mohawk*, *Northwest Passage*, *Swanee River*, and *Typhoon* had all used the improved stock.

53. *American Cinematographer*, "Faster Film," 356.

54. Haver, *Selznick's Hollywood*, 296.

55. Cummings, "Tampering with Tara," 122.

56. Glenn Lovell, "Frankly, My Dear, This Is No Imp
1998, 51. Lovell's description is inaccurate: Scarlett is
dress, and it is her straw hat that, by virtue of its high
track her progress as the camera pulls back.

57. For example, though faster monochrome film
opment of deep focus, David Bordwell points out tha
the 1930s retained a soft style while reducing illumina
Focus Cinematography" in *Classical Hollywood Cinem*

58. Rudy Behlmer, ed., *Memo from David O. Selzni*
190.

59. *Time*, "Guide to Cinema, G with the W," Dec

60. *Technicolor News and Views*, "'Black and Whi

Chapter Eight

1. Lea Jacobs, "Belasco, DeMille, and the Dev
Film History 5, no. 4 (December 1993): 416.

2. Fourteen full-color live-action Technicolor
fifteen in 1941, and thirteen in 1942. From 1943 o
production each year. Twenty-two features were
1944, thirty in 1946, thirty-two in 1947, and forty-
this project, I considered features before 1943. I
here continued through the 1940s, but I have no
the period.

3. *American Cinematography*, "Photography o
Book, May 1942, 208; review of *Chad Hanna*, Jan

4. Ibid., review of *That Night in Rio*, April 19

5. Ibid., review of *Louisiana Purchase*, Janua

6. Ibid., review of *Aloma of the South Seas*,

7. Ibid., review of *Blossoms in the Dust*, July
South Seas.

8. Ibid., review of *Blood and Sand*, June 194

9. Ibid., review of *Billy the Kid*, June 1941,

10. Ibid., review of *The Jungle Book*.

11. Ibid., review of *Louisiana Purchase*.

12. For a close analysis of Technicolor de
Scott Higgins, "Color at the Center: Minnelli'
Louis," *Style*, Fall 1998, 449–470.

13. Debra Kaufman, "The Post Process: C
Cinematographer 83, no. 3 (March 2002): 14.

sociated with Hollywood filmmaking, in particular the need to test and integrate color technologies, encourage this aesthetic renewal.

35. Shklovsky, Victor, "Art as Technique," in *Russian Formalist Criticism,* ed. and trans. by Lee Lemon and Marion Reis (Lincoln: Univ. of Nebraska Press, 1965), 13.

36. For a discussion of the institutional pressures that led to the wide adoption of color, see Brad Chisholm, "Red, Blue, and Lots of Green: The Impact of Color Television on Feature Film Production," in *Hollywood in the Age of Television,* ed. Tino Balio, 213–234 (Boston: Unwin Hyman, 1990).

Appendix One

1. Schmit, "Imbibition Process," 4–6. Schmit discusses, without reference to particular dates, Technicolor's continual efforts to improve the process by simplifying dye components, controlling the contrast characteristics of the matrix stock, and increasing the effectiveness with which dye was held to the release stock. A more detailed discussion of the process is offered at the start of Chapter 2.

2. Schmit, "Imbibition Process," 7; Haines, *Technicolor Movies,* 24; Cornwell-Clyne, *Colour Cinematography,* 465; May to the author, 1996. These commentators differ about the date that the black-and-white key image was phased out. Schmit and Haines suggest that the practice continued until the 1950s. Cornwell-Clyne, writing in 1951, suggests that the practice had been eliminated. May suggests that the black-and-white key was used until around 1944 and then phased out.

3. Paolo Cerchi Usai, "How Color Movies Think: What Happens While They Are Seen" (paper presented at the Univ. of Chicago Film Studies Center Auditorium, February 20, 1998).

4. Haines, *Technicolor Movies,* 31.

5. For a detailed description of the process of color-positive printing, see Ralph Evans and Woody Omens, *Exploring the Color Image* (Rochester, N.Y.: Eastman Kodak, 1996), 30–43.

6. Goldberg interview, July 1996.

7. Ibid. Dr. Goldberg notes that this was a problem for Eastmancolor particularly during its early development and use.

8. Ibid.

9. The Harry Ransom Humanities Research Center of the University of Texas at Austin holds original Technicolor prints of both *A Star Is Born* and *Gone with the Wind,* but neither is available for viewing or analysis.

10. Concerning *Becky Sharp,* Barry Salt noted that in modern prints, "the reds and yellows are more intense and the blacks are not so black," though he admits that the colors tend to be "fairly close in general" to the originals. Salt also noted that "the image definition of this class of modern reprints is often *better* than that of the original prints" (*Film Style and Technology,* 200).

11. May to the author, 1996.

Works Cited

Ager, Celia. "Mamoulian (with 'Becky Sharp' Just About to Premiere) Sees, in Color, the Approach to the 'Perfect' Film." *Variety,* June 19, 1935: 2, 20.

Albers, Joseph. *Interaction of Color.* Rev. ed. New Haven, Conn.: Yale Univ. Press, 1975.

Allen, Leigh. "New Technicolor System Tested by Directors of Photography." *American Cinematographer,* December 1950: 414, 424.

Aller, Herbert. "Color Marches On." *International Photographer,* May 1936: 17, 26.

American Cinematographer. "Faster Color Film Cuts Light a Half." August 1939: 355–356.

———. "The Future of Filmmaking: The Future as Seen by Cinematographers." September 2000.

———. "Is All This Color Ballyhoo Justifying Itself?" September 1936: 373, 378.

———. "Just What Is So Mysterious about Color?" October 1936: 414, 424–426.

———. Photography of the Month. Review of *Aloma of the South Seas.* October 1941: 502.

———. Photography of the Month. Review of *Billy the Kid.* June 1941: 273.

———. Photography of the Month. Review of *Blood and Sand.* June 1941: 272.

———. Photography of the Month. Review of *Blossoms in the Dust.* July 1941: 326.

———. Photography of the Month. Review of *Chad Hannah.* January 1941: 19.

———. Photography of the Month. Review of *The Jungle Book.* May 1942: 208.

———. Photography of the Month. Review of *Louisiana Purchase.* January 1942: 19, 31.

———. Photography of the Month. Review of *That Night in Rio.* April 1941: 169.

———. "Why All This Hubbub regarding Color?" August 1936: 327, 334–345.

American Film. "Lookin' Sharp." July–August 1985: 9.

Argy, Stephanie. "Cinematographer's Computer Age: Cinematographers and Visual Effects Experts Assess the Impact of Digital Technology on the Creative Process." *American Cinematographer* 80, no. 8 (August 1999).

Arnheim, Rudolf. *Art and Visual Perception: A Psychology of the Creative Eye; The New Version.* Berkeley: Univ. of California Press, 1974.

Balio, Tino, ed. *Grand Design: Hollywood as a Modern Business Enterprise, 1930–1939.* New York: Scribner's, 1993; Berkeley and Los Angeles: Univ. of California Press, 1995.

Ball, Joseph Arthur. "The Technicolor Process of Three-Color Cinematography." *Journal of the Society of Motion Picture Engineers,* August 1935: 127–147; and Academy Technicians Branch. *Technical Bulletin.* Los Angeles: Academy of Motion Picture Arts and Sciences, May 31, 1935.

Basten, Fred. *Glorious Technicolor: The Movie's Magic Rainbow.* Cranbury, N.J.: A. S. Barnes, 1980.

Behlmer, Rudy, ed. *The Adventures of Robin Hood.* Wisconsin/Warner Bros. Screenplay Series, edited by Tino Balio. Madison: Univ. of Wisconsin Press, 1979.

———, ed. *Memo from David O. Selznick.* New York: Viking, 1972.

Berg, A. Scott. *Goldwyn: A Biography.* New York: Knopf, 1989.

Bernstein, Matthew. *Walter Wanger: Hollywood Independent.* Berkeley and Los Angeles: Univ. of California Press, 1994.

Betancourt, Gilbert. "Present Color Trend Is toward Subdued Hues." *American Cinematographer,* August 1937: 317, 352.

Birren, Faber. *Principles of Color: A Review of Past Traditions and Modern Theories of Color Harmony.* Atglen, Pa.: Schiffer, 1969, 1987.

Boone, Andrew. "Pictures in Full Color Open New Era in Movies." *Popular Science* 126, no. 5 (May 1935): 13–14, 116.

Bordwell, David. "Intensified Continuity: Visual Style in Contemporary American Film." *Film Quarterly* 55, no. 3 (2002): 16–28.

———. *On the History of Film Style.* Cambridge, Mass.: Harvard Univ. Press, 1997.

Bordwell, David, Janet Staiger, and Kristin Thompson. *The Classical Hollywood Cinema: Film Style and Mode of Production to 1960.* New York: Columbia Univ. Press, 1985.

Bordwell, David, and Kristin Thompson. *Film Art: An Introduction.* 5th ed. New York: McGraw-Hill, 1997.

Bosco, W. G. C. "Aces of the Camera: Winton Hoch, A.S.C." *American Cinematographer,* January 1947: 12, 31.

Bourget, Jean-Loup. "Esthétiques du Technicolor." In *La Couleur en Cinéma,* edited by Jacques Aumont. Paris: Cinématheque français, 1995.

Branigan, Edward. "The Articulation of Color in a Filmic System." *Wide Angle* 1, no. 3 (1976): 20–31.

———. "Color and Cinema: Problems in the Writing of History." In *Movies and Methods,* vol. 2, edited by Bill Nichols, 121–143. Berkeley and Los Angeles: Univ. of California Press, 1985.

Brown, Howard C. "Will Color Revolutionize Photography?" *American Cinematographer,* July 1936: 284–285, 294.

Buscombe, Edward. "Sound and Color." In *Movies and Methods,* vol. 2, edited by Bill Nichols, 83–92. Berkeley and Los Angeles: Univ. of California Press, 1985.

Chevreul, Michel-Eugène. *The Priciples of Harmony and Contrast of Colours.* Translated by Charles Martel. 2nd ed. London: Longman, Brown, Green, and Longmans, 1855. Reprint, New York: Garland, 1980.

Chisholm, Brad. "Red, Blue, and Lots of Green: The Impact of Color Television on Feature Film Production." In *Hollywood in the Age of Television,* edited by Tino Balio. Boston: Unwin Hyman, 1990.

Conant, Russell. "Basic Principles of Color Separation." *Educational Program of Lectures Given to Control Department Film Technicians by Technicolor Motion Pic-*

ture Corporation: Lecture Five, September 1955. Technicolor Collection, Herrick Library, Los Angeles.

Corliss Mary, and Carlos Clarens. "Designed for Film: The Hollywood Art Director." *Film Comment,* May–June 1978: 25–59.

Cornwell-Clyne, Adrian. *Colour Cinematography.* 3rd ed. London: Chapman & Hall, 1951.

Coulon, Henri. "Color Control for Color Film." *American Cinematographer,* May 1934: 11, 19.

Cummings, Craig S. "Tampering with Tara: The Desecration of *Gone with the Wind.*" *Big Reel,* January 1999: 122.

Davidoff, Jules. *Cognition through Color.* Cambridge, Mass.: MIT Press, 1991.

Desowitz, Bill. "GWTW: Is Brighter Better?" *Los Angeles Times,* June 7, 1998, Calendar sec.

———. "Frankly, My Dear, You're a Bit Blurry." *Los Angeles Times,* July 7, 1998, sec. F.

Edouart, Farciot. "The Evolution of Transparency Process Photography." *American Cinematographer,* October 1943: 359–362, 386.

Eiseman, Leatrice, and Lawrence Herbert. *The Pantone Book of Color: Over 1,000 Color Standards, Color Basics, and Guidelines for Design, Fashion, Furnishings, and More.* New York: Abrams, 1990.

Evans, Ralph, and Woody Omens. *Exploring the Color Image.* Rochester, N.Y.: Eastman Kodak, 1996.

Factor, Max. "Make-Up for the New Technicolor Process: An Interview with Max Factor." *American Cinematographer,* August 1936.

Farnham, R. E. "Lighting Requirements of the Three-Color Technicolor Process." *American Cinematographer,* July 1936: 282–283, 292.

Film Daily. Advertisement for *The Adventures of Robin Hood.* April 26, 1938: 3–9.

Fisher, Bob. "Black-and-White in Color: The Comedic Fantasy *Pleasantville* Provides a Unique Opportunity for the Digital and Photochemical Production Worlds to Momentarily Merge." *American Cinematographer* 79, no. 11 (November 1998).

———. "Escaping from Chains." *American Cinematographer* 81, no. 10 (October 2000).

Fortune. "What? Color in the Movies Again?" October 1934: 92, 97, 161–164, 166–168, 171.

Fox, John Jr. *The Trail of the Lonesome Pine.* New York: Charles Scribner's Sons, 1908.

Gage, John. *Colour and Culture: Practice and Meaning from Antiquity to Abstraction.* London: Thames and Hudson, 1993.

Garau, Augusto. *Color Harmonies.* Translated by Nicola Bruno. With a foreword by Rudolf Arnheim. Chicago: Univ. of Chicago Press, 1993.

Gitt, Robert, and Richard Dayton. "Restoring *Becky Sharp.*" *American Cinematographer,* November 1984: 99–106.

Goldman, Michael. "Scorsese's Color Homage." *Millimeter,* January 2005: 14–18, 20, 22, 24, 26.

Greene, William H. "Creating Lighting Effects in Technicolor." *International Photographer,* January 1937: 10–11, 25.

———. "Low Key Lighting May Be as Easy in Color as It Is in Monochrome." *American Cinematographer,* April 1938: 146, 151.

———. "Matching Technicolor Exteriors with Artificial Sunlight." *American Cinematographer,* October 1936: 418, 426.

Gunning, Tom. "Colorful Metaphors: The Attraction of Color in Early Silent Cinema." *Fotogenia,* no. 1 (1994): 249–255.

Haines, Richard. *Technicolor Movies: The History of Dye Transfer Printing.* Jefferson, N.C.: McFarland, 1993.

Hale, Karl. "Learn About Shooting Color from *Becky Sharp.*" *American Cinematographer,* July 1935: 312.

Handley, C. W. "The Advanced Technic of Technicolor Lighting." *Journal of the Society of Motion Picture Engineers,* August 1937: 169–177.

———. "History of Motion-Picture Studio Lighting." In *A Technological History of Motion Pictures,* edited by Raymond Fielding. Berkeley and Los Angeles: Univ. of California Press, 1967.

Hanson, Patricia King, ed. *American Film Institute Catalog of Motion Pictures Produced in the United States.* Volume F3, *Feature Films, 1931–1940.* Berkeley and Los Angeles: Univ. of California Press, 1993.

Haralovich, Mary Beth. "All that Heaven Allows: Color, Narrative Space, and Melodrama." In *Close Readings,* edited by Peter Lehman. Tallahassee: Florida State Univ. Press, 1990.

Hardin, C. L. *Color for Philosophers: Unweaving the Rainbow.* Indianapolis: Hackett, 1988.

Harmetz, Aljean. *On the Road to Tara: The Making of "Gone With the Wind."* New York: Abrams, 1996.

Haver, Ronald. *David O. Selznick's Hollywood.* New York: Knopf, 1980.

Herold, Don. Review of *Becky Sharp. Life,* August 1935: 43, 45.

Higgins, Scott. "Color at the Center: Minnelli's Technicolor Style in *Meet Me in St. Louis.*" *Style,* Fall 1998: 449–470.

———. "A New Color Consciousness: Colour in the Digital Age." *Convergence* 9, no. 4 (2003): 60–76.

Hoch, Winton. "Technicolor Cinematography." *Journal of the Society of Motion Picture Engineers,* August 1942: 96–108.

Holden, Lansing C. "Designing for Color." In *We Make the Movies,* edited by Nancy Naumburg, 237–248. New York: Norton, 1937.

Hollywood Reporter. "Box Office Winners for 1939." December 30, 1939: 10.

———. "Exhibitor Poll Results, the 12 Best Money Pictures of 1937." December 31, 1937: 33.

———. Review of *Becky Sharp.* June 14, 1935: 3.

———. "Robin Hood Boxoffice Natural." April 26, 1938: 3.

Houghton, Norris. "The Designer Sets the Stage." *Theatre Arts Monthly* 20, no. 12 (December 1936): 966–975.

Howe, James Wong. "Reaction on Making his First Color Production." *American Cinematographer,* October 1937: 408–412.

Huggins, L. O. "The Language of Color." *American Cinematographer,* July 1934: 108, 117, 119.

Hunter, Mary King. "Color—The Spirit of the New Age." *International Photographer,* July 1936: 12–13.

———. "The Key to Color." *International Photographer,* December 1936: 14–15, 22–23.

Huntley, John. *British Technicolor.* Foreword by Jack Cardiff. London: Skelton-Robinson, 1948.

International Photographer. "Color Make-Up: New Factor Development Solves Color Problem." June 1937: 27.

———. "Rennahan Talks Technicolor." September 1937, 24–25.

Itten, Johannes. *The Art of Color: The Subjective Experience and Objective Rationale of Color.* Translated by Ernst Van Haagen. New York: Van Nostrand Reinhold, 1973.

Jacobs, Lea. "Belasco, DeMille, and the Development of Lasky Lighting." *Film History* 5, no. 4 (December 1993): 405–418.

Jewell, Richard. "RKO Film Grosses, 1929–1951: The C. F. Tevlin Ledger." *Historical Journal of Film, Radio, and Television* 14, no. 2 (1994): microfiche supplement.

Jones, Robert Edmond. "The Crisis of Color." *New York Times,* May 19, 1935.

———. "The Problem of Color." In *The Emergence of Film Art,* edited by Lewis Jacobs, 206–209. New York: Hopkinson and Blake, 1969.

———. "A Revolution in the Movies." *Vanity Fair,* June 1935: 13, 58.

Journal of the Society of Motion Picture Engineers. "Glossary of Color Photography." May 1935: 432–449.

———. "Report of the Studio Lighting Committee." January 1937: 39–42.

Jungmeyer, Jack. "The Studios and Color." *Variety,* January 6, 1937: 4.

Kalmus, Herbert. *Mr. Technicolor: An Autobiography.* With Eleanore King Kalmus. Absecon, N.J.: MagicImage Filmbooks, 1993.

Kalmus, Natalie. "Color Consciousness." *Journal of the Society of Motion Picture Engineers,* August 1935: 139–147.

———. "Colour." In *Behind the Screen: How Films Are Made,* edited by Stephen Watts, 116–127. London: Arthur Barker, 1938.

Kaufman, Debra. "The Post Process: Control in the Digital Suite." *American Cinematographer* 83, no. 3 (March 2002).

Kaufman, Debra, and Ray Zone. "A Legacy of Invention: Cinematographers Exploring the Growing Possibilities of Postproduction Are Continuing a Time-Honored Tradition." *American Cinematographer* 83, no. 5 (May 2002).

Kienninger, John F. "Track Printing, Blank Processing, and Transfer." *Educational*

Program of Lectures Given to Release, Rush, and Answer Print Viewers by Technicolor Motion Picture Corporation: Lecture Three, February 1956. Technicolor Collection, Herrick Library, Los Angeles.

Kindem, Gorham. *The American Movie Industry: The Business of Motion Pictures.* Carbondale: Southern Illinois Univ. Press, 1982.

Koszarski, Richard. *The Hollywood Directors, 1914–1940.* Oxford: Oxford Univ. Press, 1976.

Lastra, James. "Standards and Practices: Aesthetic Norm and Technological Innovation in the American Cinema." In *The Studio System,* edited by Janet Staiger. New Brunswick, N.J.: Rutgers Univ. Press, 1995.

Levin, Meyer. "The Candid Cameraman." Review of *The Adventures of Robin Hood. Esquire,* August 1938: 82.

Linderman, R. G., C. W. Handley, and A. Rogers. "Illumination in Motion Picture Production." *Journal of the Society of Motion Picture Engineers,* June 1943: 333–367.

Lovell, Glenn. "Frankly, My Dear, This Is No Improvement." *Variety,* June 22–28, 1998: 51.

MacGurrin, Buckley. "An Artist Looks at Technicolor Cinematography." *American Cinematographer,* July 1941: 318, 346.

Malkiewicz, Kris. *Cinematography.* 2nd ed. New York: Prentice Hall, 1989.

Mamoulian, Rouben. "Colour and Emotion." *Cinema Quarterly,* Summer 1935: 225–226.

———. "Colour and Light in Films." *Film Culture* 21 (Summer 1960): 68–79.

———. "Controlling Color for Dramatic Effect." *American Cinematographer,* June 1941: 262–263, 288, 290.

———. "Painting the Leaves Black: Rouben Mamoulian Interviewed by David Robinson." *Sight and Sound* 30, no. 3 (Summer 1961): 123–130.

———. "Some Problems in Directing Color Pictures." *Journal of the Society of Motion Picture Engineers,* August 1935: 148–153.

Mathias, Harry, and Richard Patterson. *Electronic Cinematography: Achieving Photographic Control over the Video Image.* Belmont, Calif.: Wadsworth, 1985.

McDonald, Sterling. *Color Harmony, with the McDonald Calibrator.* Chicago: Wilcox and Follet, 1949.

Miller, Arthur C., and Walter Strenge, eds. *American Cinematographer Manual.* 3rd ed. Hollywood: ASC Holding Corp., 1964.

Mole, Peter. "Arc Lights for Color." *International Photographer,* October 1935: 23.

———. "Lighting Equipment for Natural-Color Photography." *International Photographer,* June 1936: 15–17, 30.

Molt, Cynthia. *"Gone with the Wind" on Film: A Complete Reference.* Jefferson, N.C.: McFarland, 1990.

Morrison, Denis. "Color at the Crossroads." *Variety,* June 2, 1937: 5, 19.

Mosher, John Chapin [writing as "J.C.M."]. The Current Cinema. Review of *Becky Sharp. New Yorker,* June 22, 1935: 53.

Munsell, Albert. *A Color Notation.* 7th ed. Baltimore: Hoffman Brothers, 1926.

Neale, Steve. *Cinema and Technology: Image, Sound, Colour.* Bloomington: Indiana Univ. Press, 1985.

Neupert, Richard. "Technicolor and Hollywood: Exercising Restraint." *Post Script,* Fall 1990: 21–29.

Nugent, Frank. "One More Word on Color." *New York Times,* June 9, 1935.

———. Review of *The Adventures of Robin Hood. New York Times,* May 13, 1938.

———. Review of *Gone With the Wind. New York Times,* December 20, 1939.

Oppenheimer, Jean. "Toying with Visuals in Post." *American Cinematographer,* 81, no. 9 (September 2000).

Palmer, Ernest. "The Inkie's Place in Technicolor Lighting." *American Cinematographer,* July 1941: 323, 348–349.

Palmer, Raymond. "Technicolor on the Way to Its Greatest Triumph in *Trail of the Lonesome Pine.*" *International Photographer,* January 1936: 20.

Pavlus, John. "High Life." *American Cinematographer* 86, no. 1 (January 2005).

———. "No Holds Barred." *American Cinematographer,* 83, no. 11 (November 2002).

Petrie, Duncan. *The British Cinematographer.* London: British Film Institute, 1996.

Probst, Christopher. "New Products and Services: A Digital Revolution." *American Cinematographer* 81, no. 9 (September 2000): 151–152, 154.

Ramsaye, Terry, ed. *International Motion Picture Almanac, 1937.* New York: Quigley, 1937.

Rennahan, Ray. "Natural Color Cinematography Today." *American Cinematographer,* July 1935: 288, 294.

Riley, Charles A., II. *Color Codes: Modern Theories of Color in Philosophy, Painting, and Architecture, Literature, Music, and Psychology.* Hanover, N.H.: Univ. Press of New England, 1995.

Rossotti, Hazel. *Colour.* Princeton, N.J.: Princeton Univ. Press, 1983.

Ryan, Roderick. *A History of Motion Picture Color Technology.* New York: Focal Press, 1977.

Salt, Barry. *Film Style and Technology: History and Analysis.* 2nd ed. London: Starword, 1992.

Sargent, Walter. *The Enjoyment and Use of Color.* New York: Charles Scribner's Sons, 1923. Reprint, New York: Dover, 1964.

Sennwald, Andre. Review of *Becky Sharp. New York Times,* June 14, 1935.

Shklovsky, Victor. "Art as Technique." In *Russian Formalist Criticism,* edited and translated by Lee Lemon and Marion Reis. Lincoln: Univ. of Nebraska Press, 1965.

Skall, William. "Artificial Sunlight Simplifies Technicolor Exteriors." *International Photographer,* October 1936: 14, 24.

———. "Simplifying Color Lighting." *International Photographer,* March 1936: 12, 20, 31.

Slide, Anthony. "*Becky Sharp.*" In *Magill's Cinema Annual 1982,* edited by Frank Magill. Englewood Cliffs, N.J.: Salem, 1982.

———. "The Return of *Becky Sharp.*" *Films in Review,* March 1985: 148–153.
Slifer, Clarence. "Creating Visual Effects for *G.W.T.W.*" *American Cinematographer,* August 1982: 835–848.
Smith, Nancy. "The New Max Factor Technicolor Make-Up." *International Photographer,* June 1936: 10.
Society of Motion Picture and Television Engineers. *Elements of Color in Professional Motion Pictures.* Los Angeles: SMPTE, 1957.
Squire, Marion. "The Girl's Eye View." *Variety,* February 23, 1938: 6.
Stull, William. "Explanation of the Trichrome Technicolor." *American Cinematographer,* January 1935: 8–9, 12–14.
———. "A New Three Color Process." *American Cinematographer,* April 1936: 140–141.
———. "Process Shots Aided by Triple Projector." *American Cinematographer,* August 1939: 363–366, 376.
———. "Technicolor Bringing New Charm to Screen." *American Cinematographer,* June 1937: 234–237, 242.
———. "Will Color Help or Hinder?" *American Cinematographer,* March 1935: 100, 106–108.
Surtees, Robert. "Color Is Different." *American Cinematographer,* January 1948: 10–11, 31.
Technicolor News and Views. "Audiences Becoming 'Black and White Conscious.'" January 1940: 1, 3.
———. "Color Director's Work Important." May 1939: 3.
———. "Importance of Color Control Service Growing." February 1941: 1, 3.
———. "New High Speed Film Is Now in Use." April 1939: 2.
———. "New Negative Is Predicted." November 1939: 2.
———. "Rising Tide of Color Seen in Comment on Technicolor Price Reduction and Annual Report." May 1940: 1.
———. "Special Award Bestowed for Color Process." March 1940: 1, 3.
———. "Technicolor Expansion Program in Operation." April 1939: 1, 3.
———. "Three Technicolor Pictures Lead Exhibitor Poll." January 1940: 1.
Thompson, Kristin. *Breaking the Glass Armor: Neoformalist Film Analysis.* Princeton, N.J.: Princeton Univ. Press, 1988.
Time. "Guide to Cinema, G with the W." December 25, 1939: 23.
———. "Whitney Colors." May 27, 1935: 28–34.
Ungar, Arthur. "Analysis of Top Films and Stars." *Variety,* January 4, 1939: 5, 10–11, 22.
Valentine, Joe. "Lighting for Technicolor as Compared with Black and White." *International Photographer,* January 1948: 7–10.
Variety. Advertisement for *A Star is Born.* May 12, 1937: 14.
———. Advertisements for *The Trail of the Lonesome Pine.* January 1, 1936: 20; and February 26, 1936: 11–14.

———. "Color Has Producers on the Fence; Paint Brush Boys Future Big Shots?" June 19, 1935: 1, 67.
———. "Color's Future Depends on Costs." July 13, 1935: 5.
———. "Picture Grosses." March 18, 1936: 6, 8, 9, 13.
———. "U.S. Evaluations of Box Office Picture, 1937's Top Pix Grossers." January 5, 1938: 1.
———. "Wanger's First for UA All Set." July 15, 1936: 5.
———. "Writers Turned Loose on *Goldwyn's Follies.*" June 2, 1937: 5.
Variety Film Reviews. Vol. 2, 1921–1925. Vol. 3, 1926–1929. Vol. 4, 1930–1933. Vol. 5, 1934–1937. New York: Garland, 1983.
Vertrees, Alan David. *Selznick's Vision: "Gone with the Wind" and Hollywood Filmmaking.* Austin: Univ. of Texas Press, 1997.
Wear, Mike. "What Color Has Meant So Far." *Variety,* January 6, 1937: 4.
Williams, David E. "Firepower in Post." *American Cinematographer* 83, no. 2 (February 2002): 50.
Woolsey, Ralph A. "Lighting and Exposure Control in Color Cinematography." *Journal of the Society of Motion Picture Engineers,* June 1947: 548–553.
Zelanski, Paul, and Mary Pat Fisher. *Color.* 2nd ed. Englewood Cliffs, N.J.: Prentice Hall, 1994.

Unpublished Papers and Interviews

Belton, John. "Color and Realism." Paper presented at the Society for Cinema Studies Conference, Univ. of Southern California, 1992.
Gitt, Robert. Interview with the author. Hollywood, Calif., August 31, 2005.
Goldberg, Richard. Interview with the author (tape recording). Los Angeles, Calif., July 19, 1996.
———. Telephone interview with the author, September 16, 1996.
Harris, Robert. Interview with the author (written notes). Bedford Hills, N.Y., March 24, 2004.
Legato, Robert. Telephone interview with the author, February 15, 2006.
May, Richard. Interview with the author (written notes). Los Angeles, Calif., July 18, 1996.
———. Letter to the author. April 17, 1996.
Schmit, Joe. "History of the Technicolor Imbibition Process for Color Motion Pictures." Paper presented to the Hollywood Section of the Society of Motion Picture and Television Engineers, June 25, 1991.
Usai, Paolo Cerchi. "How Color Movies Think: What Happens While They Are Seen." Paper presented at the Univ. of Chicago Film Studies Center Auditorium, February 20, 1998.

Archives

David O. Selznick Collection. Harry Ransom Humanities Research Center. University of Texas at Austin.

Technicolor Collection. Margaret Herrick Library, Academy of Motion Picture Arts and Sciences, Los Angeles.

United Artists Corporation Collection. Wisconsin Center for Film and Theater Research. State Historical Society, Madison.

UCLA Film and Television Archive, Los Angeles.

Warner Brothers Features Collection. Wisconsin Center for Film and Theater Research. State Historical Society, Madison.

Index

Italic page numbers refer to figures.